CREATION'S JOURNEY

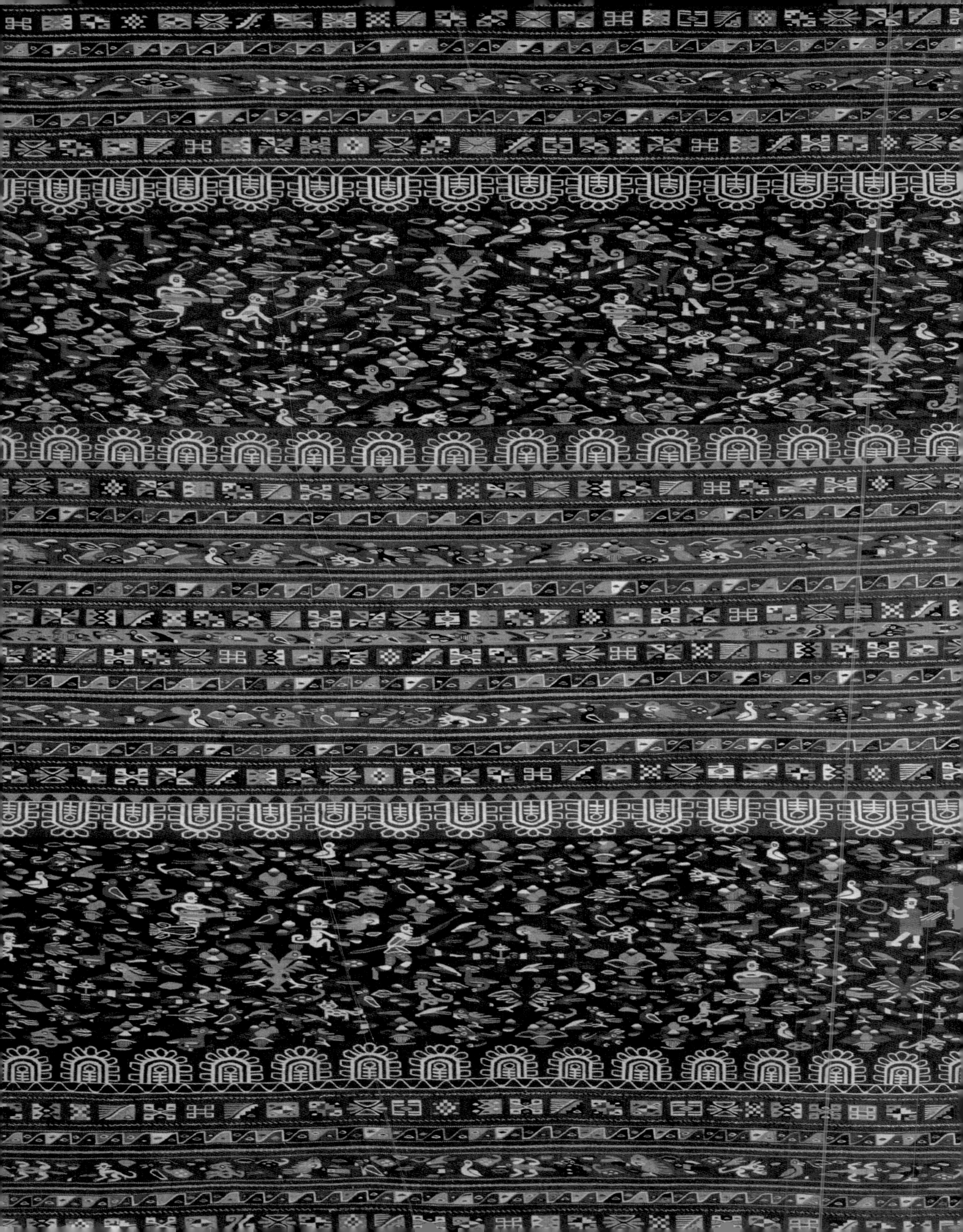

CREATION'S JOURNEY
NATIVE AMERICAN IDENTITY AND BELIEF

Edited by
Tom Hill and Richard W. Hill Sr.

Published by Smithsonian Institution Press
Washington and London

in association with the
National Museum of the American Indian
Smithsonian Institution

COVER: *PROCESSION BEFORE WAR DANCE*, CA. 1910. EARNEST L. SPYBUCK (1883–1949),
ABSENTEE SHAWNEE. WATERCOLOR ON PAPERBOARD, 44.2 X 63.9 CM (2.5735)

PAINTED AND FEATHERED DUCK DECOY AND PLAIN DUCK DECOY, CA. A.D. 200. FOUND
IN LOVELOCK CAVE, HUMBOLDT COUNTY, NEVADA. LENGTH 26.5 CM AND 27 CM
(13.4512D AND 13.4513)

MICMAC BIRCHBARK BOX WITH QUILLED DECORATION (DETAIL), EARLY TO MID-19TH C.
28 X 23 X 19 CM. (10.96)

GRASS BASKET WITH SKOKOMISH DESIGN, 19TH C. COLLECTED IN THE QUINAULT
VILLAGE OF TAHOLAH, WASHINGTON. HEIGHT 25.4 CM (5.9453)

INKA MANTA, PROBABLY LATE 18TH C. LAKE TITICACA, BOLIVIA. 118.9 X 109.5 CM (5.3773)

MIXTEC GOLD FILIGREE RINGS, A.D. 1450-1521. VALLEY OF OAXACA, MEXICO.
DIAM. 1.8 CM AND 2.2 CM (16.3447 AND 16.3417)

BEADED MOCCASINS, CA. 1860. UPPER MISSOURI RIVER.′LENGTH 27.9 CM (8.8057)

Published in conjunction with the exhibition *Creation's Journey: Masterworks of Native American Identity and
Belief*, on view at the National Museum of the American Indian, George Gustav Heye Center, Alexander
Hamilton U.S. Custom House, New York City, 30 October 1994–1 February 1997.

Library of Congress Cataloging-in-Publication Data
Creation's journey : Native American identity and belief / edited by Tom Hill and Richard W. Hill, Sr.
p.   cm.
Published in conjunction with an exhibition held at the National Museum of the American Indian,
New York City, Oct. 1994–Feb. 1997.
Includes bibliographical references and index.
ISBN 1-56098-453-8 (cloth : alk. paper).—ISBN 1-56098-454-6 (paper : alk. paper)
1. Indian art—North American—Exhibitions. 2. Indians of North America—Material culture—Exhibitions.
3. National Museum of the American Indian (U.S.)—Exhibitions. I. Hill, Tom. II. Hill, Richard W., Sr.
III. National Museum of the American Indian (U.S.)
E98.A7C74   1994
745′.089′97073—dc20   94-4757

British Library Cataloguing-in-Publication Data is available

Manufactured in the United States of America
01 00 99 98 97 96 95 94   5 4 3 2 1

∞ The paper used in this publication meets the minimum requirements of the American National Standard for
Permanence of Paper for Printed Library Materials Z39.48-1984.

For permission to reproduce illustrations appearing in this book, please correspond directly with the National
Museum of the American Indian. The Smithsonian Institution Press does not retain reproduction rights for
these illustrations individually.

Creation's Journey: Native American Identity and Belief has been made possible in part through the
generous support of the Merck Family Fund.

Terence Winch: Acting Head of Publications
Holly Stewart: Editor / Patricia Upchurch: Production
Design by Roger Gorman, Reiner Design Consultants, Inc., New York
Typeset in Waldbaum and Lithos and printed on 80# Consoweb Dull
Color Separations and Pre Press by Computer Color Corporation, Lexington, KY
Printed and bound by R. R. Donnelley & Sons Company, Willard, OH

The National Museum of the American Indian, Smithsonian Institution, is dedicated to working in collaboration with the indigenous peoples of the Americas to foster and protect native cultures throughout the Western Hemisphere. The museum's publishing program seeks to augment awareness of Native American beliefs and lifeways, and to educate the public about the history and significance of native cultures.

CONTENTS

HURON PIN CUSHION DECORATED
WITH MOOSE-HAIR EMBROIDERY
AND GLASS BEADS, 19TH C.
WIDTH 7.5 CM (22.4677)

CERAMIC FIGURE OF A WOMAN, CA.
300 B.C.–A.D. 600. JAMA–COAQUE
CULTURE, CENTRAL COAST OF
MANABI, ECUADOR.
HEIGHT 46 CM (24.8408)

FOREWORD

Museums, perhaps more than any other institutions, have shaped broad public perceptions and understandings of native cultures—in a variety of ways and from a diversity of perspectives. From their beginnings in the nineteenth and early twentieth centuries, collections of native cultural patrimony in museums of natural history, anthropology, civilization, and art have profoundly affected non-native and, for that matter, native views of the indigenous cultures and peoples of the Western Hemisphere.

As the only national institution in the United States whose exclusive mandate covers the entirety of the native cultures of this hemisphere, the National Museum of the American Indian bears a unique responsibility for addressing important issues of cultural interpretation and representation. Moreover, with its vast and brilliant collections that stretch, literally, from Tierra del Fuego in the south to the Arctic Circle in the north and span ten millennia, this institution has an extraordinary capacity for doing so. *Creation's Journey: Native American Identity and Belief*, along with the associated exhibition of masterworks, is the museum's important first effort to re-examine old conceptions and come to new understandings of native cultures and peoples, past, present, and future.

To comprehend where we are going with this inquiry, however, we first must explore more carefully where we have been, and "where we have been" is as diverse as the wide range of interpretive voices themselves and as varied as the span of time over which the interpretation has occurred. To be sure, the representational focus almost always has begun—and, unfortunately, often has ended—with native material culture, to the sometime exclusion of the complex native thinking that produced the objects in the first instance. This statement has been particularly true where a conventional European art history analysis has been employed that emphasizes aesthetics rather than cultural context. On the other hand, disciplines such as anthropology, while approaching native material from the standpoint of its context, sometimes have minimized its aesthetic qualities, which are often considerable. The debate about whether native cultural material is "art" or "artifact" has its origins in these very different approaches to cultural interpretation and representation.

As a Southern Cheyenne, I am bemused by the sometimes thunderous academic salvos that go back and forth between the art historians and anthropologists in this argument. Ironically, it is not the making of native peoples themselves, who had little to do with defining the terms of the debate. To the contrary, the whole discussion derives from intellectual constructs and systems of academic analysis that came from Western Europe.

From a native perspective, objects of material culture are viewed rather differently. In the Cheyenne language, for example, no word for "art," as that term is understood in Western culture, even exists. Furthermore, for most native peoples, the process of creating objects has always has been as important as—and perhaps more important than—the end product, the art object itself. I remember a passage in a recent memorandum written by Jacki Rand, a colleague of mine at the museum, that speaks directly to this point:

> [T]he native artist . . . [values] the creation [of art] . . . over the final product. Process speaks to historical or cultural significance because it is testimony to cultural continuity and change. It is the evidence of lost traditions, innovations, preserved cultural knowledge, historic perspective, and vision of the future. . . . It takes into account a sort of "spiritual evidence" that is integral to the creative process. The integrity of the creative process is foremost. The object is meaningless without it.

In other words, through the millennia those natives we now call "artists" were not so much in the business of producing art objects per se—

icons—as they were in creating aesthetically remarkable material that grew directly from their own cultural experience, context, and world view.

Although this juxtaposition of methods of interpretation and diverse readings of objects of native material culture raises a host of issues that deserve our thoughtful attention, from my personal point of view three stand out above the others. First, at the very least museums need to confront honestly the question of whether native cultural material, depending upon the speaker, is subject to multiple meanings and interpretive "truths" rather than the mythic and singular "objective" meaning. Second, museums must ask themselves whether, in representing native cultures, substantial interpretive value is added by integrating, along with the interpretive methodologies that historically have typified museum presentations of native material culture, the views and perspectives of native peoples themselves. Finally, notwithstanding the potential conflict among these widely variant interpretive practices and approaches, museums should not fear asking whether new understandings—new paradigms of interpretation and representation—regarding native cultures and peoples are possible even if they involve the relinquishment of long established museological methodologies.

Indeed, I believe museums should embrace this important and precedent-setting inquiry. *Creation's Journey: Native American Identity and Belief* represents the National Museum of the American Indian's sincere and, I hope, thoughtful contribution to this most worthy of intellectual and cultural quests.

✳

This book and the associated exhibition could not have been produced without the talents and efforts of many people. The museum is also grateful to the Merck Family Fund, whose very generous support helped make the production of this book possible.

In editing this volume, Tom Hill (Seneca) and Rick Hill (Tuscarora) shared not only their scholarly insights into the objects discussed, but also their personal responses to Native American creativity. The museum greatly appreciates the assistance provided to Tom by the staff of the Woodland Cultural Centre, in particular the Research Department—Sheila Staats (Mohawk) and Winnie Jacobs (Ojibway)—and typist Simone Henry Greene (Cayuga). Contributing writers Diane Fraher (Osage/Cherokee), Ramiro Matos (Quechua), John C. Ewers, Dorie Reents-Budet, Mari Lynn Salvador, Duane King, Mary Jane Lenz, Eulalie H. Bonar, Nancy Rosoff, and Cécile R. Ganteaume researched and wrote the interesting detailed captions for the objects. They were supported by curatorial assistant Andrea Gaines, Mary B. Davis and Catherine McChesney of the Huntington–Free Library, and archivists John Barbry and Allison Jeffrey, as well as by their colleagues at other institutions, many of whom are named in the contributors' acknowledgments toward the end of the book. Clara Sue Kidwell (Choctaw/Chippewa), Assistant Director for Cultural Resources, reviewed all text for content and clarity.

Terence Winch, Acting Head of Publications, managed complex contract negotiations and provided guidance and editorial direction for this project. Holly Stewart edited the text with dedication and tenacity; Lou Stancari and Ann Kawasaki helped with the many details involved in a book of this complexity. Alice Powers proofread the galleys. Publications interns Mara Furnas and Roberto Rodriguez contributed fresh minds to the project in its late stages.

Art director Roger Gorman, mountmaker Elizabeth McKean, and photographer David Heald worked together to bring the objects on these pages to life; Roger is responsible for the wonderful design of the book, as well. Tim Johnson (Mohawk) and Danyelle Means (Oglala Lakota) researched historical photographs. Sharon Dean, Janine Jones, Pamela Dewey, Karen Furth, Laura Nash, and Shilice Clinkscales were

CHEROKEE (?) BANDOLIER BAG, EARLY 19TH C. EMBROIDERED DEDICATION "TO GENERAL JACKSON FROM SAM HOUSTON." LENGTH CM 70.5 (17.9690)

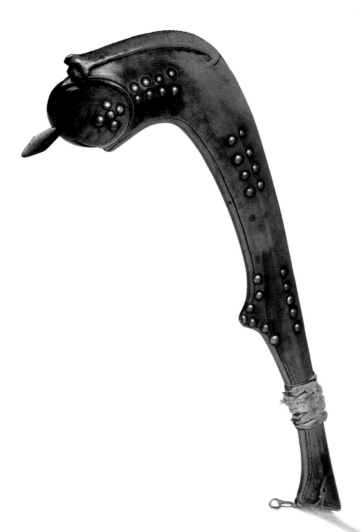

OTO OTTER EFFIGY WAR CLUB,
19TH C. LENGTH 59.7 CM (3.3555)

instrumental in coordinating photo shoots and providing images and information from the museum's Photo Archives.

The museum is pleased to collaborate on this book with the staff of Smithsonian Institution Press, in particular Daniel Goodwin, Amy Pastan, Hilary Reeves, and especially Patricia Upchurch, who met an impossible production schedule.

The exhibition, too, is the product of many of talented and dedicated contributors. Nearly every member of the museum's staff played a part. Jim Volkert guided a diverse team through a complex undertaking. Evi Oehler created the exhibition design and oversaw its production. Jacki Rand (of Choctaw descent) contributed valuable insights into the issues raised by objects so rich with meanings. Elizabeth Weatherford and Carolyn Rapkievian helped shape the exhibition and the public programs that complement it. Jennifer Miller provided administrative support.

Several departments of the museum prepared objects for study, photography, and exhibition. Special thanks are due to Collections Manager B. Lynne Harlan (Cherokee) and Mark Clark, Dwayne A. Sylvester (Seneca), Tim Ramsey, and Wiley Stephen Thornton of her staff; Registrar Lee A. Callander and Mary Nooney, Kevin De Vorsey, Margaret Cintron, Ann M. Drumheller (Onondaga), Lucia Belci, Milly Herron, and Seth Richardson of Registration; Chief Conservator Marian Kaminitz and her colleagues Scott Merritt, Leslie Williamson, Monica DiLisio, and Birgit Katzenbach; and Heye Center Exhibition Curator Peter Brill and his assistants Kelton Bound and Terry West.

This exhibition and the inauguration of the George Gustav Heye Center in New York would not have been possible without the extraordinary assistance of offices and individuals throughout the Smithsonian Institution.

Finally, I particularly want to thank the native leaders and other consultants who advised the museum on the propriety of exhibiting and publishing objects of great cultural and spiritual sensitivity; these counsellors include Porfirio Ayala (Zenú, Organización Nacional Indígena de Colombia), Aurelio Carmona (Quechua, Universidad Nacional San Antonio Abad del Cuzco), René Cibanacán Marcano (Nación Taína), Joseph Dishta (Head Councilman, Pueblo of Zuni), Alejandro Flores Huatta (Quechua), Jorge Flores Ochoa (Universidad Nacional San Antonio Abad del Cuzco), Oscar Fonseca Zamora (Universidad de Costa Rica), Leigh Jenkins (Cultural Presentation Office, the Hopi Tribe), Robert E. Lewis (Governor, Pueblo of Zuni), Victor José Loperena Mindiola (Wiwa, Organización Nacional Indígena de Colombia), Linda Manzanilla (Universidad Nacional Autónoma de México), Rigoberta Menchú (Maya), Rufo Mendoza López (Nahuatl, Teotihuacan, Mexico), Jorge Morales (Universidad de los Andes, Colombia), Salvador Palomino Flores (Quechua, Movimiento Nación Quechua), Manuel Ríos Morales (Zapotec, Centro de Investigaciones y Estudios Superiores de Antropologiá Social, Oaxaca), Reginald T. Pasqual (Governor, Pueblo of Acoma), Troy W. Poteete (Cherokee National Historical Society), Manuel Puwainchir (Shuar–Achuar Radio Education System, Ecuador), Guillermo Rodríguez Romero (Consejo para la Defensa de los Derechos Indígenas, Costa Rica), Ferrell Secakuku (Chairman, the Hopi Tribe), Felipe Tsenkush (Federación Interprovincial de Centros Shuar–Achuar, Ecuador), Manuel Turpo (Quechua, Altamisa de Ocongate, Cuzco), and María Vásquez (Maya).

W. Richard West Jr., Director
(Southern Cheyenne and member of the Cheyenne
and Arapaho Tribes of Oklahoma)

The National Museum of the American Indian wishes to thank the following individuals and organizations for their gifts in honor of the masterworks within the *Creation's Journey* exhibition and of the native people who created them.

Through their contributions, these individuals and organizations are helping to meet the fundraising goal of the museum's National Campaign. As mandated by Congress, the Smithsonian Institution must raise one-third of the cost of construction of the National Museum of the American Indian on the National Mall in Washington, D.C., before federal funds will be released. The Smithsonian has set a fundraising goal of $60 million to fund construction costs as well as an endowment for ongoing educational and outreach programs.

The museum gratefully acknowledges the following:

Charmay B. Allred
Chumash basket with Spanish coin design
Page 133

Ann Simmons Alspaugh
Kiowa beaded cradle
Page 35

JoAnn and Bob Balzer
Chilkat Tlingit *shadakookh*
(crest hat) of a Bear
Page 122

Barbara and James Block
Aztec figure of Xipe Totec
Page 210

Harvi and Robert Bloom
Gold mask with serpents, Nazca culture
Page 167

Meredith and Tom Brokaw
Ledger drawings by Red Dog, Lakota
Page 141

Sheila and David Burns
Painted, quilled, and beaded shirt,
upper Missouri River
Page 65

Dianne and Berry Cash
Innu (Naskapi/Montagnais) caribou-skin
coat and leggings
Page 192

Wahleah Faulkner Davis
In Memory of Dave Faulkner, Cherokee
Cherokee (?) bandolier bag
Pages 10 and 11

Valerie and Charles Diker
Unangan (Aleut) basket and cover
Page 117

Margot and John Ernst
Navajo sarape poncho
Page 147

Gerald J. Ford
Painted, feathered duck decoy and plain
duck decoy
Page 143

George Gund III
Raven Stealing the Moon by
Robert Davidson, Haida
Page 127

Loretta and Victor Kaufman
Polychrome pottery vessel by
Rachel Nampeyo, Hopi
Page 209

The Seymour H. Knox Foundation, Inc.
Micmac women's caps
Pages 70–71

Mr. and Mrs. Robert Krissel
James Krissel and Dina Krissel
Girl's dress, northern Plains
Page 39

Iara Lee
Haida house posts
Page 46

Masco Corporation
Absaroke (Crow) sword scabbard
Pages 134–135

Samuel Merrin/The Merrin Gallery
Colima effigy vessel in the form of a dog
Page 152

Morning Star Gallery
Assiniboine antelope-horn headdress
Page 81

Neutrogena Corporation
Blackfeet perforated buckskin shirt
Pages 190–191

Nancy and Morris W. Offit
Procession before War Dance
by Earnest L. Spybuck, Absentee Shawnee
Page 184

PaceWildenstein
Micmac birchbark box with
quilled decoration
Page 115

The Pickelner Family
In Honor of David J. Pickelner
Tapestry by Evelyn Curly, Navajo
Page 147

Margaret and Lewis Ranieri
Maya sculpted and carved ceramic bowl
Page 161

In Memory of Eleanor Houghton Anderson Ray
Tsistsistas (Cheyenne) feather bonnet
Page 89

The Slovin Family
Feather cape (?), upper Ucayali River, Peru
Pages 18–19

Doris Stone
Siberian Yupik parka
Page 41

Ellen and William Taubman
Tsimshian mask
Page 128

Eileen A. Wells
Black-on-white pottery jar by Lucy Lewis,
Acoma Pueblo
Page 208

Elaine and James D. Wolfensohn
Inupiaq kayak
Pages 118–119

Anonymous
Beaded moccasins, upper Missouri River
Page 7

Anonymous
In Honor of Futures for Children
Unangan (Aleut) model *ikyak* (baidarka)
Page 40

MIXTEC SHIELD INLAID WITH
TURQUOISE MOSAIC, 15TH C.
PUEBLA, MEXICO. DIAM. 31.8
(10.8708)

INTRODUCTION
A BACKWARD GLIMPSE
THROUGH THE MUSEUM DOOR
TOM HILL

In museums and Native American communities across the Americas, significant changes are taking place. There is fundamental new thinking about issues of cultural rights and responsibilities—about who, if anyone, can speak for the carvers and basket-makers, weavers and bead-workers, potters and painters whose work has been collected and studied for the past 150 years. As Nancy Mitchell, an Apache anthropologist, has put it, "The meaning of acquiring and interpreting ethnographic objects is no longer as clear and obvious a practice as it was in the past; Native Americans are asserting their right to manage their cultural patrimony."[1]

This book is a work-in-progress about issues that will engage our intellect and emotions well into the next century. It is also a personal account of the journey Rick Hill and I took through the collections of the National Museum of the American Indian, a journey that reawakened our senses to values, beliefs, and practices that once prevailed on this continent—and that still prevail within many communities. We have written from our experiences as museum professionals and as artists. Most of all, we have written as Native Americans living in the late twentieth century, with contemporary understandings of the spiritual ways of our forebears.

At times, our observations challenge the scientific interpretations of our colleagues, the museum's anthropologists, whose scholarship is also reflected in these pages. In some instances, we have simply added our own understandings to theirs; in others, we have noted where the views derived from their training differ from those offered by our traditions. What Native

Americans know of the past depends partly on what has survived in our cultures to this day and partly on our personal emotions, intuitions, and experiences, which have been shaped by our cultures. We have tried to include the perspectives of other Indians, as well, through their songs, poems, memoirs, and historic records.

The difficulties of learning to see with fresh eyes became obvious when we began to work from photographs of objects that had been removed from their original environment and placed in the museum. We yearned to penetrate the haze of past museum practices and public attitudes that had accumulated around the objects over time and to ask new questions about them. We tried to see the objects in the context of art, an exercise that revealed the inadequacy of existing museum documentation to encompass Native American artistic traditions. We found ourselves frustrated as well by our inability to escape the vocabulary of European-American art history and criticism.

Perhaps our goal of creating a new, Native American criticism was impossible from the start: collecting objects from other cultures is a Western concept, whether the objects are to be admired for their aesthetic power or studied for what they reveal about the cultures that produced them. As we struggled to express our thoughts, we found ourselves drawn back into the Western mind-set. Yet rather than forcing us to surrender our Native American consciousness, this struggle sharpened our awareness and offered us new insights, new historical perspectives.

✳

What has the relationship between Native Americans and museums (and their visitors) been in the past? During the nineteenth century, as the frontier advanced across native lands, collectors and museums in North America and Europe acquired colorful and exotic pieces from Indians who had been displaced and impoverished. What began as a hobby or a means to satisfy public curiosity, however, was given legitimacy through the rise, in the second half of the century, of a new social science: anthropology.

Anthropology lent credibility to collecting and justified investment in museums. Ethnocentric bias—including the notion that cultures evolve from primitivism to civilization, or, more basic still, the idea that science and scholarship, rather than faith, experience, or imagination, are the keys to understanding cultures—was institutionalized. Museums and universities decided upon the essential training and work of anthropologists: the collection, classification, and display of material culture, with occasional interviews to aid in understanding the origins and uses of artifacts.

Museums soon accommodated immense collections of "scientific specimens" and "artifacts of primitive peoples." Objects seized as pagan idols and superstitious nonsense and clothing that was ridiculed and, in some cases, prohibited from being worn in towns and on reservations, were put on proud display in prominent institutions. These anthropological collections became the primary sources of public information about and exposure to the indigenous

CHEROKEE DEERSKIN COAT, CA. 1800. LENGTH 101 CM (2.353)

SHELL MOUND. LAUDERDALE COUNTY, ALABAMA. PHOTOGRAPH BY THE WORKS PROGRESS ADMINISTRATION. (N41581)

cultures of the Americas. Indeed, scientifically catalogued artifacts—stripped of their spirits and their connection to the people who made and used them—became the means through which cultures were defined. Dr. Bea Medicine, a Lakota anthropologist, calls this once-popular methodology "laundry-list anthropology. . . . The material goods assumed more dynamic qualities than the people themselves."[2]

Whatever the vast volumes of anthropological investigation were worth to European-Americans, they were of little value to native communities. Research findings seldom made their way back to communities that had given generously of their time and hospitality to the inquisitive strangers in their midst.

Behind glass in museum cases, Native Americans were frozen in the past. European-Americans stopped wearing knickers and three-cornered hats without losing their identity. Yet native people who evolved, adapted, and made creative accommodations to the passage of time were disparaged as not being "real Indians." Ironically, this happened at the same time governments, churches, and other social institutions were making every effort to force us to cease "being Indian."

The public, educated about Indians by dime novels, the press, advertising, tourism, and, later, Hollywood, went to museums to see more of the same: the stereotype, the exotic, the scalp, the tomahawk—images and stories that excited European-Americans and confirmed their impressions of their own history. The noble savage, the bloodthirsty warrior, the "Vanishing American," the Mongolian crosser of the Bering Straits—all were presented as unchanging realities, incapable of meeting the advance of civilization and progress, trapped in the time-warp of exhibition dioramas.

In all this, there was no shortage of good intentions. The Indian past, actively being extinguished in the world, would be preserved—half relic, half trophy—in the museums of the extinguishing culture. But there could be no question about the fact that Indian culture was to be displayed and studied as a thing of the past, and the recent past at that. The Indian world was to be described in the simple past tense, lacking both a long history and a viable future. Perhaps Vine Deloria summarizes this attitude and its effect on living peoples most succinctly: "The American public feels most comfortable with the mythical Indians of stereotypeland. . . . To be an Indian in modern American society is in a very real sense to be unreal and ahistorical."[3]

It was not until the 1960s and the rise of political activism, among Native Americans no less than in the rest of society, that important shifts in museum practices began to occur. Museums, which had considered themselves above criticism, came under attack from traditional Native Americans, tribal leaders, and militant chapters of the American Indian Movement (AIM). Archaeologists were halted in mid-shovelful at their excavations. Native Americans were tired of being treated by museums as if they were extinct. At a recent conference at the University of Toronto, Mohawk art historian Deborah Doxtator explained the Indian reaction: "The very presence of religious objects on display in museums symbolized the power and control of white society over native peoples." Anthropological exhibits displaying skeletal remains in the name of science, she says, drove the point home.[4]

In 1969, the press—and all of North America—was forced to confront these issues after armed Indians seized Alcatraz, in San Francisco Bay, and proclaimed it Indian land. "We moved into Alcatraz Island because we feel that Indian people need a cultural center of their own," the occupiers announced. "For several decades, Indian people have not had enough control of training their young people. We hope to reinforce the traditional Indian way of life by building a cultural center on Alcatraz Island. We hope to build a college, a museum, a center of ecology, and a training school."[5]

That cry for cultural revitalization and self-determination was dealt with as criminal conduct. Nineteen months after the occupation of Alcatraz began, it was put down by the U.S. Coast Guard and federal marshals. But in 1972, a group under the banner of "The Trail of Broken Treaties" led a massive occupation of the headquarters of the Bureau of Indian Affairs in the heart of Washington. Later, protestors from the First Nations occupied the headquarters of the Canadian Minister of Indian Affairs, Jean Chrétien, now Canada's Prime Minister.

The modern-day Indian protest with the greatest impact, however, took place in 1973. Following a number of Indian beatings and deaths throughout the Plains, Native Americans from across the continent mobilized in a series of events that led to a confrontation with federal marshals at Wounded Knee, on the Pine Ridge Reservation in South Dakota. At the site of the infamous massacre of the Sioux in 1890, members of AIM faced the most heavily armed force of white soldiers to confront Native Americans in this century.[6] For both militant and moderate, things would never be the same after this cultural and political reawakening.

Museums were not immune from native activism. In 1970, the Six Nations Iroquois Confederacy petitioned the courts for the return of twenty-six wampum belts held by the New York State Museum in Albany. In 1971, as a partial response to Indian protests, California passed legislation granting a moratorium on the excavation of burial sites abandoned for less than two hundred years. Archaeologists learned that what was scientific research to one culture was grave-robbing to another.

The National Congress of American Indians, founded in 1944 to promote self-government, headed a moderate political front that persuaded the Nixon administration to adopt a plan for Indian self-sufficiency. Under the plan, several nations built new museum facilities. The rationale behind creating these cultural institutions may have been to stimulate economic growth, yet the museums also helped native groups regain control over their own heritage and develop a sense of themselves as nations. In Canada, Indian-led cultural institutions took shape during the 1970s. And Pacific Coast nations began their efforts to recover potlatch treasures and gifts confiscated by the Canadian government during the decades when native ceremonies were banned.

James Hanson, in his article "The Reappearing Vanishing American," noted the manner in which native museums fostered "group pride, intercultural understanding, and positive self-image. . . . These museums," he wrote, "serve important psychological needs and provide stability and security."[7]

Somehow, during this period of consciousness, energy, and determination, Native Americans found a way to move toward seemingly contradictory objectives: they developed a pan-Indian identity that emphasized intertribal unity, particularly in the cities, and, at the same time, they reaffirmed traditions unique to their own tribes and nations. Nations restored their former names. In Canada, "Indians" became "natives," then "First Nations," and then, at least for the time being, "aboriginal people." In the United States, the term "Native American" came into use.

The impact on European-American institutions of this

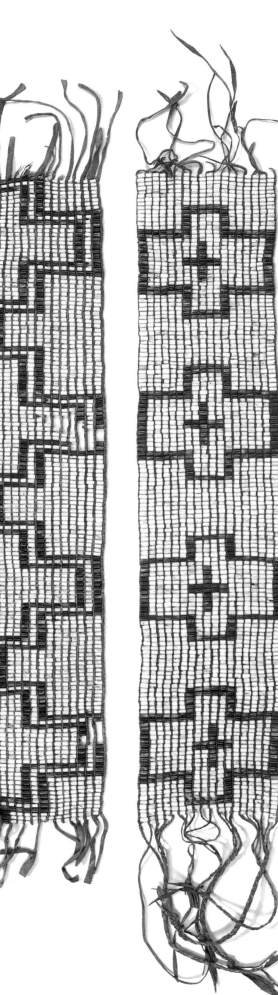

WAMPUM BELTS, 18TH C. (?).
EASTERN WOODLANDS.
LENGTH 100.3 AND 97.8 CM
(5.3150 AND 5.3151)

spontaneous renewal of the Native American spirit has been positive, but slow to effect change. Museums and universities, at first resistant to—even angry over—intrusions into their domain, have begun increasingly to support cultural self-determination by the original peoples of this hemisphere. New theories within anthropology call into question the once-assumed objectivity of museum exhibitions that present native material. Art history now accommodates interdisciplinary methods and less hierarchical, more socially contextualized interpretations. Emerging scholarship more closely reflects Native Americans' traditional notions of artistic expression, in which art is an integral element of life.

This renewal is sustained by tribal communities and cultural leaders—as well as by individual artists who seek ways to express native ideals in their work. After all, the arts, which epitomize human achievement, have always played an essential role in helping us understand the world in which we live.

✳

Let me take one last glimpse through the museum door into the past. When I was growing up, a family elder, Ezekiel Hill, was a speaker at the Sour Springs Longhouse. He was also a member of the False Face Society. I remember he kept the masks entrusted to him hanging behind his woodstove. He never used them to frighten me, and I learned by his example to treat them with great respect. These powerful presences came from a distant realm of the human past. They made an indelible spiritual impression on me, especially when I saw them during the ceremonies, in the presence of my family and our community. In those ceremonies, the masks' power was integrated with the energies of those who wore them in a timeless ritual of healing.

Ezekiel told me about the masks, but only when I asked. "Why is the nose crooked?" I would ask. Or, "What do you feed them?" And Ezekiel would explain. He told me how the masks were carved from living trees that consented to sacrificing a part of themselves. He reaffirmed my confidence in what I had seen and experienced: that, in the ceremonies, the masks had the power to focus the attention of all who saw them on natural forces that we experience but cannot understand. Through the masks, I learned about good and evil, the Creation, healing, and respect. They gave me a sense of history, too, a feeling of being part of a long chain of life.

I realized later that Ezekiel was not the only one who had masks: museums found them irresistible public favorites, amusing displays. But these exhibitions never captured the masks' spirit. Whenever I see a mask in a museum, I think how different it is from those that hung by Ezekiel's stove. Behind glass, they become objects. I feel insulted and denigrated by the way they are treated, and I can understand how they have become emotional symbols of cultural control and loss. Some Iroquois enjoy seeing a connection between the fire that ravaged the New York State Museum many years ago and the power of the masks imprisoned there.

Strangely, I think some anthropological pioneers, including Franz Boas and Claude Levi-Strauss, although collectors to the core, began eventually to understand the meaning and purpose of ceremonial art. In the early 1960s, Levi-Strauss set out to write about the savage mind, but he ended up with a realization of how complex and subtle that mind could be:

A vase, a box, a wall are not independent, pre-existing objects which are subsequently decorated. They acquire

their definitive existence only through the integration of the decoration with the utilitarian function. Thus, the chests of the Northwest Coast are not merely containers embellished with a painted or carved animal. They are the animal itself keeping an active watch over the ceremonial ornaments which have been entrusted to its care. Structure modifies decoration, but decoration is the final cause of the structure, which must adapt itself to the former. The final product is a whole: utensil–ornament, object–animal, box that speaks.[8]

I think the false faces would not mind being described in similar terms—as spiritual unities.

*

Despite experience, many Native Americans wish to transcend the past and join with others in building for the future. Those who were formerly mere objects of study are inviting anthropologists and museum professionals to be their partners in that work.

Institutions, too, are taking clear steps toward partnership with Native Americans. The legislation creating the National Museum of the American Indian (1989), the Native American Graves Protection and Repatriation Act (1990), and Canada's Task Force on Museums and First Peoples (1991) outline principles and recommendations to address past inequalities between museums and Native Americans and establish excellent guidelines for future cooperation. Regarding the National Museum of the American Indian's collections—founded, ironically, on the great wealth of native objects acquired by George Gustav Heye (1874 to 1957), perhaps the epitome of the obsessive collector—policy explicitly states: "All Native American materials, including human remains, funerary objects, ceremonial and religious objects, and communally owned property, together with all culturally specific information, must be treated as the sole property of the affected Native American culturally affiliated group and with the utmost respect by scholars and interpreters of those cultures, whether in collections research, scientific study, exhibitions, or educational programs."[9] The Canadian Task Force has called for new partnerships between institutions and First Peoples to be based on such principles as mutual appreciation, the recognition of shared interests, and full involvement by Native Americans in the development of policies and programs. All this is a far cry from the practices of the past.

This book documents Rick Hill's and my own creative journey as we tried to describe the elusive spirits of native objects and the lessons they may have for us today. Whether we acknowledge it or not, each of us is on such a journey. We live in a world filled with contradictions—rich in possibilities, yet beset by tragic social problems. Perhaps the values expressed in a cradleboard, a mask, or a lovingly made coat can help guide us toward solutions. Children raised in the worlds of these objects and the beliefs they embody understood that life moves in a circle and that all creation is related. That knowledge led them to take responsibility for how they lived on the earth.

Traditional native values can help guide museums as well. No longer monuments to colonialism, these institutions may be led to a truly new world in which cultures have genuine equality and creators and creations can be seen whole. We hope readers will join in the effort to construct new cultural paradigms for the twenty-first century. Museum doors, like all doors after all, have two sides. After this brief glimpse backwards to the past, let us refocus our vision on the future.

FEATHER CAPE (?), EARLY 20TH C.
COLLECTED ON THE UPPER
UCAYALI RIVER, PERU.
LENGTH 80.5 CM (19.5983)

GROWING UP INDIAN
TOM HILL AND RICHARD W. HILL SR.

The native understanding of the world begins with the Creation. Elaborate Creation stories are told all over the hemisphere and provide the best means to understand our world views and traditions—and, thus, our arts. Origin stories teach us what kind of people we hope to become, what kind of contribution we hope to make, what kind of legacy we hope to pass on to our children. In some ways, life's journey is an effort to keep the wisdom from the time of Creation a part of our everyday existence.

Iroquoians, like many other natives, believe that the Creation is ongoing and that people were placed on earth to re-create the Creator's good works—that is, to be creators. The Iroquoian Creation, like all such stories, is a complex epic. It would be a mistake to assume that our synopsis here includes all the truths that have evolved through its retelling over time.

In the beginning, people lived beyond the sky, because deep waters covered the entire earth. Then, a pregnant woman fell from the Sky World toward the water. All the water animals, such as the beaver, otter, and muskrat, saw her fall reflected in the water, and they argued over whether she was coming up from the watery underworld. The ducks and geese, however, believed she was falling from the sky. They flew up to break her fall with their overlapping wings, protecting her from the terrors of the water. They carried her to the Great Turtle, master of all animals, who told them to set her down on his strong back. First, however, he ordered the water animals to dive to the bottom of the water and bring up some earth that had

LAKOTA TURTLE AMULETS, LATE 19TH/EARLY 20TH C. 22.5 X 19.0 X 2.8 CM (12.2273)

HOPI GIRL HOLDING KATSINA DOLL, AUGUST 27–28, 1938. ARIZONA. PHOTOGRAPH BY HAROLD KELLOGG.

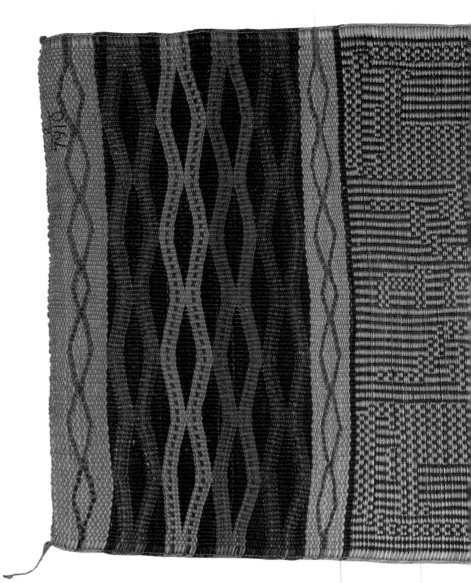

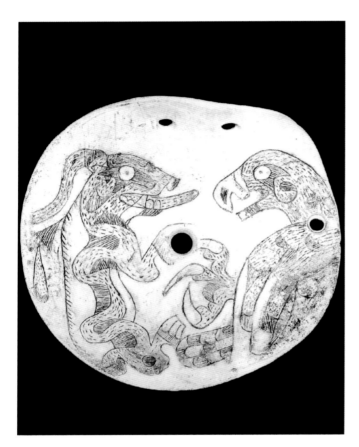

SHELL GORGET WITH UNDER-
WATER PANTHER AND CELESTIAL
BIRD, CA. A.D. 1200–1500. TEXAS.
DIAM. 14 CM (22.7574)

WHITE BREAST'S FAMILY,
MESQUAKIE. TAMA, IOWA. (35631)

MESQUAKIE RUSH MAT AND DETAIL
OF PANTHER, LATE 19TH C.
182 X 92.5 CM (2.7910)

fallen from the sky with the woman. When this magic earth was placed on his back, the woman was told to dance upon it in a sunwise circle. As she did, the Great Turtle began to grow into a large island.

Eventually, the woman gave birth to a daughter, who in turn gave birth to twin sons: Teharonhiawako, born naturally through the birth canal, was responsible for all good things that grew, such as corn, fruit, and tobacco; his brother, Sawiskera, born through the mother's armpit, was responsible for weeds, vermin, and other earthly evils. Sawiskera, the evil-minded one, would continually disrupt or alter the creations of Teharonhiawako: Teharonhiawako would create a rose and Sawiskera would add thorns. The brothers fought, and eventually Teharonhiawako banished his twin into the dark and night.

Many native cultures explain the universe in this way, as a layered structure, with the earth suspended between the vault of the Sky World and the murky realm of the Underworld, entered through the deepest lakes and rivers. Humankind must mediate between the Sky World and Underworld in order to preserve the well-being of the earth. The slightest change in the harmony and balance of the natural world would summon the powers of these antithetical forces.

The Sky World and Underworld are personified by a pair of mythical beings—a celestial bird or thunderbird and an underwater

panther or water serpent—who are engaged in a life and death struggle. Images of these two beings appear on objects from very early times. A stylized panther confronts a fierce bird of prey on a shell gorget made by an engraver from the Mississippian culture (A.D. 700 to 1500). Perhaps a thousand years later, a Mesquakie weaver in Iowa created a composition of ideal balance depicting the supernatural panther in his underwater realm.

✶

Children are born within circles of tradition that define the world views of their communities. For example, an Iroquoian child's first moccasins are punctured to keep the relationship between the child and the earth intact. Traditional birth, with the mother squatting down to deliver her baby, symbolically pulled the child to the earth.

  Each culture has a distinctive philosophy about how to raise children. Many native groups, however, used cradleboards. Strapped in their vertical cradles, children saw the world from the same viewpoint as adults. This Mohawk cradle (p. 24) has a stiff back to support the child, a footrest for the baby to push against, and a curved bow to protect the baby's head if the cradleboard should fall. The baby would be wrapped in a cloth beautifully beaded with designs the child would later wear on his or her clothing. Sometimes silver brooches were pinned to the wrap.

  Even more important than these manifestations of love and protection is the symbolism of the cradleboard's decoration.

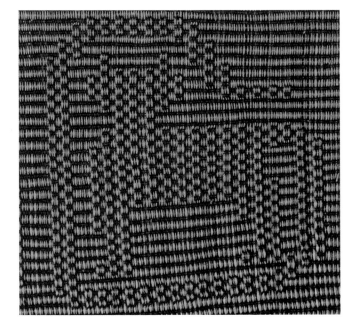

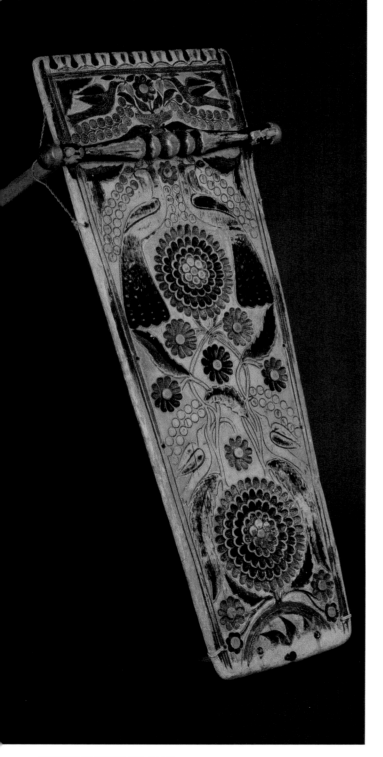

The backs of many Iroquois cradleboards are carved and painted with designs that include a flowering tree holding a mother bird feeding her young. The Iroquois believe that such a tree, full of flowers, fruits, and bright lights, exists in the Sky World. Arches representing the Sky World and images of the celestial tree were sewn onto the beaded skirts mothers wore as well.

Another tree, the white pine, is a metaphor for the Great Law of Peace, the constitution that united the five original Iroquois Nations—the Seneca, Cayuga, Onondaga, Oneida, and Mohawk—into a confederacy during the late sixteenth century. (A sixth nation, the Tuscarora, joined in the early eighteenth century.) People were encouraged to sit at the base of the tree if they sought peace in their lives. Images of the tree often show roots spreading in the four cardinal directions. People understood that if they grasped the white roots and followed them back to the tree, they would find peace and unity. Secure in an Iroquoian cradleboard, the child was symbolically tied to all the traditions its imagery represents.

Sometimes, too, a turtle—an important symbol to the Iroquois and many other peoples—sits at the base of the flowering tree. Or, instead of a turtle, the carver may add the clan animal of the mother—as that is also the clan of the child—or clan effigies of both parents. The clan remains a primary level of identity in many native cultures. The clan system connects the child to other people within the community, and, among the Iroquois, links the Six Nations. Clan ties extend to distant nations as well. The child is a new voice that will carry on the traditions of the clan.

After the early twentieth century, few families used cradleboards. Many non-Indian health officials claimed that cradleboards caused physical deformities. Since the 1970s, however, there has been a resurgence in the use of cradleboards, and today they are again symbols of the strong bond between children and traditions. In every Iroquois community, cradleboards can be found in the homes of younger families, and babies are often introduced to their neighbors from their cradleboards.

*

Children learn by observing. They learn through the rhythms of the community, the songs, dances, and annual cycles of rituals and events. Iroquois women are encouraged to dance when they are pregnant so that their children will feel the rhythms of life. Children who can't dance well are said to have come from mothers who didn't dance when they were pregnant. The cadences of songs, stories, drums, flutes, and rattles are soothing to children.

Among many native groups, there was, traditionally, a seasonal calendar for storytelling, setting a rhythm of learning. In some cultures, winter was a time for stories; in others, stories about history might be told anytime, but other stories were reserved for special times. Through stories, the ways of the ancestors were made real for children, and the world around them became a powerful place. Stories taught problem-solving and lessons about life. There were humorous stories and adventure stories of great deeds. There

MOHAWK CRADLEBOARD (BACK),
19TH C. LENGTH 78.7 CM (18.7090)

were stories just for children. Some stories could be animated with miniature figures.

Learning to tell stories starts with learning to listen. To show respect for storytellers and other speakers, children were taught not to interrupt. Turn-of-the-century Oglala Lakota elder Standing Bear wrote that children learned to use all their senses "to look when there was apparently nothing to see, and to listen intently when all seemingly was quiet."[1]

*

Traditional native toys reaffirmed the child's identity, rather than taking him or her away from the family's world. Elaborately decorated dolls encouraged children to respect the ways of their people. Old-fashioned Iroquois cornhusk dolls—like dolls from many other cultures—were dressed in clothing like that worn by adults, and some carried cornhusk babies in miniature cradleboards. These dolls traditionally had no faces. People believed that children would see the faces the Corn spirit wanted them to see—that the Corn spirit would nourish their imaginations. Other toys were smaller versions of the things used by adults, often made with the same care. For many groups, children's things had special spirits.

*

Try to imagine what it was like to grow up in a time when making things was a never-ending part of daily life. Household goods, hunting equipment, clothing, and religious objects were produced within the community. Every day included artistic creation and spiritual expression. Children were surrounded by artists.

Imagine the time after trade goods became available, when people were introduced to new tools, materials, and ideas. Metal kettles, knives, and other tools made daily life easier. Glass beads, trade cloth, steel needles, spun thread, mirrors, and other new goods challenged people's imaginations and enriched their creativity.

Think of what childhood must have been like for the Seminole or Miccosukee boy who wore a colorful shirt his mother had made him, so much like his father's shirt. Or for the Alaskan children who watched their father carve his bow drill, knowing he was sharing with them his happiness in his life, pride in his work, and love of the world.

These worlds of creativity and imagination still exist. Many native households today make traditional clothing for powwows and ceremonies, utensils for rituals, objects of spiritual faith and power. Some Indians make native objects and artworks for sale; in supporting their families, they bring new skills and ideas to ancient arts. Today, as in the past, nearly every native person is related to an artist. The creative process is still an integral part of growing up Indian.

KIOWA GIRL WITH TOY CRADLE-BOARD, CA. 1890. PHOTOGRAPH BY IRWIN AND MANKINS.

You day-sun
Circling around
You daylight
Circling around
You night-sun
Circling around
You poor body
Circling around
You wrinkled age
Circling around
You spotted with gray
Circling around
You wrinkled skin
Circling around

—SEMINOLE BIRTHING SONG

Miccosukee women began making patchwork clothing during the early decades of the twentieth century. By incorporating bands of simple patchwork designs into their families' clothing, they created a textile art that was to flourish, among both the Seminole and Miccosukee, throughout the twentieth century.

Until the 1920s, the Miccosukee and Seminole—descendants primarily of Creek Indians who settled in Florida beginning in the 1700s—lived in relative isolation. Their camps were made up of *chickees*—thatched-roofed, open-walled houses—built around a communal fire. Practically all household activities centered on the family chickee. There, Miccosukee and Seminole mothers and daughters sewed *foksikco.bi*—big shirts—for their husbands, fathers, sons, and brothers, and long skirts and capelike blouses for themselves.

These two big shirts are fine examples of patchwork designs from the mid- to late 1920s, when patchwork was becoming popular. This boy's big shirt is made from calico and has a single row of patchwork in the skirt, blouse, and each sleeve. Notice the care the maker took to match the sawtooth patchwork pattern on the sleeves and body. The man's big shirt has two rows of patchwork in the skirt, blouse, and each sleeve, as well as stripes and rickrack.

By the turn of the century, nearly every Miccosukee and Seminole family owned a sewing machine. Before they began making patchwork, women and girls decorated their families' clothing with appliqué and ruffles. At first, their patchwork bands were relatively uncomplicated. Later, women developed more intricate patterns, incorporating a greater number of colored cloths into each piece of clothing.[1]

In 1928, with the opening of U.S. Route 41 linking Tampa and Miami, tourists began to visit Miccosukee and Seminole camps. Eventually, the Miccosukee and Seminole set up craft shops. The palmetto doll shown here is typical of those made for sale. While the production of patchwork soon became a commercial enterprise and an important source of income, this distinctive textile art remains an expression of cultural identity, as well as of family love and care. Today, while store-bought clothing is worn every day, on special occasions such as the Green Corn Ceremony or for tribal gatherings, the Miccosukee and Seminole almost always wear patchwork, whether it's a patchwork vest or baseball cap.

C.R.G.

MICCOSUKEE–SEMINOLE BOY'S
FOKSIKCO.BI (BIG SHIRT), CA.
1925–1935. LENGTH 36 CM (20.3627)

MICCOSUKEE–SEMINOLE MAN'S
FOKSIKCO.BI (BIG SHIRT), CA.
1925–1935. LENGTH 152 CM (19.5115)

SEMINOLE WOMAN IN TRADITIONAL
DRESS. FLORIDA. (P14116)

MICCOSUKEE–SEMINOLE DOLL, CA.
1935. HEIGHT 38.1 CM (22.1549)

PRAIRIE POTAWATOMI DOLL, LATE
19TH/EARLY 20TH C. HEIGHT
25.8 CM (24.1799)

HUICHOL DOLLS, FIRST HALF OF
THE 20TH C. HEIGHT 35.8 CM AND
37.5 CM (20.8070 AND 20.8071)

These dolls, from cultures half a continent apart, exemplify rich and complex traditions. Familiar and appealing as children's toys, they also remind us of the imagination that all people share. Yet they are mysterious as well, suggesting unseen worlds of belief.

The doll at left, made of hide with painted features almost obscured by time and wear, is dressed in a fashion worn by women of the Great Lakes, the original home of the Potawatomi Indians before some of the tribe was relocated to Kansas in the mid-nineteenth century. Her brooches and earrings, the property of a wealthy woman, are replicas of nineteenth-century jewelry stamped and engraved by native smiths from rolled sheets of a copper, zinc, and nickel alloy known as German silver. Her bear-claw necklace is a symbol of sacred power. She also wears a beaded bag for sacred medicine, a faithful copy of a full-size bag down to the different designs on the front and back (in this case, on the back, a blue and white checkerboard). She carries a leather paint bag, probably for vermilion used in curing. The stick in her belt may represent a prescription stick marked with formulas for administering sacred medicines.

In the past, every young Potawatomi was encouraged to undertake a vision quest for a manitou, a spirit that would be his or her lifelong protector. Many designs on clothing and personal possessions such as medicine bags refer to this spirit. Individuals fortunate enough to acquire a powerful manitou became wealthy not only in worldly goods, but also in spiritual power, and were accorded great respect. Potawatomi culture remains highly spiritual, and some young people today embark on vision quests.

The worn, soiled surface of these Huichol dolls from western Mexico—a family made of cornhusks and cardboard, realistically painted and wrapped in beautifully woven textiles—attests to the fact that they were loved and cuddled. But these dolls, too, are more than toys. They are one way a mother communicates Huichol values to her child.

Weaving is an integral part of Huichol culture. When a woman passes her treasured designs to her daughters and granddaughters, she gives them important information about their place as women within Huichol society.[1] Young girls learn that they will be highly respected if they become accomplished weavers, able to bring the powers of the supernatural world into their textiles.[2]

A weaver conceives new designs through dreams, peyote visions, and the study of live reptiles. The eight-pointed star or *toto* flower depicted on these dolls, one of the most popular Huichol designs, is associated with peyote. Through this process of creating, a woman achieves a deeper understanding of her physical, social, and spiritual world. By weaving the images she has seen into textiles, she preserves her insight for future generations. Women thus become keepers of sacred knowledge essential to the well-being of Huichol culture.[3]

M.J.L. and N.R.

The American flag motif, a striking design element on this bandolier bag, is not unusual on objects of native manufacture, especially those dating to the turn of the century. In fact, around that time, a relatively large number of objects incorporating American flag motifs were produced, due, quite possibly, to the growing importance among native peoples of Fourth of July celebrations. During the late 1800s, the U.S. government discouraged or outlawed many Native American celebrations. The Fourth of July became one of the few opportunities for Indian peoples to come together to dance, feast, and publicly observe their traditions.

Many activities, such as giveaways, distinguished Indian Fourth of July celebrations. A giveaway is held by family members to honor a relative. During giveaways, gifts—often elaborate, exquisitely wrought, and extremely valuable items, such as bandolier bags—were presented to friends and neighbors. Today, star quilts and Pendleton blankets are popular giveaway gifts.

Bandolier bags have a long history throughout much of native North America. Among the peoples of the western Great Lakes, early bags were made of darkly dyed hides decorated with porcupine quillwork. Bags with fabric foundations and woven beadwork panels, attached to woven beadwork baldrics or bandoliers, became common only in the latter part of the nineteenth century.[1] Although originally catalogued as Chippewa (Ojibwe), this bag has since been identified as Winnebago; Winnebago bandolier bags are distinguished by their loose-warp technology, bandoliers made from one, rather than two sections, and offset straps.[2] In addition to its nine sets of crossed American flags and twelve smaller flags, this bag is decorated with wool tassels, faceted glass beads, and red, white, and blue silk ribbon.

Among the various Great Lakes groups, beaded bandolier bags were considered essential items of ceremonial dress. They were not, however, primarily functional. These bags signified prestige, and it was not unusual for a man or woman to wear two or more bags at a time. This finely woven Winnebago bandolier bag may well have been made to be worn—or presented as a gift—at a Fourth of July celebration.

C.R.G.

WINNEBAGO (?) BANDOLIER BAG, LATE 19TH C. 86.3 X 37.8 CM (19.3217)

LAKOTA BEADWORK MADE FOR SALE: "JOE CLAYMORE BEADWORK EXHIBIT, FIRST PRIZE," CA. 1915. FORT YATES, NORTH DAKOTA. PHOTOGRAPH BY FRANK B. FISKE.

OSAGE CHILDHOOD
DIANE FRAHER

*The female Red Bird replied, I shall
    cause your children to have bodies
    from my own.
My left wing shall be a left arm for
    the children.
My right arm shall be a right arm
    for them.
My head shall be a head for them.
My mouth shall be a mouth for them.
My forehead shall be a forehead
    for them.
My neck shall be a neck for them.
My throat shall be a throat for them.
My chest shall be a chest for them.
My thighs shall be thighs for them.
My knees shall be knees for them.
My heels shall be their heels.
My toes shall be their toes.
My claws shall be their toenails.
You shall live forever without
    destruction.
Your children shall live as human
    beings.
The speech of children I will bestow
    on your children.*

—FROM THE CHANT OF THE RED EAGLE CLAN, OSAGE

WAH-ZAH-ZHE (OSAGE) HA-A-HEAN
(RIBBONWORK BLANKET),
20TH C. 181 X 155 CM (23.6986)

WAH-ZAH-ZHE (OSAGE) W'ON-DOP-SHE
(CRADLEBOARD), EARLY 20TH C.
108 X 35 X 34 CM (23.6985)

OSAGE GIRL IN RIBBONWORK BLANKET
WITH TRADITIONAL PATTERN, "FROM
HANDS THAT LOVE YOU TO YOUR HANDS."
LOUISIANA PURCHASE EXPOSITION,
ST. LOUIS, MISSOURI, 1904.

Among the Osage or Wah-zah-zhe (Children of the Middle Waters), some of the old people said that when the cradleboard was empty, the bentwood bow must be pushed down flat or else it was bad luck. That might be your first experience of culture: your family lovingly taking care to protect you from harm. From then on, grandparents, aunts, and even other siblings traditionally take part in teaching you who you are.

Almost as important as the elders' instruction is a child's participation in the I'lon-ska ceremonial dances. Through these dances you receive your name and traditional clothes, including your blanket. The ribbonwork pattern and colors worn on your clothes become outward symbols of your identity. Only you may wear your blanket.

Ribbonwork is done in a variety of patterns. There are individual family patterns and clan patterns and even patterns from the two major divisions of the tribe. This woman's blanket is a Turtle pattern from the Hunka division. The inner border of double sawtooth is unusual and was made with great care. Both sides of each sawtooth were folded under and held in place simultaneously by hand as they were stitched. The exact symmetry of this piece also testifies to its maker's skill. Traditionally, the wool broadcloth used to make a blanket denotes a child's place within the family: the eldest son or daughter wears red; the second son, a combination of red and blue; all other sons and daughters wear blue. (All children are loved equally, but older sons and daughters have greater responsibilities within the family.) The ribbons on this blanket are pure silk moiré. Osages are extremely fond of royal purple and delight in using it in their ribbonwork.

Before you may dance, you must have your Indian name. Once you receive your name from a clan elder, other clan members become your relatives. When people die, the Creator calls them up by their Indian names.

The old people, born before the turn of the century, are gone, but their wisdom is still followed. Today, some elders say that they do things a little differently in their district or their clan, but interpretation is as unique as identity. During the nineteenth century, the Osage people moved west from their ancestral home along the Mississippi River in Missouri to reservations in Kansas and finally Oklahoma, where this cradleboard and blanket were made. Great flexibility and pragmatism were keys to the culture's survival, as they are today. This way of being is something you wrap around yourself and wear like a blanket. When you are away from home, the identity given to you by your people protects and comforts you, for you always know who you are.

Sleep, sleep,
it will carry you into the land of
* wonderful dreams,*
and in your dreams you will see
* a future day*
and your future family.

—YUMA LULLABY

YUMA CRADLE, LATE 19TH/EARLY
20TH C. LENGTH 58 CM (8.8621)

KIOWA BEADED CRADLE, CA. 1910.
104 X 30.5 X 27.5 CM (2.8380)

MOTHER AND CHILD, BLACKFEET.
GLACIER NATIONAL PARK,
MONTANA. (P21544)

Many kinds of baby carriers were used throughout native North America. At home during much of the day, babies were swaddled in soft wrappings, secured in simple hammocks, or carried about on their mothers' backs snugly wrapped in shawls. At other times, babies were placed in cradles of more elaborate construction, like this beaded Kiowa cradleboard (right). Unique in the repertoire of Kiowa beadwork—which is usually restricted to small, intricate motifs—cradles frequently display bold geometric or abstract floral designs. This cradle, dating to the early twentieth century, is remarkable in the variety of images its maker created—American flags, antlered elk, and numerous buildings. The hourglass-shaped figures near the bottom on each side derive from stylized bison hides painted on the buffalo robes of an earlier generation.

A rigid cradle of wood, rawhide, or basketry served many purposes. Well-wrapped and secure within the frame of the cradle, a baby could be hung from a saddle while traveling or suspended from a nearby tree while the mother worked away from home. The projecting rim or hood protected the baby's head in the event of a fall and supported a covering that could be draped over the baby's face to ward off sun, wind, or insects.

Cradles provided spiritual protection as well. For the Arapaho, neighbors of the Kiowa, each element of a traditional cradle referred to an aspect of the sacred cosmos, and together the decorations constituted a visual prayer for a long life. Cradles were passed down from one child to another, unless a baby died. Then, the cradle was considered unlucky and was discarded or placed in the child's grave.

In addition to their protective properties, cradles were important social markers. In societies in which the bonds of family are paramount, a child holds an important position linking the kinship networks of the mother and father. Among the Arapaho, Lakota, Atsina, and Cheyenne cultures of the central Plains, cradles were given to an expectant mother as gifts from the father's family. They symbolized the family's respect for her and their future support for her child. There was great prestige associated with receiving many cradles, demonstrating that the child was born into a large group of kin and one with the resources necessary to celebrate important life events. Gifts from the mother's family did not carry the same prestige, as their support for her was already assumed.

Great care was taken in making cradles. Enriched by their association with the bonds of kinship, they came to be given as honoring gifts on occasions other than births.

The use of elaborate cradles declined in the early twentieth century, although they are still made on a limited scale, principally for gift-giving and for display in craft shows. It is the simpler home traditions of baby care that continue today, as do the strong and complex ties of kinship into which each child is born.

J.C.E.

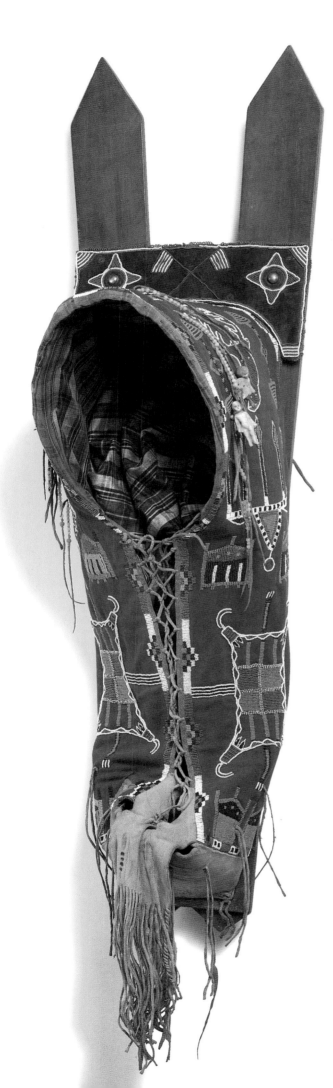

"My mother used to tell me that when I was still a baby in the cradle, she would strap my cradle to her saddle and drive a herd of ponies across the prairies, sometimes all day long."

—ARAPAHO WOMAN, CA. 1930

"When I was little I stayed with my grandfather. . . . He told me to always get up early in the morning. He said that when I grew up to be a man, always get up early and feed and water the horses. He said to take care of the horses and keep them fat, because they would take care of me and help me find something to eat. . . . He said that there were many ways to use corn and that there were going to be many more, and that was why I should never forget to raise it. . . . He told me always to give blessings for food and be thankful for my home."

—JIM WHITEWOLF (BORN CA. 1880), KIOWA APACHE

Kiowa women wore small beaded bags, heavily fringed with metal cones, or tinklers, hanging from their belts. Together with a knife sheath and awl case, these bags held all the small items a house-wife and mother of an earlier time might need on a moment's notice to care for her family—sinew for sewing, tinder and steel for starting a fire, and so on. Men carried similar containers tied to their bows to meet their needs when away from home. After the reservation system was established, the same bags were used to keep government ration tickets.

Belt bags are among the few Kiowa objects covered with solid areas of beadwork, often in complex geometric, abstract, or semirealistic designs. (In contrast, narrow bands of tiny geometric forms were applied around the borders of clothing.) The Kiowa may have learned these patterns, as well as beading techniques to create curved lines, from eastern tribes such as the Lenape (Delaware) after the government moved them to Indian Territory in present-day Oklahoma.

Although all women were expected to be competent at beading, a few individuals in each generation were recognized within their communities as master bead-workers, and for a girl to be trained by one of them was an honor. Working within the broad canons of tribal style and current fashion, individuals sought to create new patterns through the harmonious use of color and form. Women owned the designs they created. A pattern could not be copied without the owner's permission, although it might be given away, particularly to a young relative whom the bead-worker was training, thus becoming, in effect, a family design. Similar rights of authorship applied to other craft products—for example, silverwork patterns—as well as to nonmaterial arts such as songs and stories. Today, creativity and innovation in beadwork are still esteemed, and Kiowa women still wear three belt cases symbolically designated for sinew, knife, and awl when they put on traditional dress.

J.C.E.

KIOWA BEADED BAGS, EARLY
20TH C. 47 X 11 CM AND 43 X 10 CM
(2.4378 AND 10.5403)

KIOWA GIRLS IN TRADITIONAL
DRESS. (36370)

HUNKPAPA LAKOTA GIRLS. (37975)

"Two teeth remain after everything else has crumbled to dust . . . and for that reason the elk tooth has become an emblem of long life. . . . When a child is born . . . an elk tooth is given to the child if the parents can afford the gift."

—OKU'TE, LAKOTA ELK DREAMER, EARLY 20TH C.

The elk-tooth dress was a garment of particular prestige throughout the Plains. Indeed, among the Crow (Absaroke), elk-tooth dresses became impressive gifts, appropriate for the formal exchanges associated with the settlement of conflicts, transfer of ceremonial prerogatives, or celebration of marriage.

Elk teeth were used primarily as decoration on women's dresses. As each elk has only two teeth of the type used for adornment, scarcity made them valuable. The Swiss collector Rudolph Kurz, who visited the Crow in 1852, reported that one hundred elk teeth cost as much as a pack horse. Some dresses were adorned with hundreds of teeth.

This dress was collected on the northern Plains around 1855 by Thomas S. Twiss, the Indian agent for the upper Platte district, which included the territory of the Lakota, Cheyenne, Arapaho, and other tribes. Its construction is typical of the northern Plains style in which the design and decoration are closely tied to the natural shape of the deerskin from which it is made. Two hides are required for such a dress, one forming the front and the other the back. The pieces are sewn together at the shoulders, with the hind portions of the hide folded over to create a yoke, the tails serving as pendants on the breast and back. The sides are seamed below large cape sleeves formed from the hind legs, and the neck and forelegs create a deeply scalloped hem. Heavy fringes and rows of beadwork emphasize the garment's structural lines.

The earliest glass trade beads to reach the Plains were large, suitable for use as pendants or strung into necklaces. By the early decades of the nineteenth century, beads about an eighth of an inch in diameter, often called pony beads, were widely available. These small beads could be sewn to garments as a form of embroidery, and creative native craftswomen quickly developed techniques for their use, based on established traditions of embroidery with dyed porcupine quills. In addition to narrow bands of beadwork around the edges of garments, bands were sometimes placed side-by-side to cover larger surfaces such as the yoke of a dress. By mid-century, even smaller beads in a greater variety of colors became available; these seed beads largely replaced pony beads, except among the groups of the northwestern Plains and the adjacent Plateau region where the older style of beads long remained popular. Following the adoption of seed beads, designs became more complex and the amount of beadwork placed on garments increased.

J.C.E.

GIRL'S DRESS, CA. 1850. NORTHERN
PLAINS. LENGTH 107 CM (5.3776)

Miniature models of kayaks, often fitted out with figures and equipment, have long been popular mementos for travelers visiting the Arctic. This one was collected in the Kuskokwim area of western Alaska, an important intertribal trading center.[1] It depicts a three-man Aleut *ikyak*, or baidarka, with three sea otter hunters wearing painted wooden hunting hats.

The Aleuts—whose name for themselves is Unangan—have lived for perhaps eight thousand years in small settlements along the shores of the foggy, windswept, and treeless Aleutian Islands. Kayak hunting on the open sea, out of sight of land, navigating by winds and ocean currents, demands supreme physical and intellectual skills. Young boys are trained very early in strength, agility, observation of animal behavior, and understanding of the frequently shifting weather patterns of the Aleutian Island chain.

The Aleut baidarka is the fastest and technically most sophisticated sea-hunting kayak ever invented, uniquely adapted to heavy seas and foul weather. Its distinctive shape—a two-part bow and square stern—has both practical function and symbolic meaning. The flared baidarka bow allows the craft to ride over waves rather than plunging directly into them, while the square stern provides stability. Symbolically, the craft is said to resemble a sea otter swimming on its back with forepaws to chin. Sea otters, seen as transformed human beings, fond of finery and adornment, were important in traditional belief. Carved sea otter images helped protect hunters.

Early accounts indicate that hunters wore elaborately painted and decorated wooden hats to honor the spirit of the sea otter and entice him close to the baidarka. It has also been suggested that the hats functioned as masks, hiding the hunters' human identity and changing them into beings with special powers and vision. Such hats were the property of wealthy and important men.

In the traditional societies of the Arctic the creation of clothing was a woman's responsibility, and wives were skilled in fashioning garments that were not only water- and weatherproof, but also beautiful. Little girls learned very early, often by making doll clothes, the sewing techniques that would provide warm, dry clothing for their families. This gutskin parka, made to be worn by a hunter while paddling a kayak, exemplifies both beauty and utility.

Gutskin parkas are fashioned from long strips of seal or walrus intestine sewn together in folded seams to ensure that the garment will be watertight. The sinew thread swells slightly when wet, adding to the parka's waterproofing. The seams are often decorated with cormorant feathers and pieces of auk beaks. The bottom edge of the parka fastens around the cockpit of the kayak, making the hunter and his boat virtually one.

Model baidarkas have been found in archaeological sites and may at one time have had ritual significance. Since the late eighteenth century, they have been made as curios, and they continue to be made as souvenirs today.

M.J.L.

"We're not just Eskimos anymore. That's what my grandmother told me. . . . She said I'd be lucky if I even remember when I'm older what it used to be like in our village. . . . Then she told me what my mother did at my age—the same thing her mother did."

—NATIVE ALASKAN GIRL, 1970s

ESKIMO MAN IN BAIDARKA.
COOK INLET, ALASKA. (36097)

SIBERIAN YUPIK PARKA,
LATE 19TH/EARLY 20TH C.
LENGTH 116 CM (6.8652)

The man who engraved the handle of this bow drill succeeded in creating, with a few simple strokes, scenes from a life filled with work, play, music, danger, and domesticity. Bow drills are sturdy and cleverly designed tools, useful not only for drilling holes, but also for starting fires by friction. Engraved walrus-ivory bows have been made and used throughout the Arctic since ancient times. Thousand-year-old bows from the Thule period, found in archaeological sites, reveal the same rich variety of forms and activities seen in bows from the nineteenth century. We do not know why they were decorated. Perhaps they illustrate personal histories or record hunters' tallies; perhaps they are artistic expressions, pure and simple. Whatever their purpose, they reveal an ability to create art despite the most difficult living conditions. And as windows onto the past, they reveal a world that surrounded children in the Arctic for hundreds of years.

The principle of the bow drill is ingeniously simple. The cap piece is held between the teeth—leaving a hand free to steady the material being worked—while the shaft is inserted into a hollow in the cap. A cord is wound around the shaft, and as the bow is sawed back and forth it causes the drill to rotate. The drill, made of stone or metal, is hard enough to drill holes in ivory, bone, antler, or wood.

The images engraved on three sides of this bow span the yearly range of activities. The first portrays hunting scenes: four hunters drag the carcass of a walrus, while three other hunters in kayaks, armed with spears and throwing boards, pursue a group of seals. The second side shows a settlement with three large skin tents, a kind of dwelling used on both sides of the Bering Strait. A man appears to be calling a dog. Two watercraft, kayaks or umiaks—open boats—are stored on racks. The antlered animals may be Alaskan caribou, but are more likely Siberian reindeer. The third side shows a pair of winter houses. Meat racks outside keep supplies out of the reach of hungry dogs. A man standing on the roof appears to be adjusting a line, which holds a fur pelt. In another winter scene, three drummers provide music for dancers, whose arms are flung into the air as they dance with joyous abandon. In the next scene the season has shifted to a summer tent, fish drying on a rack, and the frame of an umiak in storage with its cover removed. Finally, a hunter is engaged in combat with a bear.

Engraving on ivory became a popular form of tourist art in the 1890s during the Alaska gold rush. Miniature images decorated pipes, cribbage boards, jewelry, and other kinds of curios. Yet the carvings on bow drills have a particular, personal appeal, for each is a statement about how one man saw his life—busy, energetic, joyous, and brave.

M.J.L.

The lands around my dwelling
Are more beautiful
From the day
When it is given to me to see
Faces I have never seen before.
All is more beautiful,
All is more beautiful,
And life is thankfulness.
These guests of mine
Make my house grand.

—IGLULIK POEM

INUPIAQ BOW DRILL, LATE 19TH/
EARLY 20TH C. LENGTH 48.2 CM
(BOW), 15.9 CM (MOUTHPIECE),
24.8 CM (DRILL) (9.4635)

MAN USING BOW DRILL TO MAKE
CRIBBAGE BOARD, CA. 1902-1903.
ST. MICHAEL'S, ALASKA.
PHOTOGRAPH BY MILES BROTHERS.

CHILKAT TLINGIT TUNIC WITH
BEAR DESIGN, 19TH C. LENGTH
96 CM (7076)

Sometime in the early decades of the nineteenth century, women in the northern part of the Northwest Coast developed a way to re-create in wool and shredded cedar bark complex and beautiful crest designs that men painted on wood and hide. This new technique is known as Chilkat weaving—after the Chilkat division of the Tlingit, whose women were its most prolific masters—although oral tradition credits Tsimshian weavers with its invention. Fringed Chilkat dancing blankets were widely traded up and down the coast. Far fewer Chilkat tunics were made. This extremely fine example, described in museum records as depicting a Bear, is clearly the work of a master weaver.

Chilkat blankets and tunics are ceremonial dress, worn on important occasions such as potlatches, formal gift-giving ceremonies that confirm their hosts' generosity and social rank. Their crest designs entail family histories told to children through folktales, songs, and oratory.

Russian and European explorers who ventured into Prince William Sound and Tlingit and Haida territory along the coast during the eighteenth century—before the invention of Chilkat weaving—described high-ranking, wealthy persons wearing robes of a distinctive zigzag weave known today as *yeil koowu*, or Raven's Tail. This pair of dance leggings is made from a cut-up yeil koowu robe. During the nineteenth century, and apparently earlier as well, blankets were sometimes cut into pieces and distributed as potlatch gifts. The pieces were usually fashioned into leggings, bags, hats, or decorative strips for clothing.

Both yeil koowu and Chilkat weaving are made with mountain goat wool, but they differ in several ways. Yeil koowu uses as many as nine twining techniques, while Chilkat weaving uses only three. Chilkat weaving incorporates yellow cedar bark in the warp strands. Clearly, though, the most visible difference is in the style. Yeil koowu echoes the linear designs on baskets, also produced by women. Chilkat weavers followed the curvilinear crest designs that men painted for them on pattern boards.

Knowledge of yeil koowu seems to have disappeared from memory in the late eighteenth or early nineteenth century. Today only eleven early yeil koowu weavings are known to exist in museum collections, some in fragments. Another four appear in early artists' renderings or photographs. Through the efforts of several weavers, however, the techniques of Raven's Tail weaving have been rediscovered and revived and the pattern is again being worn for ceremonial occasions.[1]

M.J.L.

If I do not take anything to the party
I shall be ashamed.
I shall be ashamed.
Little girls, listen.
—TLINGIT CRADLE SONG FOR A GIRL

CHILKAT DANCERS. HAINES,
ALASKA. (P20128)

DANCE LEGGINGS MADE OF A YEIL
KOOWU (RAVEN'S TAIL) ROBE,
EARLY 19TH C. COLLECTED FROM
THE NISGA'A VILLAGE OF GITLAK-
DAMIKS. LENGTH 31 CM (1.4177)

Why does he cry softly?
Why does he wriggle as he sits?
He wriggles and cries for
grandfather's house.

—HAIDA CRADLE SONG

These two Wolf figures, carved of cedar wood and placed within a traditional Haida clan house, are symbols of clan and lineage history, a history that claims ancient relationships with natural and supernatural beings and forces. The house posts would have been commissioned by a wealthy house-owner, carved by an artist of the opposite side of the Haida, and dedicated with feasting, masked dancing, recitations of clan histories, and a potlatch in which the host presented valuable gifts to the guests.[1]

Two centuries ago, a child born in a Haida village, on the Queen Charlotte Islands or the Northwest Coast mainland nearby, grew up witnessing constant, visible reminders of his or her place in the social hierarchy, the natural world, and the mythical timeless past and future. The huge winter house of cedar planks reflected, physically and spiritually, these several worlds. It had been built by the wealthy chief who occupied the highest-ranking place, against the back wall, marked by emblems such as these Wolf posts. The several families sheltered within its walls, related by clan membership or marriage, acknowledged their place in the social order by where they slept—high-ranking families close to the house-owner, poor relations and slaves near the door.

A house, like the lineage it sheltered, was considered immortal. Just as each child was the reincarnation of an ancestor and so named, the name of a house was also passed down.[2] During long, dark winter nights the house became a ceremonial space, sheltering dancers, drummers, singers, and speakers who brought to life ancient stories and ancestral spirits.

The entrance to a Haida house often displayed a giant totem pole carved from a red cedar tree. Many Haida poles were topped with small crouching figures wearing high-crowned hats. Known as watchmen, they had special powers and could warn the house-owner of approaching danger. The figures on the pole also depicted family crests and histories, including incidents from the mythic past.

During the nineteenth century, the Haida people suffered devastating population losses, primarily from epidemics of smallpox and other diseases. By 1900, most of the great beamed communal houses and carved totem poles had fallen into ruin, replaced by European-style frame dwellings. The last quarter of the nineteenth century was a time of intense museum collecting on the coast, and a number of carvers were commissioned to produce models of houses, totem poles, and canoes as a way of recording a traditional life that was perceived as having passed away.[3]

Through the efforts of a few Haida artists, a cultural revitalization began in the 1960s, marked in 1969 by the artist Robert Davidson's carving of the first totem pole to be erected in ninety years at the Haida village of Masset. A carved and painted house built in memory of the artist and chief Charles Edenshaw, Davidson's great-grandfather, was dedicated there in 1978. Another house and pole were later built at Skidegate. Today dances, songs, and ceremonies are again performed in the old way.

M.J.L.

HAIDA HOUSE MODEL, LATE 19TH C.
HEIGHT (TOTEM POLE) 90 CM
(7.3031)

HAIDA HOUSE POSTS, 19TH C.
HEIGHT 2.3 M (17.6682 AND 17.6683)

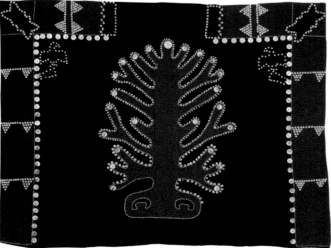

During the Kwakiutl Tseyka or Red Cedar Bark Dances, young men of noble families are initiated into the prestigious Hamatsa or Cannibal Society with songs and rituals passed down from their ancestors. The ceremony reenacts a novice dancer's kidnapping, his reappearance as a wild man-eater, and his eventual capture, taming, purification, and return to the human world. Part of the Hamatsa ritual is the entrance of dancers dressed in cedar bark and wearing masks of giant man-eating birds, with great beaks that snap open and shut. The mask shown here depicts the Cannibal Raven, servant of the Cannibal-at-the-North-End-of-the-World. The dramatic effect of these great birds, seen only by firelight in the great room of the bighouse, swaying to drumbeats and songs and snapping their beaks ferociously, can only be imagined in a museum setting.

Native observances like the Red Cedar Bark Dance were banned by law in Canada from the late nineteenth century until 1951. Yet the Kwakiutl never stopped performing their rituals. The ceremonies flourish today, together with the custom of distributing potlatch gifts to guests to affirm the family treasures and privileges being celebrated.

Beautiful robes, called button blankets in English, are worn at potlatches and other ceremonial occasions along the Northwest Coast. These robes have been referred to as "totem poles on cloth,"[1] for, like totem poles, many display family crest designs that proclaim hereditary rights and obligations. The design of this Kwakiutl blanket, however, is shared by many families. It is known as Gwa'ka'lee'ka'la, or Tree of Life, and, like the name of the Red Cedar Bark Dances, refers to the sacred importance of the cedar tree for Northwest Coast people. The red flannel border on this, and many, button blankets is also said to depict red or yellow cedar.

First created in the nineteenth century, when trading was well established along the Northwest Coast, button blankets have from the beginning been made almost entirely of foreign trade goods: English broadcloth, often in the form of Hudson's Bay blankets; mother-of-pearl buttons imported from China and Europe; and red wool flannel. From these nontraditional materials the artists of the Northwest Coast fashion designs of great beauty, grounded in centuries-old family, clan, and tribal histories and traditions.

Turn-of-the-century museum collectors passed button blankets by, considering them less authentic than things made of indigenous materials. Since then, we have come to recognize that culture and identity live on despite foreign contact and change. Today button blankets are worn not only on traditional occasions, but to mark contemporary milestones, including museum exhibition openings. One church uses a button blanket as an altar cloth, while in 1992 a hospital in Alaska was presented with a button blanket at a gathering of communities from Juneau and elsewhere to celebrate native heritage.

M.J.L.

Look at me, friend!
I come to ask for your dress,
For you have come to take pity
    on us;
For there is nothing for which
    you cannot be used, . . .
For you are really willing to give
    us your dress,
I come to beg you for this,
Long-life maker.

—KWAKIUTL PRAYER TO THE CEDAR TREE

KWAKIUTL MASK REPRESENTING
RAVEN, LATE 19TH/ EARLY 20TH C.
LENGTH 89 CM (1.2180)

KWÁGHITOLA, KWAKIUTL ARTIST,
CA. 1960. BRITISH COLUMBIA.
(P19648)

KWAKIUTL BUTTON BLANKET, LATE
19TH/EARLY 20TH C. 182 X 139.7 CM
(11.5129)

POLES IN CHIEF'S HOUSE CHILKAT.

GIVING THANKS FOR WHAT WE HAVE AS INDIANS

RICHARD W. HILL SR.

In 1989, as part of a group of elders, I visited Haida Gwaii, on the Queen Charlotte Islands off the British Columbian mainland. Great feasts were held for us. After we were seated, a song started, and in danced the women carrying large wooden trays of salmon, seaweed, and clams, proudly showing the food to all. Each dancer wore a decorated button blanket. As the dancers danced around the tables, swinging their trays from side to side, their blankets gently twirled, and you could see the striking images of their family crests, outlined in mother-of-pearl buttons against dark blue, black, or bright red backgrounds. It was the first time I had seen the blankets worn; before, I had only seen them displayed on flat boards, under glass, at an angle dictated by museum conservation concerns.

The feasting ended with dances by the children of the community. As the hand drums began to beat, the young dancers prepared to enter the dance, their robes swinging around their shoulders. Three or four dancers entered together in a line, and you could see that the same animal was treated differently on different blankets. You could also see the community aesthetic at work, all the designs that together make up Haida art.

To see people wearing these "robes of power" (as my friend Doreen Jensen, a Gitksan artist, has called them) was something I will never forget. The older dancers swung their shoulders to make their blankets open. Eagles appeared to soar; the Raven mimicked their actions. Bears stood proud.

Somehow, seeing the young and old dancing that night, I felt that the animal spirits would be proud of their people, for surely the dancers showed their thankfulness to those spirits. It was at that moment that I realized clothing was a form of visual prayer, a way to give thanks for what we have as Indians by proudly wearing the symbols of that connection. I went home and began to make our daughter her own dress, in the style of our ancestors. I had sewn the designs before—the sky dome, the celestial tree—but now the designs meant more to me. Each bead, every stitch, each design carried more weight.

In November 1992, my family attended the opening of an exhibition I had worked on at the Custom House in New York City. Our daughter wore her beaded dress at the powwow to celebrate that opening. After the powwow, we went up to the top of the Empire State Building, and I pointed out to our kids all the buildings that were built by Iroquois ironworkers. When we returned to the car, someone had broken into it and stolen the bag with our daughter's dress, as well as the traditional clothing of our two sons.

Our daughter was heartbroken. She said that she could never dance again. She was six years old. I felt so defeated, wondering what I had done wrong that the Creator would let such a thing happen. My wife and I had spent months sewing the beadwork on those clothes. I woke early the next morning after a restless night. I prayed to the Creator, reminding him how much that dress meant to all of us. For some reason, I went back to where the car had been parked and walked around for two hours, searching every garbage can, every alley, everywhere, hoping against all odds that I would find the clothing thrown away. I wondered if the dress would mean anything to whoever stole it. As I was about to give up, I walked down one final alley. There was an old street guy, holding up our daughter's shawl as if he was trying to figure out what it was. Over his arm was our son's ribbon shirt. I said, "Excuse me, but those are mine." He showed me where he'd found them. To my surprise, laid out all over the sidewalk, were our daughter's beaded skirt, her overdress with large brooches, her leggings and bead crown; our sons' clothing and moccasins were there as well. I was so happy, I shoved a bunch of money in that old man's hand and jumped in a cab.

When I returned to the hotel and gave our daughter her dress, I nearly cried. The Creator wanted our daughter to have her dress. I figured that he must like the way she looks when she dances in that dress.

CHILKAT GIRL WEARING BUTTON BLANKET. ALASKA. PHOTOGRAPH BY LLOYD WINTER AND PERCY POND.

SENECA SILVER BROOCHES, 18TH/EARLY 19TH C. MADE BY NATIVE AND NON-NATIVE SILVERSMITHS. HEIGHT 2.5 TO 6.1 CM (2.9711)

YOUNG SENECA WOMAN.

Before the development of a non-Indian market for baskets in the mid-nineteenth century, basketweaving among the Yurok, Karuk, and Hupa peoples of northwestern California served everyday needs. Women made pack baskets, food-processing baskets, cooking and serving baskets, water containers, ceremonial baskets, basketry caps, and trinket baskets. A well-provisioned family needed six baskets just to store seeds.[1]

Close-twined conical baskets like this one were used for gathering seeds. Women bent grass stems over the mouth of the basket and beat them with a wicker beater or stick. The seeds were parched over hot coals before they were stored or ground and eaten.

A young girl learned to weave baskets by watching the older women in her family. At first she would play at copying their work; later her mother, grandmother, or aunt might start a root basket for her. By the age of ten or twelve, a child would be making baskets for household use.

Baskets were space- or close-twined and were generally made from hazel or willow rods with flexible root twining materials. Decorative patterns were created with overlays of white grass, black maidenhair fern, and *Woodwardia* fern dyed reddish brown. Experienced weavers knew how to shape each basket to conform to standard proportions and how to place the designs properly; they also knew which color combinations were appropriate. Not only weaving, but all the processes of gathering, preparing, sorting, and storing basketry materials are included in a single Hupa word that means *make*.[2]

Working in horn and bone was another skill used to produce traditional tools and utensils. Men ate acorn mush, a favorite dish, with spoons they carved from elk horn, as here, or, occasionally, deer horn or wood; women ate with mussel shells or pieces of undecorated elk horn or deer bone. Both men's and women's spoons were stored in small, open twine baskets hung in the plank house where the family gathered for meals.

The Hupa, Karuk, and Yurok lived in towns along the lower Klamath and Trinity Rivers, a heavily forested, mountainous region. Although they spoke unrelated languages, they shared many political, economic, and religious institutions and beliefs; they attended each other's dances, traded, and followed nearly identical lifestyles and customs. In fact, although this basket is catalogued as Hupa, it may be Yurok or Karuk, so similar are the designs and techniques.

The introduction of metal pans and commercial containers eventually rendered most utilitarian baskets obsolete. In the late 1920s, Yurok and Karuk weavers said that seed baskets had not been made for years and that old ones were now used exclusively to gather herbs for the Brush Dance, a curing ceremony. These baskets were never sold, although a weaver might make a replica on order. Today, elk-horn spoons, too, are collector's items. Acorn mush, however, is still eaten on special occasions by the Hupa.

E.H.B.

POMO WOMAN GATHERING SEEDS, EARLY 1920S (?). YOKÁYA, CALIFORNIA. PHOTOGRAPH BY EDWARD S. CURTIS.

KARUK ELK-HORN SPOONS, LATE 19TH/EARLY 20TH C. LENGTH 12 CM TO 18.3 CM (5.2311 [3], 18.9665, AND 18.9666)

HUPA DANCERS IN JUMPING DANCE,
1893. YUROK TOWN OF PATWIN,
KLAMATH RIVER, CALIFORNIA.
PHOTOGRAPH BY A.W. ERICSON.

HUPA ELK-HORN PURSES, LATE
19TH/EARLY 20TH C. LENGTH 15.8
CM, 12.7 CM, AND 16.2 CM (1371,
8847, AND 10.8164)

TOLOWA ELK-HORN PURSE, LATE
19TH/EARLY 20TH C. LENGTH 16 CM
(5.4496)

HUPA STRUNG DENTALIUM SHELLS,
LATE 19TH/EARLY 20TH C. LENGTH
70 CM AND 65 CM (2585 AND 8141[2])

Elk-horn purses were used to store strings of dentalium shell beads, the most common form of currency used by the Hupa, Tolowa, and their neighbors. Wealth was of great religious and social importance to the peoples of northwestern California and further north along the Pacific coast. Although he had no formal authority, the man with property settled feuds, negotiated the marriages of his relatives, shared his money and food with his kin and followers in times of need, and organized communal fishing and hunting. The more generous his expenditures, the greater his standing within the community—and the greater his responsibilities as well. He not only provided the woodpecker-scalp headdresses and other treasures worn at the dances, but also, with his family, all the food for the annual feasts.

Men crafted purses from elk or deer antler, carving a slit down one side of a section and scraping out the porous core. A small splint was placed over the opening and the whole piece wrapped with a strip of buckskin. Decoration included grooves rubbed with pigment and blackened incised triangles and zigzags. Dentalia—thin, tubelike shells—were sometimes wrapped with tiny strips of snake- or fish skin with tufts of red woodpecker feathers fastened at the tips.

Each dentalium shell had a fixed value according to size, although shells shorter than about one and seven-eighths inches were not considered currency and were left undecorated. Standardized systems for counting shell money existed throughout the region. A Hupa man would measure individual shells against the creases of his left hand. Or he might measure a string of five equal-sized shells against a series of lines tattooed on the inside of his left forearm.

Other valuables were also used for exchange, including scarlet-feathered woodpecker scalps, albino deerskins, and large chipped red and black obsidian blades. Like dentalia, these things had to be acquired through trade, a factor that increased their worth. Festivals provided a wealthy man with the opportunity to display his treasures. In the Jumping Dance, a ceremony held by the Hupa to ward off famine and other misfortunes, participants wore buckskin headbands decorated with rows of red woodpecker scalps. Men performing in the White Deer Dance held albino deerskins high on long poles and carried obsidian blades tied with buckskin.

Although wealth was inherited in the male line, it could be acquired in other ways as well. Shamans collected high fees from their patients. Wrongs ranging from personal insults to injury or homicide could be settled only by paying reparations to victims or their families. Marriage, too, could increase property; wives produced foodstuffs and gave birth to daughters who, in addition to contributing their labor, might one day command high bride prices. Wealth itself was used to acquire additional wealth: trade was one possibility; gambling, another. Every transaction was based on the complex significance of wealth.

E.H.B.

Although their precise origin is not known, woven beadwork T-necklaces have come to be an essential part of girls' ceremonial dress among the Tonto, Cibecue, San Carlos, and White Mountain Apache of east central Arizona. Distinctive to these peoples, T-necklaces have been worn by Apache girls since the early twentieth century. The necklaces shown here are typical of that period and are woven in peyote stitch. Since that time, T-necklaces have become longer, wider, and more ornate. Many today are decorated with figures—perhaps eagles or mountain spirits—or are composed of large, beaded medallions.

T-necklaces are always worn in the four-day Sunrise, or Na-ih-es, Ceremony. Held the summer after a girl's first menstrual cycle, the Sunrise Ceremony prepares her for adult life by calling on the spiritual presence of Changing Woman, who is also called White Painted Woman or White Shell Woman. Nowadays, the Sunrise Ceremony begins on Friday. Before sundown, the girl is ceremonially dressed by her godmother, while the medicine man directs the placement of ritual articles he has blessed, including an abalone shell, which identifies the girl with Changing Woman, an eagle feather, a reed drinking tube, and a scratching stick.

Early Saturday morning, the Sunrise Dance takes place. Blankets covered with a buckskin are laid on a specially prepared dance ground: cartons or burden baskets filled with candy, fruit, and coins have been placed to the east; a basket or abalone shell filled with sacred yellow pollen, to the west. The medicine man, singers, and drummers stand behind the buckskin, facing east. The girl, accompanied by a friend, stands in front of them. When the singing begins, the two girls dance in place, stepping gently from one foot to the other. Together, they dance to songs that tell of the creation of the universe and of Changing Woman. As these sacred songs are sung, the girl receives the power of Changing Woman and becomes holy. She will remain holy for the next four days.

Dressing and performing the Sunrise Dance are only two of several elements of the Sunrise Ceremony. And although the ceremony is intended to grace an adolescent girl with the gifts of Changing Woman, including physical and spiritual strength, the presence of Changing Woman touches the entire community. During the four days following her dance, while the girl is invested with special spiritual powers, people line up to bless her with yellow pollen and pray for her. She, too, blesses and prays for them. In this way she learns to share in the life of her community and is brought to maturity.

C.R.G.

WHITE MOUNTAIN APACHE BEADED T-NECKLACE, EARLY 20TH C. 29 X 26 CM (9.4608)

WHITE MOUNTAIN OR SAN CARLOS APACHE BEADED T-NECKLACE, EARLY 20TH CENTURY. 29 X 27 CM (10.5586)

WESTERN APACHE COUPLE, CA. 1884. (P6788)

"It is dancing day. All the people are very happy. They have brought some corn and watermelons for the children. . . . In the afternoon, just when the kachina stop dancing, for their dinner, there is a big rain storm. As soon as they eat their dinner, they start dancing again. It is still raining. Everybody gets wet, the kachina also. The water is running. We can see the water everywhere, the water is running all over the fields. So we are very glad. . . . In the evening the kachina bring some dolls and arrows and bows for the children."

—CROW-WING
PUEBLO INDIAN JOURNAL
JULY 27, 1921

The name Hopi, from Hopisinom, signifies to the Hopis a life of peace, harmony, tranquility, and fellowship with every living being. Katsinas represent the life spirit of all things; the earth, wind, the entire cosmos is represented through the katsinas. They are messengers, intermediaries who take the prayers of the people to the forces of nature to bring rain for the crops, children, and long life.[1] For half the year, the katsinas live in the Hopi villages, pueblos on three great mesas rising above the high desert of northeast Arizona; then they return to their home in the peaks of the San Francisco Mountains.

Long before the Emergence—the time when the ancestors climbed up into this world—the katsinas taught the Hopis their dances, still performed today. Dancers represent these katsina deities; carved and painted *tithu* (katsina dolls) represent the dancers. Dancers give the dolls as gifts to the children of the pueblo, especially to little girls. Since the late nineteenth century, katsina dolls have also been made for sale.

The tihu to the near left represents Taawa, the Sun katsina who warms the crops in the fields below the Hopi mesas. He carries several ears of corn and a pouch of sacred meal. Taawa appears at the village of Oraibi on Third Mesa during the winter solstice festival called Soyalangwu, when prayers are sent to bring the sun back from his journey to the north. The ceremony marks the beginning of the new year and of the new katsina season.

Mongkatsina (right) represents the highest katsina priest-hood. The slat of wood in the tihu's hand represents a chief's badge. Mongkatsina is the leader of the katsinas at the late winter ceremony called Powamuy, also known as the Bean Dance, when the katsinas make their annual return to the village. As part of this ceremony, the katsinas bring bean plants to the people, a blessing that symbolizes the germination of crops in the spring.[2]

Mosarusmana—Buffalo Maiden (far left)—is seen with Buffalo Youth in the Momsayrutu, or Buffalo Dance, a social dance. She wears a fringe of hair over her eyes and a symbolic squash blossom with two eagle feathers on her head; her dance kilt is decorated with cloud and falling rain symbols.

At the Ninan ceremony, following the summer solstice, the katsinas distribute the first corn of the season and depart for their homes in the springs and mountains to the west. Tithu made throughout the year are hung on the walls of Hopi homes, although children also play with them.

E.H.B.

HOPI MONGKATSINA TIHU (CHIEF KATSINA DOLL, ABOVE), LATE 19TH C. HEIGHT 35 CM (18.4594)

HOPI TAAWAKATSINA TIHU (SUN KATSINA DOLL, LEFT), LATE 19TH C. HEIGHT 42 CM (18.6259)

HOPI MOSARUSMANA TIHU (BUFFALO MAIDEN DOLL, FAR LEFT), LATE 19TH/EARLY 20TH C. HEIGHT 30 CM (19.4052)

The Kaapor (Wood-Dwellers)—erroneously known as the Urubu (Vultures)—who live in the lush tropical forests of northeastern Brazil, are known for their spectacular feather ornaments, which they refer to as *putir*—flowers. Kaapor children learn when they are very young that featherworking is a source of great pride. Men and women alike devote much of their time to making feather ornaments, particularly before ceremonial feasts. Truly elaborate pieces bring prestige to the wearer; community leaders and heads of important families often have the finest featherwork.[1]

The right to wear certain ornaments depends on age and gender. For example, a few days after a male child is born, his lower lip is pierced and a small feather is placed in the hole. About the same time, the ears of both boys and girls are pierced, and they begin wearing miniature earrings. As children get older, they wear larger ornaments.[2]

This necklace (right), called a *tukaniwar*—adornment of the toucan—is worn exclusively by women and consists of a thick strand of small orange toucan feathers and a mosaic pendant of iridescent blue and red cotinga feathers. Miniature versions of the tukaniwar are made for young girls. The *rembe-pipo*—tongue feather—is worn by men and consists of four scarlet macaw feathers that serve as a base for a mosaic of blue and black cotinga feathers. The contrast of colors is striking on both ornaments—in effect, they resemble stylized birds.[3]

Elaborate ornaments like these are worn by adults for ceremonial occasions, the most important of which is the naming feast. When a child is three months old, he or she is officially presented to the community. Frequently on the same day, boys and girls who have reached puberty are initiated into the community of adults.[4]

Maíra, the culture hero of the Kaapor, is responsible for creating the world and all its peoples, and it is through his legendary exploits that the origin and nature of things is explained. Through the stories told about him, children learn the symbolic importance of feather ornaments. For example, blue feathers evoke the sky and the supernatural beings who live there. In origin myths, Maíra wears the same types of ornaments. To the Kaapor, feather ornaments not only identify them as true Indians, but also represent the ideal of being *hantan*—hard—and strong like Maíra.[5]

N.R.

KAAPOR TUKANIWAR (WOMAN'S FEATHER NECKLACE, RIGHT), 20TH C. 16 X 23 CM (23.3269)

KAAPOR REMBE-PIPO (MAN'S LABRET), 20TH C. 12.3 X 30.2 CM (23.3267)

The oldest known ceramics in the Americas were made circa 3200 B.C. by people of coastal Ecuador. Fragments of figurines like those shown here lie scattered in great numbers along the beaches near the Valdivia archaeological site. Children who find small figures in the sand are unaware of their significance. They think the figurines look like toys and often sell them to eager tourists.

Most of these ancient figurines are female; perhaps they represent the ideal woman of that time. They are highly stylized— trapezoidal and solid, with prominent breasts, short arms often crossed below the breasts, and fat legs. The heads are more individual and realistically modeled, with flat faces, long necks, and elaborate, carefully executed coiffures. The eyes and eyebrows are incised, perhaps by the makers' fingernails. Most of the figurines are nude, revealing their sex. Red paint on a few of them suggests body-painting.

The figurines were not made in molds, but were produced by hand on a large scale. There is great variety in their proportions, facial expressions, and remarkable hairstyles. It is not clear what these differences indicate; perhaps they are changes in style that took place over time.

The figurines are usually found in fragments. This has led some scholars to theorize that they were used in fertility rites or prayers to the earth for a good harvest, then thrown on the ground as offerings. Others believe that the figurines were made for healing ceremonies, after which they were thrown away to get rid of bad spirits. The shamans and healers of some Indian groups in Colombia today use small wooden figures in a similar way; while the figures play an important role in the ceremony, they lose their power afterward. Another hypothesis is that Valdivia figurines were offerings to Pachamama (Mother Earth) and Taita Orccu (Father Mountain), in the same way that, much later, the Inka offered small human and animal figures to these spirits.

For centuries people have gathered Valdivia figurines as souvenirs or for good luck. Knowledge of their original use and the traditions surrounding them has been lost, perhaps forever. But we can still appreciate their form. And by comparing contemporary native customs to these archaeological remains, we can try to understand their meaning.

R.M.

CERAMIC FIGURINES, CA. 3200 B.C.
VALDIVIA, ECUADOR. HEIGHT 8.5 TO
12.7 CM (24.8400, 24.8401, 24.8404,
24.8726, AND 24.8727)

TUSCARORA AND MOHAWK BEADED
HATS, 19TH C. HEIGHT 14.5 AND 10.5
CM (3.2302 AND 19.5729)

VISUAL PRAYERS
TOM HILL

Plains Indians painted images from dreams and visions on their clothing as a way to pay tribute to spirit forces. Designs became metaphors for beliefs. Symbolic objects, too, were attached to clothing; these objects added strong elements of design and form, as well as meaning. Clothing like this painted, quilled, and beaded warrior's shirt became the first multimedia art among Indians, a form of collage that influenced early cubist artists.

✳

Image-making among the Plains Indians—with their direct and distinctively painted art forms—perhaps comes closest to Western ideas of art. Robes, tipis, shields, and rawhide containers known as parfleches were painted with pigments applied with porous buffalo bones. Specific people, known as paint-gatherers, collected and prepared minerals and other sources of pigment. Many native place names refer to pigments found in the rocks or plants there.[1] With European Contact and trade, commercial colors became available on the Plains as early as the 1770s; many native communities also learned to extract dyes from trade cloth.

The desire to communicate psychological insights was one impetus behind the image-making of Plains Indians—as it is for all people—and perhaps their use of color was an integral element of that process. Anthropologists and art historians have not adequately explored this area. Bernelda Wheeler, a Cree writer and broadcaster, recalls stories from her past of how women—mothers, aunts, grandmothers, and friends—besides giving a name and guardian spirit to a newborn baby, would also select a color to influence the character or reflect the

PAINTED, QUILLED, AND BEADED
SHIRT, MID-19TH C (?). UPPER
MISSOURI RIVER. LENGTH 134 CM
(17.6345)

SLEEPING BEAR, OGLALA LAKOTA,
CA. 1900. NORTH DAKOTA. (17671)

OTO AND MISSOURI DELEGATION
TO WASHINGTON, BEFORE 1894.
PHOTOGRAPH BY J.K. HILLERS.

personality of the child. Women would use those colors predominantly in making the child's clothes and other things. From Wheeler's oral histories, we can imagine the child's environment as a sensuous world, with women providing not only for the child's physical and nurturing needs, but for his or her emotional, spiritual, and psychological needs as well, through the use of color.

There was a clear division of responsibility by gender in Plains culture. While women enriched the world with their arts, embellishing clothing and household objects, men painted the religious symbols that appeared on the outside of tipis and produced objects for war, hunting, and ceremonial use. Robes, however, were painted by both men and women. Men decorated robes with realistic exploits of war or the hunt or depictions of ritual visions. Women produced abstract designs, which have been described by scholars as box and border, border and hourglass, horizontal stripes, bilateral symmetry, and feathered circle, shown on the robe in this chapter.[2] Both men's and women's designs—created for protection, ritual use, or as expressions of personal spirituality—were usually impotent and meaningless unless they were accompanied by the proper songs, dances, and stories.

The meanings of many abstract designs have been lost to time. It is unlikely, however, that these abstractions were frivolous. Rather, they may have had their beginnings in the maker's attempt to represent sensations or emotions within the context of religious belief and practice.

✳

Plains art—abstract and realistic, symbolic and decorative—was centered in religion and influenced by visions, dreams, and meditations. Plains people had a holistic world view. As John Snow, chief of the Stoneys of Alberta, explains:

> Our philosophy of life sees the Great Spirit's Creation as a whole piece. If something in the environment harms man, it is reasonable that the Creator provided a specific herb to cure the sickness or has given some person the wisdom to heal. Man is a complex being of body, mind, and spirit. Prayer is the essential part of all medicine; it puts the person troubled by illness into a proper relationship to the Great Spirit and his Creation.[3]

Early anthropological studies of Plains Indians indicate that each individual was protected by a guardian spirit—in addition to tribal spirits—with whom he or she could communicate. A young Blackfeet Indian, for example, might seek the identity of his individual guardian by fasting and praying in a secluded place of spiritual significance; frequently the spirit was revealed through a trance or vivid dream.

Plains cultures were not pantheistic. They believed in an all-watchful Sky Father who resided in the high realm. Individuals sought spiritual guardians in the middle realm—the domain of eagles, thunder, lightning, sun, stars, and moon. Among some Plains societies, the earth was also a central power and presence in the universe. An exhibition at the Glenbow Museum in Calgary described Grandmother Earth as "the great mother source and protector of all living things. She gave to the people both the buffalo and corn, as well as the sacred colors used in the art of the Plains people. The Cheyennes addressed her as Eschehman; the Sioux called her Maka; from her hands came the materials and the ideas that produced the sacred art of the Plains."[4]

✳

Language, like religion, both shapes a culture's world view and is shaped by it. At a recent conference, "The Mythical Indian," Dr. Leroy Little Bear of the University of Lethbridge, Ontario, pointed out that Plains languages are verb-oriented and focus on action (as opposed to English, which is noun-oriented and focuses on the object). In Plains languages—and therefore in Plains thought—everything is in constant flux or motion. Everything is animated, everything is equal to the person, everything has a spirit. To Plains artists and their communities, the designs on objects were vital, having life and spirits all their own.

In such a world, the making of art becomes a process of mediation between natural phenomena and spiritual presences. Objects and designs are go-betweens or messengers acting on their makers' behalf. The most powerful images might even prevent death.

This vitalistic aspect of art is evident in the creation of war shields. Made of thick animal hides laced to wooden hoops, these shields protected warriors from enemy arrows and lances with the power inherent in their imagery. The half-spirit, half-human figure painted in black on the vibrant red shield of the nineteenth-century Crow chief Arapoosh represents the moon, who came to Arapoosh in a vision and gave him the shield. Feathers and charms attached to the shield and rituals governing its use heightened its potency. Like war shields, Plains clothing was charged with intensely personal symbolism, often discovered through visions. The Ghost Dance movement of the late nineteenth century provides a tragic example of faith in the power of image-making. Ghost dancers believed that their shirts would protect them from the bullets of the U.S. Army.

With the exception of Ghost Dance shirts, clothing was crafted primarily by women, while ornaments were made by men. Often, the work was sacred. Some tribes formed societies and guilds whose members fulfilled these spiritual tasks. In traditional times, clothing designs were usually completed in porcupine quills, which were dyed with mineral and plant colors and embroidered directly onto clothing. Geometric patterns were the most common, but with the arrival of trade beads on the Plains during the nineteenth century, curvilinear patterns began to appear, perhaps borrowed from Eastern Woodlands floral motifs.[5]

✳

TSISTSISTAS (CHEYENNE) DRAGONFLY HAIR ORNAMENTS, CA. 1885. 33 X 25 AND 63 X 13.5 CM (24.2440 AND 24.2441)

"Acculturation" is a word often used in the discussion of Native American history to suggest debasement. In the arts, acculturation began at the time of Contact with Europeans and the introduction of new materials and technologies. By 1670, the spread of European influence along the Atlantic coast, and to a great extent in the Eastern Woodlands, had largely been completed, and the effects of European technology were being felt more or less intensely at least as far west as the Rocky Mountains. By 1750, nearly seventy percent of the household objects used by the Iroquois were of European manufacture. Change for Native Americans was inevitable, although aspects of culture that were firmly rooted in world views—like the art of the Northwest Coast—showed greater resistance to change. In some cases, materials changed faster than techniques—as on the Plains, when trade beads replaced porcupine quills in the decoration of clothing. In others, techniques changed faster than concepts—as in the Eastern Woodlands, when people began using metal drills to fashion shell wampum. At times, concepts changed faster than traditions—perhaps best exemplified by the addition of European Christian and military practices to some traditional rituals. Yet, Native American arts endured, sometimes alongside European counterparts, sometimes as whole new art forms.

One such art form, illustrated at the beginning of this chapter, is the making of beaded caps by the Tuscarora and Mohawk. Fashioned from cotton-lined velveteen and elaborately beaded with floral motifs in both raised and couched beading techniques, the caps are evidence of Native Americans' vigorous assertion of identity during the Victorian era. These caps were sometimes known as Glengarry caps for their similarity to Scottish military headgear. In fact, the skullcap form was more reminiscent of a traditional Iroquoian *gustoweh* without the feathers. With their resemblance to fashionable hats worn by Victorian ladies, these caps were probably more popular with Native American women than men. However, my grandmother, a seamstress in turn-of-the-century Ohsweken, recalls making beaded skullcaps for the Mohawk chief George Martin Johnson, who, according to her, wore them to cover his bald spot.

*

Traditionally, among Indians, clothing was an expression of how we felt about ourselves and the world in which we lived. It signified, to knowing receivers, our age, status, region, and religion. It satisfied the wearer's personal aesthetic and spiritual needs. In its artistry, spirituality, and intense subjectivity, it was often seen as a form of prayer.

Today, when the global village has replaced the tribal village, you can still see Native Americans wearing elements of this ancient artistic heritage. Many of the ideas embodied in native clothing were never lost. They are still acknowledged in communities throughout North, South, and Central America where traditional religious practices are observed. Powwows, too, encourage us to revive old rites and celebrations and to synthesize traditional and

contemporary values to create new forms of wearable art—ribbon shirts, beaded baseball caps, fluorescent-hued Fancy Dance dress, beaded sneakers, and iconography ranging from images of Sitting Bull to Mickey Mouse. Born out of intertribal gatherings among Plains tribes over the course of hundreds of years, these powwows are our modern-day celebration of what we, as Native Americans, share. They address our need to interact and to maintain our identities. They embody the ideas, beliefs, images, assumptions, anxieties, and hopes that make up our situation and our destiny. They are our community's new wordless prayer to our past, present, and future.

TAPESTRY PONCHO, 500-100 B.C. PARACAS CULTURE, PERU. 31 X 104.2 CM (23.7299)

WIFE OF WATÁNGAA, SOUTHERN ARAPAHO CHIEF, 1901.

TZOCH, A CIBECUE APACHE SCOUT, 1880s.

OMAHA OR CROW BELT DANCE, 1892. PINE RIDGE, SOUTH DAKOTA. PHOTOGRAPH BY JAMES MOONEY, BUREAU OF AMERICAN ETHNOLOGY.

MICMAC WOMAN'S CAP, 19TH C.
HEIGHT 39.3 CM (3.2085)

MICMAC WOMAN'S CAP, LATE
19TH C. HEIGHT 37.5 CM (17.6423)

MICMAC WOMAN'S CAP, 19TH C.
HEIGHT 37.5 CM (17.6452)

MR. AND MRS. ANDREW JOE,
MICMAC, 1951. CONNE RIVER
RESERVE, NEWFOUNDLAND.
PHOTOGRAPH BY FREDERICK
JOHNSON. (20277)

Sixteenth-century French fur traders who encountered the Micmac—hunting people of what is now northeastern Canada and New England—told of their "fantastic ornamentation." Native decorative techniques, they wrote, were "so lively that ours seem in nothing to be comparable to them."[1] The Micmac clothing admired by the French was made from mammal, bird, and fish skins; many kinds of bark and plants; feathers, fur, and quills; and beads made of copper, shell, and stone—all used in a variety of ways. There were, for example, six different methods for working porcupine quills. And clothing was painted or otherwise adorned in graceful patterns the French called "lacelike."

Before marriage, a young Micmac woman was required to make a full set of clothing for her husband-to-be, as proof of her skill. Creating such beautiful garments must have been a source of pleasure and pride. But the elaborate designs on ceremonial clothing had meanings beyond beauty, for they were sources of protective power.

We know this early Micmac clothing only through written accounts. Micmac artisans eagerly adopted European trade goods, particularly cloth, silk ribbon, and glass beads. European beads required no preparation, offered a wide variety of colors, and allowed great freedom in design. White and blue beads were in use as early as 1606. By the 1700s, tiny seed beads were available;

seamstresses threaded them on moose hair—the only thread fine enough—laid them out on cloth in designs, and stitched them down after every second bead with cotton or linen thread.

By 1750, virtually all Micmac clothing was made from trade goods, albeit in old patterns. Peaked caps for women seem to have been a new creation, however, possibly derived from French hats. These caps became popular not only with the Micmac, but also with their neighbors, the Maliseet of Canada and the Penobscot and Passamaquoddy of Maine. There are two types of decoration on Micmac caps. One is done with tiny strips of ribbon appliqué. The other uses beads in what is today called a double-curve. These designs may reflect the lacelike patterns described by the French two centuries before. Double-curve motifs are used by many of the peoples of the Northeast and may be very old; they can be seen on petroglyphs in the area and certainly predate European Contact.

By the middle of the nineteenth century, the Micmac wore Western-style clothing almost exclusively. Traditional garments, however, including these old-style caps, were saved and worn on special occasions such as St. Anne's Day.[2] They became, and remain today, symbols of Indian identity and testaments to superlative artistic achievement.

M.J.L.

In the early 1900s, life for the Mississippi, Louisiana, and Tennessee Choctaws centered not only on subsistence agriculture and seasonal hunting, but on stick ball, social dancing and music, their native language, and traditional foods and dress. For the most part, the Choctaws' everyday clothing was indistinguishable from that of their neighbors. But at traditional gatherings, the Choctaws dressed in a style that blended European-American influences with distinctively Choctaw attire and design elements. For special occasions, Choctaw men typically wore store-bought trousers; commercial or native-made shirts embellished with finely cut and stitched appliqué; cotton hunting coats with ruffled collars and cuffs, also decorated with appliqué; wide-brimmed black hats with native-made silver bands; glass-bead necklaces; native-made silver earrings; and magnificent beaded bandoliers—sashes worn across the chest and over the shoulder or as belts. Women wore one-piece cotton dresses and ruffled aprons, both finely decorated with appliqué worked in contrasting colors; shawls; ornamental hair combs; several glass bead necklaces; and, again, beaded bandoliers.

Finger-woven bandoliers and belts incorporating beads were common throughout the Southeast, but those made from red wool trade cloth and decorated with bead embroidery in geometric designs, like the bandoliers illustrated here, are most frequently associated with the Choctaw, Koasati, and Alabama Indians.

The Choctaws were the first of the "Five Civilized Tribes"— the Choctaws, Cherokees, Chickasaws, Creeks, and Seminoles— selected for the government's westward removal of Indian peoples living east of the Mississippi River.[1] Beginning in the winter of 1831–1832, the majority of the Choctaws were moved west to Indian Territory (now Oklahoma). Landless and impoverished, the Choctaws who remained behind became squatters, eking out their existence on marginal farmlands. Remarkably, by the turn of the century, these isolated people had formed rural communities with schools and churches.

Around that time, non-Indians began yet again to pressure the eastern Choctaws to leave their homelands and move west— ostensibly, to take part in the assignment of allotments of Indian land. In 1887, Congress had enacted legislation calling for the distribution of tribal lands in Indian Territory to individual Indian households. The Five Civilized Tribes challenged this policy. But in 1898, Congress dissolved their tribal governments and extended allotment to their lands, helping pave the way for Oklahoma statehood nine years later.

The bandoliers shown here signify the determination of the eastern Choctaws—who successfully resisted two removal efforts— to retain not only land in their traditional territories, but their distinct cultural identity.

C.R.G.

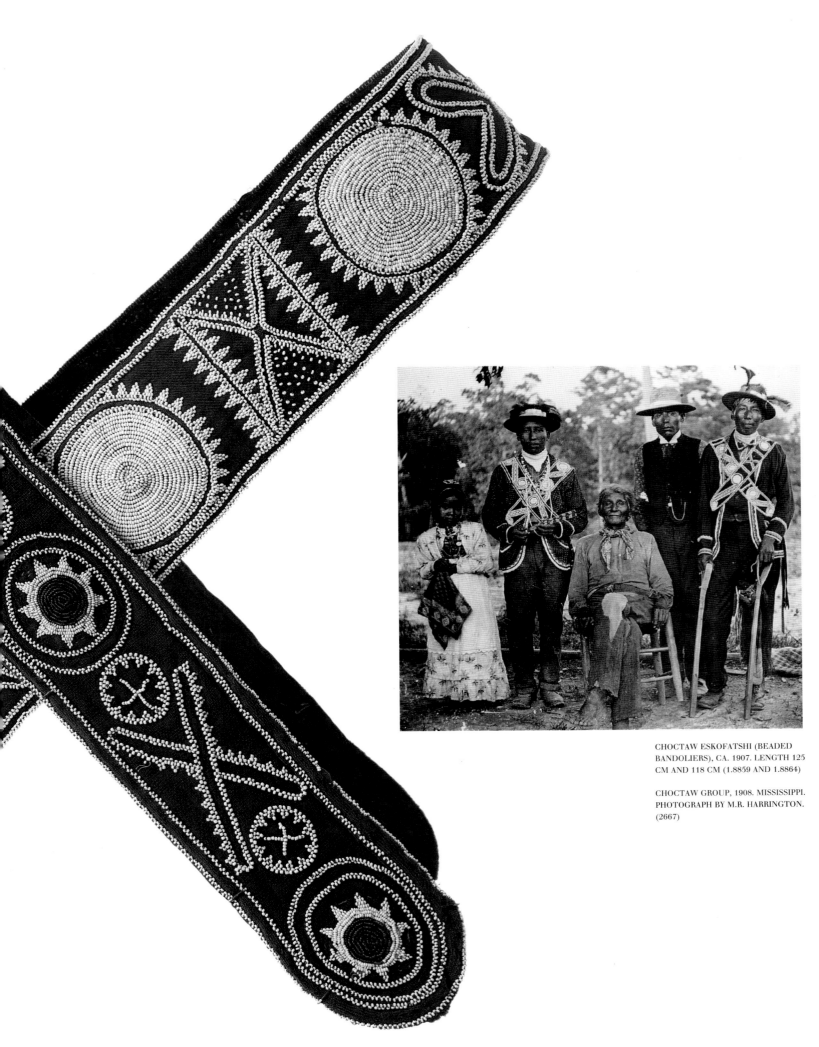

CHOCTAW ESKOFATSHI (BEADED
BANDOLIERS), CA. 1907. LENGTH 125
CM AND 118 CM (1.8859 AND 1.8864)

CHOCTAW GROUP, 1908. MISSISSIPPI.
PHOTOGRAPH BY M.R. HARRINGTON.
(2667)

This lavishly beaded inner parka, collected near Chesterfield Inlet on the west coast of Hudson Bay, is made of caribou skin with the fur inside. It would have been worn for special occasions with an outer parka that had the caribou fur turned to the outside. Beaded decoration became popular in the area about 1860 when whalers who were well supplied with trade goods began to winter in the bay. Known as *sapangaq* (precious stone), trade beads used in large quantities became a sign of wealth and prestige. The heart and the floral designs on this parka may show European influence. Other motifs—rows of triangles and multiple lines of beading—may be very old, from the time of the Thule ancestors of the Inuit, who moved into the eastern Arctic a thousand years ago.

Traditionally, throughout the eastern and central Arctic, a woman's parka or *amautik* exemplified both her skills as a seamstress and her role as a woman, a hunter's wife, and a mother. A fine seamstress enjoyed genuine esteem, and the wrists of a baby girl were wrapped with strips of caribou skin in the hope that she would become skilled in the complex cutting and sewing required to create warm clothing for her family.[1]

The most distinctive feature of the amautik is the *amaut* or carrying pouch in the back, designed to hold a baby nestled close to the mother's warm body. The garment's shoulders are loose and wide to allow the mother to bring her baby to her breast while still protecting the child from the cold.[2]

The construction of the amautik is rich with references to a woman's role as a giver of life. The front apron flap or *kiniq* may be a symbol of childbirth, seen in the word *kinersertoq* for a pregnant woman.[3] The long back tail calls to mind animals, the source of food, furs and skins, bones and ivory, and oil. The placement of the beaded designs on the wrists and shoulders suggests tattoos.[4]

Women's sewing, like men's hunting, was permeated with ritual and spiritual belief and with rules and practices intended to encourage success in the hunt. Seasonal cycles separated hunting land animals, such as caribou, from sea animals, including seal and walrus. Sewing was forbidden during the hunting season, and new clothes were made only in late autumn, when families moved into their new snow houses. If sewing was not finished by the time the family had moved onto the sea ice and begun to hunt there, a special hut had to be built on shore where the work was completed.

A little girl's amautik was made like her mother's, with a small pouch to carry a doll, a puppy, or a baby brother or sister. When the child matured into an adolescent, her parka was made without a pouch, calling attention to her unmarried status.

Today only a few women make elaborate beaded amautiks, turning their talents instead to wall hangings and other art forms. But contemporary parkas made of duffel cloth still follow the traditional designs that embody the multiple meanings of an Inuit woman's life and her connections with generations gone before.

M.J.L.

"When a woman has her first child, her mother and her grandmother help her to make her amautik. That's how we start to learn. . . . When we make an amautik, we have to do a lot of trying on to see how it will fit. Even if the amautik is completely finished, we have to take it apart if there is even one little mistake. We can't leave mistakes to spoil the amautik."

—ELISAPEE KILIUTAK, INUIT

AIVILINGMIUT IGLULIK AMAUTIK
(WOMAN'S PARKA), EARLY 20TH C.
LENGTH 123.5 CM (13.7198)

INUIT WOMEN ONBOARD SHIP, CA.
1903–1904. CAPE FULLERTON,
NORTHWEST TERRITORIES.
PHOTOGRAPH BY A.P. LOW.

NEZ PERCE CORNHUSK BAG, LATE
19TH C. 26 X 26 CM (13.8632)

WALLA WALLA CORNHUSK LEGGINGS,
LATE 19TH C. 67 X 40 CM (10.8091)

Flat, rectangular bags made of twined Indian hemp and other native grasses and decorated with dyed cornhusks served basic needs on the Columbia and Snake River Plateau, in present-day Oregon, Washington, and Idaho. These bags were almost always used for harvesting, storing, and trading foodstuffs. The Nez Perce, for example, traded cornhusk bags full of berries or camas and other roots to the Crow for meat stored in parfleches (untanned hide containers). Occasionally, individual Plateau women adapted these bags to quite different ends. By cutting a twined hemp and cornhusk bag in two and embellishing its halves with red trade cloth, blue ribbon, black velvet, rabbit fur, and hide fringe, a Walla Walla woman transformed a storage container into an extraordinary and extremely rare pair of leggings—a testament to her creativity, as well as her resourcefulness.[1]

Plateau women were highly skilled fiber artists; according to archaeologists, the technique used to make twined bags dates back several hundred years. This Nez Perce bag is classic in both construction and decoration, although it was made relatively recently and most likely was used to store personal belongings. Its geometric designs are done in a technique known as false embroidery: when the maker wove the bag, she wrapped strips of natural or dyed cornhusks around the outside weft (or horizontal fiber) as she crossed it over the warp (vertical fiber). Typically, the front and back of a bag are decorated with different patterns executed in different color combinations.[2] Depending upon whether she used natural or dyed cornhusks—or later, commercial worsted yarn—the weaver created effects ranging from subtle to quite vivid. For all their beauty, though, cornhusk bags were durable and highly utilitarian containers.

Although cornhusk bags are the most common twined basketry made by women throughout the Plateau, they are most frequently associated with the Nez Perce. Perhaps this is because, in the early nineteenth century, the explorers Lewis and Clark saw the bags in use among the Nez Perce and mentioned them in their journals.

C.R.G.

The most remarkable leader of the small Hidatsa tribe during the second half of the nineteenth century was Poor Wolf, who occupied the position of second chief throughout most of this period and lived on into the first decade of the twentieth century. As the composition at right testifies, Poor Wolf presented a striking figure when he appeared unclothed from the waist up, for his entire right arm and the right side of his body were tattooed. He underwent that ordeal when he was a young man, to provide protection in battle. In this he seems to have followed the example of his uncle, Addih-Hiddisch (Road Maker), chief of the village of Awachawi, who had similar extensive tattooing on his upper body when he posed for his portrait by the young Swiss artist Karl Bodmer in 1834.

The Hidatsa, along with the other small farming tribes of the middle Missouri, the Mandan and Arikara, suffered heavy losses in the smallpox epidemic of 1837. By 1845, for their mutual protection against the hostile Sioux and Assiniboine, these three tribes united in one large, fortified village of earth-covered lodges—Like-a-Fishhook, near Fort Berthold, the American Fur Company post in what is now North Dakota.

As a young man, Poor Wolf gained recognition as a successful warrior and one who carried the pipe—that is, led expeditions—against his people's enemies. As second chief he gained the respect of traders and government officials for his sharp bargaining and wise diplomacy.

This drawing illustrates but four of Poor Wolf's exploits—which were well known to other members of his tribe—including two war actions (at left in the drawing) in which he killed two Sioux. The central figure shows him dancing and counting his coups after returning from a fight in which he had killed a Sioux. The illustration at the upper right portrays Poor Wolf administering justice to the abductor of his brother's wife, while the one at the lower right portrays an example of his generosity: "Poor Wolf kills a buffalo cow, and gives his entire equipment to the first man who comes to him, because his heart feels good."

Poor Wolf himself made drawings of his war actions and of various tribal activities. Most of them bear his unique pictorial signature, a lightly penciled and very thin wolf. This drawing appears to have been the creation of another, and probably a younger, Hidatsa.

In his old age, Poor Wolf became a convert to Christianity and assisted in pioneer studies of the Indian sign language. Missionaries, historians, and anthropologists found him to be their best source of information on the history and traditional culture of the Hidatsa.

J.C.E.

THE EXPLOITS OF POOR WOLF, HIDATSA SECOND CHIEF, EARLY 20TH C.(?). ARTIST UNKNOWN, HIDATSA(?). CRAYON, WATERCOLOR, AND INK ON PAPER, 43 X 56 CM (4.2446A)

POOR WOLF (RIGHT) AND CROW'S BREAST, TWO PRINCIPAL CHIEFS OF THE HIDATSA, 1872. LIKE-A-FISH-HOOK, DAKOTA TERRITORY. PHOTOGRAPH BY STANLEY MORROW.

Prominent warriors of many Plains tribes wore headgear with animal horns attached. Most commonly these were buffalo horns—or thin sections of horns—paired, one at each side of the headdress. Perhaps the headdresses were intended to impart to their wearers the qualities of strength and courage of the buffalo.

The headdress at right, however, is made with antelope horns, and perhaps the power it carried into combat was the antelope's speed and elusiveness. Although it was called Nez Perce when it was catalogued by the museum, it is definitely of the old Assiniboine style. Indeed, during the summer of 1831, while at Fort Union near the mouth of the Yellowstone, Karl Bodmer painted a portrait of Noapeh (Troop of Soldiers), an Assiniboine warrior, wearing a headdress very like this one. It features a pair of antelope horns that have been cut, thinned, and tipped with dyed horsehair. Between the horns is a crest of clipped black feathers. The horns and feathers are fastened to a leather strap that secures the headdress to the head. From this strap is suspended a long fringe of buckskin, each strand of which is bound intermittently with porcupine quills. Bodmer's employer and traveling companion, Maximilian, a natural scientist as well as the prince of a small Prussian state, sought in vain to purchase this headdress for his collection.

As early as 1819, David G. Burnett observed that the headdress of a noteworthy Comanche chief on the Texas frontier "was a cap made of the scalp of a buffalo bull, with the horns attached in proper position." On the upper Missouri during the summer of 1832, George Catlin painted the portraits of leading warriors from the Sioux, Blackfeet, and Mandan tribes wearing buffalo-horn headdresses. One of them was Four Bears (Mato Tope), second chief of the Mandans, who claimed to have the best war record of any man of his tribe. His headdress had thin vertical sections of horn, tipped with dyed horsehair, attached to either side of a skin bonnet covered with short strips of white weasel.

J.C.E.

TANTAN'KA HOKS'ÍLA (BUFFALO BOY), 1912. STANDING ROCK AGENCY, THE DAKOTAS. PHOTO-GRAPH BY FRANCES DENSMORE.

ASSINIBOINE ANTELOPE-HORN HEADDRESS, MID-19TH C. LENGTH 84.5 CM (10.8302)

Indian women used a number of ingenious techniques to decorate clothing and other things with porcupine quills. One quite distinctive method involves wrapping quills around a core or filler of horsehair. Crow women in particular—the native name for their tribe is Absaroke (Children of the Large Beaked Bird, later mistranslated as Crow)—made beautiful decorations in quill-wrapped horsehair on clothes and moccasins.

This shirt has quill-wrapped horsehair bordered by beads of several colors on the over-shoulder and over-sleeve strips. It is also decorated with a V-shaped neck-panel of red cloth and cut buckskin fringe. Several white (winter) weasel-skin pendants add to its striking appearance.

This shirt, like several other examples of quill-wrapped horsehair, was recorded as Nez Perce. But whether the Nez Perce received it in trade or as a gift from their Crow allies, or whether the shirt was created by a Nez Perce woman in imitation of Crow work, we do not know.

We do know that the head chief of the Mountain Crow, Sits-in-the-Middle-of-the-Land, was wearing a shirt bearing a quill-wrapped horsehair decoration when he was photographed during a visit to Washington as a member of the first Crow delegation to travel to the capital in 1873.

Similarly, these moccasins are credited to the Piegan people of the Blackfeet, rather than to the Crow, but there is no substantiating evidence that Blackfeet women used quill-wrapped horsehair in their craftwork. It seems more likely that the moccasins are Crow.

They are quite fine—made in the old style, with side seams and soft soles. The decoration is confined to the area over the toes, comprising three double lanes of quill-wrapped horsehair in natural-colored quills, with accents in red and brown dyed quills. The quillwork is bordered with blue and white pony beads. Although these moccasins may be more than 150 years old, they are in excellent condition.

J.C.E.

ABSAROKE (?) (CROW [?]) QUILL-WRAPPED- HORSEHAIR MOCCASINS, MID-19TH C. 27.9 X 11.3 CM (17.8027)

SITS-IN-THE-MIDDLE-OF-THE-LAND, HEAD CHIEF OF THE MOUNTAIN CROW, AND HIS WIFE, 1873. WASHINGTON, D.C.

ABSAROKE (?) (CROW [?]) QUILL-WRAPPED- HORSEHAIR SHIRT, MID-19TH C. LENGTH 106 CM (11.4243)

In pre-reservation days, a Sioux, Numakiki (Mandan), Hidatsa, or Assiniboine warrior wrapped himself in a robe made of the whole skin of a buffalo. Many robes were painted. One might bear figures of men and horses in action, representing how the owner won war honors, the scenes painted by the owner or another man whom he believed to be a more gifted artist. Or a robe might bear a large, colorful design composed of concentric circles of triangular feather motifs. This pattern was painted by women, the masters of geometric art among the Plains Indians. There is some evidence that the women did not draw all these hundreds of tall triangles freehand, but outlined them using triangular wooden templates.

Most geometrically painted men's robes had a central element, which Prince Maximilian learned in 1834 represents the sun. The concentric circles of feather elements radiating from it symbolize a war bonnet. The designs on early-nineteenth-century robes were generally painted in two colors—black or dark brown, and red—and were outlined in size, a clear, gluey liquid made by boiling hide scraps. But as the century progressed, painters tended to use more colors, obtained from traders.

The feather-bonnet motif is very clear in this robe, although it lacks the central sun element. Note that the painter added some blue and yellow to her palette. This robe was collected between 1878 and 1885 among the Mandan of Fort Berthold Reservation, in what is now North Dakota. Although the creators of feather-bonnet-painted robes appear to have been members of only the Siouan-speaking tribes mentioned above, some robes may have been given or traded to the Crow, Blackfeet, and other neighboring tribes after the intertribal wars ended during the 1880s and the tribes began to exchange friendly visits.

At least three white artists who knew the tribes of the northern Plains before 1835 sought to portray Indians wearing robes bearing this design, but only Karl Bodmer, who accompanied Maximilian to the upper Missouri, did so correctly. He pictured Two Ravens, a prominent Hidatsa warrior, wearing a war-bonnet-painted robe over his left shoulder.

J.C.E.

NUMAKIKI (MANDAN) FEATHER-
BONNET-PAINTED ROBE, CA. 1875.
254.7 X 180.5 CM (19.630)

PEHROSKA-RUHPA (TWO RAVENS),
HIDATSA. PRINT BY KARL BODMER,
PUBLISHED IN MAXIMILIAN'S
TRAVELS (PL. 17), 1834. (1842)

With its rich painting and minimal use of beaded ornamentation, this dress, dating from the turn of the century, epitomizes the restrained elegance of southern Plains clothing. Narrow bands of beadwork define rather than cover the surface of southern Plains garments, and extensive painting with rich earth pigments or paints procured from traders emphasizes the fine texture of the hides from which they are made.

The bird painted on the front of this dress is covered with spots often used to represent hail. It may be the thunderbird, which flies on the leading edge of the powerful thunderstorms that sweep the Plains in spring and summer. Revered by native people throughout North America, the thunderbird is associated with the upper world of spiritual powers. Such symbols of spiritual association were placed on both ceremonial and everyday clothing to evoke blessings. The Ghost Dance, with its elaborately painted garments, is well known, but it represents only one of many religious movements among the people of the Plains. In addition to practicing communal faiths, individuals frequently sought direct, personal spiritual revelation as well. Symbols evocative of such experience might also be painted on garments or other objects, their full meaning known to only a few.

Much of the beauty of southern Plains clothing derives from the supple leather of which it is made. Preparing hides was a women's task, and skill and industry at the difficult and laborious process could be a source of considerable prestige. While men kept count of their accomplishments in war, women proudly recorded the number of hides they had processed, maintaining tallies with lines marked on the handles of their elk-horn hide-scrapers. Scrapers were valued possessions and might be passed on from mother to daughter, well-worn but treasured family heirlooms.

Unlike the dresses of the northern Plains, which are constructed of two hides, the southern style uses three skins: two for the skirt and a third for the bodice with its wide cape sleeves. This design no doubt developed from a form of women's dress widespread in the warmer southern regions of North America, which consisted of a skirt and a separate cape or poncho. Hide skirts and ponchos are still worn for formal dress among the Apache neighbors of the southern Plains tribes. But in the mid-nineteenth century, the Kiowa, Comanche, and southern bands of the Cheyenne and Arapaho joined the two pieces into a single garment. Fashions in buckskin dresses have continued to change over the decades, however, and now Kiowa and Comanche dresses are again often made with a capelike bodice worn over a separate skirt.

Connections to the Southwest can also be seen in this southern Plains woman's footwear, which combines moccasins with leggings to create high-topped boots. A shawl worn over the shoulders or wrapped around the waist and a belt complete her outfit.

J.C.E.

The whole world is coming,
A nation is coming, a nation is
coming,
The Eagle has brought the message
to the tribe.
Over the whole earth they are
coming;
The buffalo are coming, the
buffalo are coming,
The Crow has brought the message
to the tribe.

—GHOST DANCE SONG

WOMAN'S BOOTS, LATE 19TH/EARLY
20TH C. SOUTHERN PLAINS. LENGTH
78 CM (20.7749)

DRESS, LATE 19TH/EARLY 20TH C.
SOUTHERN PLAINS. LENGTH 140 CM
(20.8052)

KIOWA DANCERS.

THE SYMBOLISM OF FEATHERS

RICHARD W. HILL SR.

For many cultures—including contemporary American culture—clothing is the first level of the extension of the self through art. Clothing reveals how individuals see themselves and relate to their communities. In native societies, however, clothing expresses more than gender, class, or personal taste. Within native groups, certain designs are elements of rituals, celebrations, and dances. Through these designs—and through the process of creating them—clothing becomes a means of spiritual communication.

One aspect of that communication is the expression of the relationship between humankind and the animals who give their flesh for food, their hides for clothing, and their power as totems. The use of feathers on clothing and ritual objects illustrates the importance of animal spirits, as well as animal materials, in native dress. For many Indians, wearing feathers celebrates an ancient connection with birds. Some cultures associate certain birds with spiritual or protective powers. Birds are believed to have delivered songs, dances, rituals, and sacred messages to humankind. Feathers worn in the hair blow in the wind and evoke birds in flight. For followers of the Ghost Dance religion of the late nineteenth century, birds became important symbols of rebirth.

✳

Among the Iroquois, the feather headdress called a *gustoweh* (real hat) is a symbol of identity. Around the time of the Revolutionary War, some Indians added silver bands to their gustowehs, modeling them after European crowns; after trade beads were introduced, people decorated the bases of their gustowehs with handsome designs similar to those on Mohawk and Tuscarora caps. Traditionally, each nation arranged the eagle feathers at the top of the gustoweh differently: Mohawks wore three eagle feathers pointing up; Senecas, one feather straight up and one lying down toward the back. The eagle feathers of the gustoweh are fastened in a way that lets them twirl in the wind. It is said that these turning feathers represent the eagle that landed in the top of the Tree of Peace at the time of the formation of the Iroquois Confederacy. The eagle flies closest to the Creator, searching out approaching danger. It is considered a protector of the people. By wearing eagle feathers, Iroquoians express these beliefs.

✳

The best-known use of feathers, of course, is the Plains feather bonnet. Although feather bonnets call up stereotyped images of Indians from popular culture, they should not be ignored, for they are truly moving sights and objects of great power.

The beliefs behind Plains war clothing are very complex. The Cheyenne warrior Wooden Leg, who fought against General Custer, explained the significance of war bonnets:

War bonnets were not worn by all warriors. In fact there were only a few such distinguished men in each warrior society. . . . The act [of putting on a war bonnet] meant a profession of fully acquired ability in warfare, a claim of special accomplishment in using cunning, and common sense and cool calculation coupled with bravery attributed to all warriors. The wearer was supposed never to ask for mercy in battle. . . . The feathered headpiece, then, was not a sign of public office. It was a token of individual and personal feeling as to his own fighting capabilities.[1]

A common misconception is that each feather in a war bonnet was earned individually. In fact, bonnets were often made with matched tail feathers from a single eagle. It is true, however, that a feather could be bestowed in tribute for a heroic deed. Plains Indians honor veterans of contemporary wars by presenting them with eagle feathers in recognition of their service to their native land.

Decorated shirts and other Plains warriors' dress conveyed another kind of courage in battle—a faith in the life to come and a desire to show respect for the Creator. Again, according to Wooden Leg:

All of the best clothing was taken along with him when any warrior set upon a search for conflict. The articles were put into a special bag and slung at one side of the horse. . . . If a battle seemed about to occur, the warrior's first important preparatory act was to jerk off all his ordinary clothing. He then hurriedly put on his fine garments. . . . The idea of full dress in preparation for battle comes not from a belief that it would add to the fighting ability. The preparation is for death. . . . Every Indian wants to look his best when he meets the Great Spirit.[2]

✳

In the past, museums have often referred to native clothes as "costumes." A brochure used to guide people through the exhibitions of native culture at the American Museum of Natural History went so far as to say: "So we see that if we wish to study the original costumes of Indians in the United States, we will, in the main, have to deal with a people who for the most part went naked and protected themselves from the cold by wrapping up in skin robes."[3]

In fact, very little clothing from the time before European Contact can be found in museum collections. Most of the clothing shown in this book was made in the last two hundred years. Yet surely these things—so rich in beauty and meaning—are products of much older traditions of artistry and faith.

My children, my children,
The wind makes the head-feathers
  sing—
The wind makes the head-feathers
  sing.

—INUNA-INA (ARAPAHO) GHOST DANCE SONG

TSISTSISTAS (CHEYENNE) FEATHER
BONNET, CA. 1870. LENGTH 198.5 CM
(20.5318)

TSISTSISTAS (CHEYENNE) FEATHER
BONNET STORAGE CASE, LATE 19TH C.
LENGTH 57.8 CM (2.8777)

SOLOMON OBAIL, SENECA.

89

Shirts like these appear in late-nineteenth-century photographs of Apache leaders who were, in one way or another, struggling to maintain their homelands.

The 1870s and 1880s were decades of turmoil and exploitation for all Indian peoples. Under a so-called Peace Policy, the government created reservations for many Indian groups, often far from their traditional lands.

The Jicarilla Apache hoped to negotiate a reservation in an area they chose, in what is now New Mexico. In 1880 Jicarilla delegates travelled to Washington, where they were photographed in both their traditional and Western store-bought clothing; the traditional shirt worn by Guerito, seated in the center, is very similar to this one in the museum's collection (right). The government often brought Indian leaders east, to impress upon them the "arts and industries of the civilized world." Typically, Indian delegates were given Western clothing to "help them onto the white man's road."[1] But the Jicarilla leaders resisted government efforts to move them to Utah or force them to live with the Mescalero Apache, and eventually they won the right to a reservation in northern New Mexico, close to their former home.

Farther west, four reservations had been established in 1871 and 1872 for Apache living within the Arizona Territory; as more and more settlers entered the territory, they demanded that the Indians be confined to these reservations. In 1877, one rancher wrote to the Arizona *Star*: "This is all wrong to have these Indians fed on the reservation at the expense of the government, and yet allowed to run at large. We insist that they be kept at home. No passes given, and if they come about our settlement, or we find them off the reservation, we would know what to do with them."[2]

In response to the settlers' demands, the government moved the San Carlos, White Mountain, Cibecue, and Tonto Apache, as well as the numerous bands comprising the Chiricahua Apache, to the San Carlos agency. Some groups, including the Cibecue and White Mountain Apache, eventually negotiated a return to their homelands. Others, particularly the Chiricahua who supported Chief Naiche and his war leader Geronimo, fled the reservation.

The Chiricahua were never defeated. But near starvation and harassed by U.S. troops guided by Apache scouts, the last Chiricahua fugitives surrendered in 1886. One U.S. Army scout, a Cibecue named Tzoch (called Peaches by non-Indians), was photographed in 1884 (see p. 68). Shirts tailored in a European style like the one Tzoch wore and this one in the museum's collection (left) are apparently unique to the Cibecue, White Mountain, and San Carlos Apache. Typically, they were stained with ocher, stitched with sinew, fringed, and decorated with distinctively Western Apache beadwork—that is, with narrow lanes of beadwork incorporating stripes and triangular designs in alternating and contrasting colors.

C.R.G.

SAN CARLOS APACHE BEADED
BUCKSKIN SHIRT (LEFT), CA. 1880.
LENGTH 108 CM (20.2049)

JICARILLA APACHE BEADED
BUCKSKIN SHIRT, CA. 1880. LENGTH
108 CM (12.3380)

JICARILLA APACHE DELEGATION TO
WASHINGTON, 1880.

Over the past one hundred years, Kuna women of northeastern Panama have brought together eclectic elements to create a style of dress unlike that of any of their neighbors. Most striking are their *molas*, beautiful traditional blouses made by cutting designs on a layer of brightly colored cloth, stitching it to the layer below, and then repeating the procedure over and over again to create reverse appliqué. They also fashion bright blue and green wraparound skirts and red and yellow scarves using print fabric from England. They wind strings of yellow and orange beads into elaborate patterns on their arms and legs. The effect is unmistakably Kuna.[1]

Mola making as it is known today is a relatively recent art form. Toward the end of the nineteenth century, Kuna women began to take centuries-old designs used for body-painting and paint them onto cotton wraparound skirts.[2] Then they cut and stitched geometric patterns in blue and red fabric around the hems of loose-fitting blouses to wear over their painted skirts. As Kuna women discovered different ways to cut and sew designs, they filled more of the blouse and created complex geometric patterns like the one shown here, which was collected in Kuna Yala during the 1920s.

Kuna men and women consider molas to be an integral part of their culture and important to their identity. Mola making is often discussed at village gatherings.[3] Women are articulate critics of their art, valuing skill in cutting and sewing, as well as design considerations like complexity and visibility, use of space, and interesting subject matter. Red, yellow, and blue—colors once used for body-painting—are still popular, and the geometric patterns they call *mugan* (grandmother designs) are made with pride to this day. Kuna women look to local plants and animals or events from traditional Kuna culture—village gatherings or girls' ceremonies, for example—for original images.[4] They also take pleasure in creating designs using comic books, greeting cards, and product labels; news of the world outside Kuna Yala, like boxing matches, circuses, or the space program; or even objects from archaeological excavations.[5]

Tension between tradition (rules, repetition, and balance) and innovation (pushing beyond the rules, use of subtle variations, and asymmetry) gives this unique art its vitality and dynamism.

M.L.S.

KUNA MOLA (WOMAN'S BLOUSE),
EARLY 20TH C. LENGTH 59.5 CM
(16.6425)

YOUNG KUNA WOMAN.

*Many pretty flowers, red, blue,
  and yellow; we say to the girls,
"Let's go and walk among the
  flowers."
The wind comes and sways the
  flowers, the girls are like that
  when they dance; some are
  wide open, large flowers and
  some are tiny little flowers.
The birds love the sunshine and
  the starlight; the flowers smell
  sweet.
The girls are sweeter than the
  flowers.*

—KUNA LOVE SONG

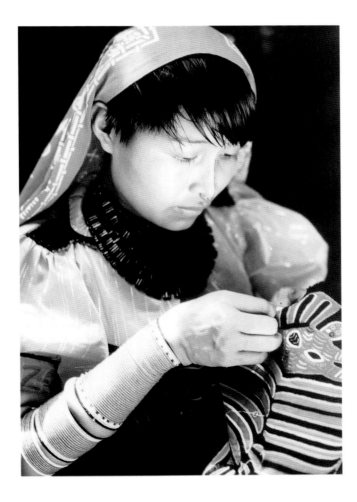

MAYA FIGURINE OF A WEAVER, A.D.
500–899. HEIGHT 15.2 CM (25.2865)

KAQCHIKEL MAYA HUIPIL (WOMAN'S
BLOUSE), EARLY 20TH C. 61 X 87 CM
(16.928)

The traditional garments or *traje* of the Highland Maya of Guatemala
tell us many things about Maya culture. For example, the distinctive
design of this *huipil* or woman's blouse—rows of dots between wider
bands of geometric patterns—indicates that it was probably made
in San Martín Jilotepeque, in the Department of Chimaltenango.
Zigzags and chevrons are popular motifs there, and they cover
almost the entire length of this blouse, front and back. The blouse's
two-panel construction and dark blue background—probably indigo-
dyed—are also characteristic of Sanmartineco huipils of the early
twentieth century.[1]

 The Maya of San Martín Jilotepeque speak Kaqchikel, and
their word for huipil is *rupan po7t*.[2] The huipil is usually the most
elaborately decorated part of a woman's outfit. This beautiful huipil
probably belonged to a woman of high social and economic status
who wore it for special occasions: it is heavily brocaded with
expensive, commercially dyed silk threads. The weaver may have
signed her work with three small bow-tie shapes near the lower edge.

 Present-day weaving techniques and clothing styles date
back to ancient Maya civilization. This ceramic figurine of a woman
weaving on a backstrap loom, found on Jaina Island, Mexico, is
from the Classic period, A.D. 500–899. Yet the weaver is using the
same basic tools her descendants use today—a backstrap loom,
spindle whorl, and warping stakes, all virtually unchanged since
pre-Columbian times.[3]

 According to Maya legend, weaving was invented by Ixchel
(Rainbow Lady), who is also the goddess of medicine and childbirth.
Weavers made offerings of beans or maize to her before beginning
new textiles. Ixchel is always depicted with a backstrap loom,
sometimes holding a weaving needle.[4]

N.R.

"We express ourselves through our designs, through our dress— our huipil, for instance, is like an image of our ancestors."

—RIGOBERTA MENCHÚ
K'ICHÉ MAYA

"*The shaman slowly turned around while the woman carefully painted his body in a dark color. The ceremony was to take place within a short time; the audience waited, tense, before the shaman began his rituals to divine and cure the patients.*"

—RUIZ BLANCO, 1712

FIGURE OF A MAN SMOKING, CA. A.D. 1000–1500. TRUJILLO, VENEZUELA. HEIGHT 26.6 CM (11.2852)

YEKUANA MUAHO (BEADED APRON), EARLY 20TH C. LENGTH 22.5 CM (16.331)

The Yekuana of central Venezuela are also known as the Makiritare, an Arawakan word meaning River People, but this is not what they call themselves; they prefer the name Yekuana (Canoe People) or So'to (True People). They live in a region of mountains and rain forests crossed by five great tributaries of the Orinoco.[1] After Spanish explorers arrived in that region in 1759, the Yekuana established extensive trading relationships with white settlements on the lower Orinoco. Yekuana women learned to use small European glass beads acquired in trade to make their decorative dance aprons, called *muaho*; earlier dance aprons may have been made of quartz and stone beads.[2]

The muaho is the most intricate item in a woman's wardrobe, worn for ceremonial occasions. She fastens the apron around her waist with a string, and as she walks or dances, the two danglers of beads and dried seeds rustle. Women weave these aprons with cotton threads on a D-shaped frame made of two sticks. The aprons are generally trapezoidal, with geometric or zoomorphic designs on the upper and lower edges. On this elaborately woven apron, however, the design fills the entire piece; it is done with blue and white beads, the most popular colors.[3] The design, which was probably inspired by baskets woven by Yekuana men, depicts Awidi, the venomous coral snake. Some scholars speculate that such imagery, incorporated into safe and familiar objects, gives the Yekuana symbolic control over the forces of death that surround them.[4]

Body-painting, once widespread throughout South America, may be another form of protection, literally, as well as by magic: plant oils of various kinds were applied to the skin as insect repellent. These oils or animal fats could be colored with dyes from fresh-cut plants, such as *achiotl*, a red pigment. Every group had its own way of body-painting and its own design preferences. The complexity of the painting reflected the status, age, and gender of the wearer. Intricate body designs were used only for certain occasions, such as dances, hunting expeditions (where designs brought luck), initiation rites, and war celebrations. Among some groups, people decorated their faces every day, but had specialists apply designs for important occasions.

The body of this seated man is almost completely covered with geometric painting. He may be a shaman, for he appears to be smoking tobacco. Tobacco, rarely smoked for leisure, was used as medicine and in magic or religious ceremonies. During these ceremonies, the shaman would go into a trance and enter another world. There he could converse with spirits who exercised powerful influences over life. Effigies like this one, found in a cave in the mountains east of Lake Maracaibo, were hidden during the colonial period to save them from destruction by the Spaniards.

Today body-painting and tattooing are still practiced by some Amazonian groups, particularly the Yanomami in Brazil and the Shipibo in Peru.

N.R. and R.M.

The Shuar and Achuar, who live in the mountainous tropical areas of southeastern Ecuador and northern Peru, share many cultural characteristics, including an appreciation of beautiful ornaments. Both men and women adorn themselves for ceremonial and special occasions, but men wear the most elaborate decorations and spend considerable time collecting materials, making ornaments, and glamorizing their appearance. The object is, of course, to make themselves attractive to women.[1]

These wing-cover ornaments or *akitiai* were made to be worn as earrings or sideburn decorations. The iridescent green wing-covers, from a beetle that the Shuar and Achuar call *wauwau*, are crowned with red and yellow toucan feathers. According to several Shuar and Achuar elders in 1992, beetlewing-cover ornaments may have been made by the Waorani and traded to the Shuar and Achuar. They added, however, that the Achuar who live in remote regions continue to make traditional ornaments because they have greater access to natural materials and have retained knowledge about making them.

Today, the Shuar and Achuar rarely wear ear and sideburn ornaments, but feather headbands are still popular. Feathers are associated with virility and spiritual power. In the past, a man's prowess was based on his success as a warrior—how many enemies he had killed. As a warrior's reputation grew, he wore more elaborate feather headdresses and other ornaments. Superior warriors eventually became informal leaders or shamans.[2]

Traditionally, feather headbands, called *tawasap* in Shuar and *etzengrutay* in Achuar, were worn by men who had achieved positions of power and leadership. Today, they are worn primarily by older men and political leaders as symbols of authority. They are made with red and yellow toucan or *tsukanka* feathers and the black feathers of a bird called *awacha*, attached to a woven cotton band.

Among the Shuar and Achuar, feather ornaments have also been associated with wealth. For example, in the past shamans were paid with highly valued goods such as shotguns, hunting dogs, blowguns, feather headbands, and Western clothing. Such valuables were also given to powerful shamans by their less powerful colleagues as signs of respect.[3]

N.R.

SHUAR TAWASAP OR ACHUAR ETZENGRUTAY (FEATHER HEADBAND), EARLY 20TH C. LENGTH 51 CM (19.4842)

SHUAR OR ACHUAR AKITIAI (EAR OR SIDEBURN ORNAMENTS), EARLY 20TH C. LENGTH 24.5 CM (18.8743)

SHUAR MAN. ORIENTE, ECUADOR. (N36823)

This drawing, copied from a fifteen-hundred-year-old ceramic vessel made by a potter of the Moche culture on the northern coast of present-day Peru, shows a workshop where women are weaving copies of small textiles that hang in front of them. Moche society had specialists for all kinds of activities, including metallurgy, architecture, and the production of ceramics, painted murals, and textiles.

Moche weavers made remarkable garments covered with small plaques of gold and silver, perhaps ritual armor for chiefs. They also knew various decorative techniques, such as embroidery and painting. The images most frequently found on their textiles are Presentation scenes (in which priestly figures make offerings to the gods), warrior figures, trophy heads, battle scenes, war prisoners, deer hunters, tule boats, and supernatural runners (mythological beings with the bodies of men and the heads, legs, and wings of swift animals).

This tapestry-weave shirt, dated to A.D. 700 to 800, combines late Moche imagery with that of the Huari culture, which flourished in the Peruvian central and northern highlands from A.D. 600 to 1000. The figure represents one of the individuals portrayed in the Moche Presentation scene. He holds a goblet in one hand and perhaps a

staff in the other. The goblet may contain the blood of sacrificed prisoners, who are shown in similar scenes in other Moche designs. The figure's long shirt and tasseled headdress are characteristic of the Late Moche style. Two crests on the headdress may represent tufts of feathers. Long sashes with serpent heads hang from the waist. The shirt ends in a fringe of beautiful, multicolored wool wefts.

This shirt may have been found at Campanario, a Moche cemetery located in the lower Huarmey Valley, Peru. The rich tombs of Sipán, Cerro la Mina, Huaca de la Luna, and other sites, have preserved few textiles, but those that remain indicate that the Moche people buried their dead in beautiful clothing, with ornaments of gold, silver, and copper. The manufacture of ceremonial garments may have been a sacred act undertaken in buildings devoted exclusively to that work; if so, the garments may have been woven by a special class of initiates who made no other textiles.

Today, in native communities of Peru, spinning takes place throughout the year. Weaving, however, tends to be done between July and November, during the dry season between harvest and planting time.

R.M.

"Finally the shirt was ready. It had been woven by one of the women in the workshop. She had in front of her a piece woven with the same designs so no mistake would occur."

—ANDEAN FOLKLORE

The art of weaving was invented in Andean societies more than six thousand years ago, long before pottery was known. Textiles were first produced from plant fibers—wild cotton and agave. Later, with the domestication of llamas and alpacas, animal wool was used in weaving. Archaeological textiles tell of particular times and societies and even of the people for whom they were made. They may express religious and political beliefs. For example, the most elaborate textiles were ritual clothing worn by an elite class of priests and chieftains.

In the Paracas culture of southwestern Peru (800 to 100 B.C.), textiles were the most important manifestations of wealth—as gold was to other societies—and Paracas weavers created fabrics unlike any others of that time (see p. 69). When a leader died, his body was wrapped in layers of beautiful garments and laid to rest in the dry soil of the Paracas Peninsula, a practice that suggests the strong Andean tradition of ancestor worship. The images on these textiles, preserved in the desert environment, reflect ancient conceptions of the natural and spirit worlds.

Priests of the Tiwanaku and Huari cultures (A.D. 600 to 900) of the central and southern Andes performed their rituals outdoors, in front of their temples, and they wore a variety of ritual garments for different ceremonies. These vestments include unusual four-cornered hats, abstractions of both the mountains and the mountain god Apu-jirca (Powerful Mountain) who dwells there. Found in coastal tombs, these hats symbolize the dominance of the Andes, even in the lowlands along the coast.

People of the Chimú culture (A.D. 900 to 1450) on the northern coast of Peru made beautiful ritual clothing of feathers from seabirds and birds of the tropical rain forests on the eastern side of the Andes. Feathers have a sacred significance in many native cultures, and textiles like this mantle were used by Chimú priests. During hallucinogenic trances, Chimú shamans transformed themselves into birds able to fly between the natural and supernatural worlds.

People of the coast and highlands of Peru, Bolivia, and Ecuador still wear feathers in their ritual dances. And other textiles created by pre-Hispanic cultures are used today by native priests and community leaders in traditional rituals. Through cloth and clothing, beliefs and symbols have been transmitted from ancient times to the present day.

R.M.

"The hats were kept in the dark temple. Only the priests knew where, and only they were allowed to wear them during the ceremonies twice a year."

—ANDEAN FOLKLORE

PILE-WEAVE FOUR-CORNERED HAT,
A.D. 600–1000. TIWANAKU CULTURE.
HEIGHT 11 CM (22.3722)

FEATHER TABARD, A.D. 900–1450.
CHIMÚ CULTURE, PERU. 76 X 65 CM
(15.9404)

The Mapuche (People of the Land) live on reservations in three different geographical zones of central southern Chile: the rolling hills of the Central Valley, the forested area along the coast, and the Andean foothills.[1] They are known for their great military prowess and for their extraordinary textiles and silver ornaments.

The man's poncho, called a *makuñ*, is probably the most striking of all Mapuche textiles, and its quality reflects the wearer's social and economic position.[2] This poncho is unusually complex, combining two different weaving designs in one piece. It alternates a *ñimin* design of complementary-warp patterned bands with a *trarikan* design of ikat patterned bands.[3] The dark blue and white trarikan design, which is associated with the authority position of a lineage head or *lonko*, symbolizes a stairway into the infinite. This stairway is somewhat similar to the ceremonial ladder or *rewe* that every Mapuche shaman carves and erects near her house as a symbol of her status and ability to communicate with the gods.[4] Ñimin and trarikan ponchos are made by master weavers, called *duwefe*, who are greatly respected for their abilities. Only relatively wealthy men can afford such ornate ponchos, and they wear them only for ceremonial occasions.[5]

Mapuche men may help with the warping of the loom, but all weaving is done by older girls and women. Training through observation begins about the age of ten. Most knowledge is freely shared. Some patterns are known by all women, although others are kept within a family.

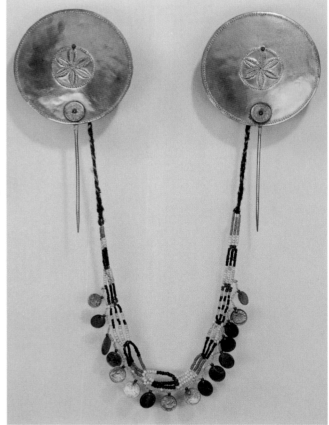

The Mapuche have been weaving for a long time, probably since before they came in contact with the Inka and began to use wool from a type of llama called *chiliweke*.[6] Their first materials may have been plant fibers. Weaving became an important activity among the Mapuche after the Spanish introduced sheep to the region. Originally, wool was colored with vegetal and mineral dyes. Today commercial dyes are preferred because they are easier to obtain and they make highly marketable, brightly colored textiles.[7]

The Mapuche began making silver ornaments at the end of the eighteenth century, using coins and other silver objects they received as trade goods from Spanish colonists.[8] Today, silver is a symbol of Mapuche identity and pride—for women, as jewelry; for men, in the form of decorated stirrups and spurs.[9] Mapuche women wear large silver brooches called *tupus* (a Quechua word)[10] to fasten their shawls. This ornament is made of two tupu pins, with strands of multicolored glass beads and Chilean coins dating from 1899 to 1922. The silver disks are embossed with a flower design.

All Mapuche women own silver jewelry regardless of their social status, and today such pieces are considered heirlooms. Although they put on Western clothes for everyday work, Mapuche women still wear traditional clothing for ceremonial occasions and when they leave their communities.[11]

N.R.

VISION AND VIRTUOSITY
TOM HILL

In many native cultures, the concept of virtuosity includes more than mastering the skills needed to realize an artistic vision. It encompasses understanding the beliefs and processes of transformation behind the creation of an artwork. In this sense, shamans were perhaps the original artists, for they pursued their beliefs into new ways of knowing, ritually transforming themselves from one shape or form of being into another to travel to the spirit world.

✳

The relationship between community aesthetics and individual creativity in native art is largely an untold story, perhaps because so little is known about the individuals who made these beautiful objects. Clearly, within many cultures, there was a responsibility to maintain the community's visual experience. But artists also brought personal creativity to aesthetic traditions. Experimentation and adaptation, grounded in the processes of quillwork and carving, painting and weaving, had significant roles in the conception and execution of many of the works in this book.

In every culture, each generation inherits the creative achievements of its predecessors, builds on its inheritance to make a new artistic legacy, and passes that legacy on to its children. In the past—as in the present—individuals had a social responsibility to contribute to the evolution of art forms. Old ideas were made new. Designs were exchanged with other tribes. In some cases, changes created tension within communities, and radical departures from norms were sometimes softened as artists understood just how far an aesthetic could be challenged or pushed. But the desire to create and transmit cultural values has always been a powerful force behind Indian art. And that force becomes stronger as artists grow in their understanding of and commitment to those values.

*

There is a spiritual dimension inherent in making art. Native Americans have often been awakened to spiritual ideals by the simple act of doing things in the old ways. Contemporary Métis artist Edward Poitras recalls his 1975 art courses at Manitou College in Quebec, where as one of his projects he constructed a pair of snowshoes. Northern Cree elders guided him through the work, which was very labor-intensive. The deceptively straightforward art of webbing rawhide to a tamarack form involved a conceptual rigor and attentiveness that Poitras experienced as highly emotive and ritualistic.

Much later, as his career flourished, Poitras credited the disciplined and spiritual process of creating traditional objects as a major influence in his contemporary art. His work, particularly his large installations, reflects a spiritualism that appears to be forever in a state of becoming. There is a hidden energy in his art that baffles the traditional community, and on a number of occasions he has stopped making pieces rather than be misunderstood by his Cree elders. As rituals did in the past, his work engages viewers as participants in visual dramas that are totally dependent on the power of new symbols he creates. His vision and virtuosity transcend time, place, and culture.

Like Poitras, many other contemporary Native American artists, including Truman Lowe, Faye HeavyShield, Bill Reid, Robert Davidson, Dorothy Grant, and James Luna, attribute the technical, spiritual, and emotional insights they bring to their work to their artistic heritage. Western art traditions center on intellectualism and the isolation of human experience outside the natural world. Native American art often expresses the opposite: spiritualism, intuitive emotionalism, and the human relationship to the environment. Native art is also characterized by its unconcern with distinctions between craft and art and by its particular aesthetics of color and space. While some contemporary Indian artists have placed native artistic values aside in order to pursue Western theories of art, many others continue to work within their traditions.

Haida artist Robert Davidson, born in 1946 in Hydaburg, Alaska, is the great-grandson of the carver Charles Edenshaw (ca. 1839 to 1920). Davidson tells about dancing at a 1990 potlatch in Haida Gwaii on the Queen Charlotte Islands, wearing a salmon mask he had created. After he danced, an old man came up to him and said that it had been a long time since he'd seen that dance. Until then, Davidson wasn't sure he'd got it right; in fact, he had no idea whether the dance had ever been done before. Davidson likes to tell the story to illustrate how cut off from Haida culture he was—and yet how traditional Haida images seemed to be in his mind unconsciously. "We all have that cosmic memory," he comments, "but artists—practicing artists—have it a lot."[1]

CREE MAN IN TRADITIONAL DRESS. (P13226)

FEAST DISH, LATE 19TH/EARLY 20TH C. CARVED BY CHARLES EDENSHAW (CA. 1839–1920), HAIDA. 43.8 X 36.2 X 15.9 CM (1.2371)

HURON MOCCASINS WITH QUILLWORK AND MOOSE-HAIR DECORATION, CA. 1830. LENGTH 22.9 CM (19.6346)

In the 1960s and 1970s, Davidson was part of a new wave of young Northwest Coast artists whose work evolved through traditional carving to producing serigraphic prints, a new art form intended primarily for the art market. His *Raven Stealing the Moon* includes highly conventionalized Northwest Coast iconography and references to mythology. But in *Raven*, Davidson also strikes out in radical new directions, manipulating space and line into an intricate, compressed image. The result is a tension-filled composition that exerts a powerful outward force: if you were to adjust the boundaries of the composition or remove one of its ovoid forms, the shapes might magically materialize and tumble out. Davidson's ability to create and sustain such expansive energies within a silkscreen print—his daring and control—testifies not only to his skill as an artist, but to his insight into the Haida tradition of innovation. "The Haida were experimenting a hundred and more years ago," he points out. "Our art has always been in a state of progression. It is a matter of being creative within known and long-established boundaries, but not a matter of being different. Too many people experiment before they have enough knowledge, but that is not innovation. It is bastardization."[2]

✳

Since the end of the eighteenth century, museums throughout the world have collected Northwest Coast material. During the 1950s, Northwest Coast artists, determined to revitalize their artistic traditions, began to look to these collections. The museums in British Columbia with the largest volume of material were particularly supportive in developing special programs to give artists access to their heritage. Master Kwakiutl carvers Mungo Martin and Ellen Neel were employed in 1949 by the Museum of Anthropology of the University of British Columbia to restore works and serve as informants. This coming together of contemporary artists with museum anthropologists would eventually influence Northwest Coast art and the international art market. By the 1970s, objects that had once been seen by anthropologists as material culture were being proclaimed by curators and collectors as high art, works from one of the great artistic traditions of the world.

In truth, of course, Northwest Coast art, and the art of other native cultures, had not gone unnoticed by the international art community. As early as 1931, John Sloan and Oliver LaFarge had organized the *Exposition of Indian Tribal Arts* in New York. Eight years later, the San Francisco Golden Gate International Exposition—a project of New Deal Indian policy—included an arts and crafts exhibition. Rene d'Harnoncourt, general manager of the U.S. Department of the Interior's Indian Arts and Crafts Board, coordinated the exhibition. In 1941, d'Harnoncourt and Frederick H. Douglas, curator of Indian art at the Denver Art Museum, followed the San Francisco exhibition with an exhibition at New York's Museum of Modern Art, *Indian Art of the United States*.

Non-native artists, as well as curators, were discovering native aesthetics. In the 1940s, the surrealist painter and sculptor

Max Ernst became intrigued with a Northwest Coast spoon he purchased from an antiquarian shop on Third Avenue in New York. Soon, a whole group of surrealists who had moved to New York from war-ravaged Europe began collecting the visual puns that are so prevalent in Northwest art. European artists—including André Breton, Yves Tanguy, Roberto Matta, and Kurt Seligman—were

fascinated by how reality was depicted in these puns: two beings, sharing various parts, realized in a single image or space. In 1946, Ernst and the abstract expressionist painter Barnett Newman mounted an influential exhibition entitled *Northwest Coast Indian Painting* at the Betty Parsons Gallery in New York. These Western artists, however, were intrigued primarily by the aesthetic theory expressed in Northwest Coast art. Kirk Varnedoe perhaps best describes what interested them: "Like many aspects of the primitivism of the 1940s, the Native American influences existed more broadly on a conceptual level in the artists' words than in specific formal terms in their paintings and sculptures."[5]

The surrealists' effort to penetrate the aesthetic mysteries of Northwest Coast art was surpassed by Haida artist Bill Reid, who began his rediscovery of Haida artistic traditions in the early 1950s. The son of William Reid, a non-native from Michigan, and Sophie Gladston, a Haida from the Queen Charlotte Islands, Reid studied museum collections and ethnographies written by early anthropologists to reconstruct formal Haida conventions. Reid mastered Haida art in all its complexity and, unlike the surrealists, had great insight into its deeper meanings. Karen Duffek, in her essay from the exhibition publication *In the Shadow of the Sun*, writes of Reid: "In essence, Reid became an 'apprentice' to his great-uncle, the late Charles Edenshaw, . . . whose work was well represented in museum collections and reproduced in books. Reid's copying of the master's art was a traditional way of learning Northwest Coast form and provided the foundation for the original works he went on to create."[4] Reid believed that the artist must master the techniques of an artistic tradition in order to contribute to that tradition in any meaningful way. He understood that art grows out of a way of life:

TSIMSHIAN MASK, EARLY TO MID-19TH C. HEIGHT 24 CM (3.4678)

THE BEACH AT KLINKWAN, 1892. PRINCE OF WALES ISLAND, ALASKA. PHOTOGRAPH BY PHOTO SHOP.

TLINGIT INDIANS IN TRADITIONAL DANCE DRESS. CHILKAT, ALASKA. (N36406)

its skills are the practical skills of a culture developed to such a high degree that a qualitative change occurs and the artist's work comes to life.

✳

The traditional cultures of the Northwest Coast—the Haida, Tlingit, and Tsimshian of the north coast; Nuxalk and Kwakiutl of the central coast; and Nuu-chah-nulth and Coast Salish of the south—shared many elements. Their ways of life, after all, were shaped by a common natural environment. But, as their art reveals, these cultures differed in many respects as well. In each, art was so interwoven with religious belief and social structure that it is difficult to ascertain where one begins and another ends.

Sculpture and two-dimensional art were the Northwest Coast's fundamental means of artistic expression. The sculpture of these cultures tends to be realistic. It is likely that their more symbolic two-dimensional art forms traditionally had a more decorative function. In two-dimensional work, as in the relief on the Tsimshian double chest shown in this chapter, symbols are dislocated into elements and redesigned according to the culture's rules of convention. Masks, like the Tsimshian portrait mask, show the masterful handling of naturalistic human forms. This piece's minimal distortion, smoothly rendered surfaces, and pure lines reflect a distinctive tribal style. But the conceptualization of the image and the subtle sculpting of facial expression give the mask its unique personality. A contemporary Tsimshian carver like Freda Diesing might refer to it as having a life all its own. It is art driven by the spirit within.

The portrait mask, double chest, and Chilkat Tlingit Bear crest hat are powerful and masterful works that transmit cultural values. Yet each also reflects an individual's vision and virtuosity, the maker's conceptual ability and technical skills.

✳

The people of the Northwest Coast may not have had words for fine art in the Western sense—art for art's sake—but their art-making clearly manifests high aesthetic standards, individual interpretation, and virtuosity. The realization that this art had commercial value to non-natives led to the development of a whole new art form—Haida argillite carving—made specifically for the tourist trade. Ironically, at the same time argillite carving was becoming successful, the potlatch law banning ceremonial traditions was being enforced in Canada.

Yet in spite of dramatic changes along the Northwest Coast—the introduction of new materials, techniques, and markets, as well as the imposition of prohibitive laws—these cultures survived. Northwest Coast artists working today continue to reaffirm the gift of virtuosity and the significance of their cultures' vision of the indivisibility of life from art.

HURON CIGAR CASES, POCKET-
BOOK, AND BOX, 18TH AND EARLY
19TH C. LENGTH 10.2 TO 14.3 CM
(19.8132, 8.6755, 16.7398 AND 17.9778)

JEREMIAH LONE CLOUD HOLDING
CRUCIFIX DECORATED WITH
QUILLWORK AND MOOSE-HAIR
EMBROIDERY.

HURON CIGAR CASE, EARLY 19TH C.
LENGTH 13.3 CM (3.4835)

These cigar cases and this box and small pocketbook were produced for sale to non-natives more than a century and a half ago. Their beautiful floral decorations are created not with silk embroidery thread, but with white hairs plucked from the mane, cheeks, and rump of the moose.

The oldest and most widespread type of moose-hair "embroidery" is appliqué, where several hairs are laid across the surface of an object and fastened down with closely spaced stitches. The technique shown here, however, is true embroidery: a needle with a single thread is sewn through the material being decorated to make a design. Because moose hairs are so short—no longer than a few inches—the needle may have to be rethreaded with each stitch. These elegant personal accessories are made of birchbark, two of them covered with trade cloth. The stiff bark closes tightly around the embroidery, holding each stitch firm. The cigar cases and the box also have birchbark linings to cover the ends of the threads, while the pocketbook is lined with cloth.

The origins of appliqué embroidery are not known, but true moose-hair embroidery can be dated to 1639, when three French nuns of the Ursuline order landed in Quebec to open the first of a number of seminaries for Indian girls. Needlecraft was an important skill for French ladies of the time, and embroidery lessons were offered to students at the convent, both native girls and the daughters of French colonists. At first, costly silk and metallic threads were imported from Europe, but dyed moose hair quickly became a cheaper substitute. In all likelihood, it was native seamstresses who taught the nuns how to work with moose hair.[1] The nuns and their students used moose-hair embroidery to decorate not only church vestments, but also objects made for sale to fur traders and other travelers.

The floral designs shown here are reminiscent of crewel embroidery patterns in seventeenth-century Europe. The centers of the flowers are done in a technique known as stump work or tufting, trimmed with imported scissors. Native women who already had great skill and a high artistic sense born of a long tradition of finely decorated clothing clearly mastered new needlework techniques very quickly.

Although women of other eastern tribes attended the convent schools, Huron women produced the most exquisite moose-hair embroidery, and by the early nineteenth century they monopolized the curio trade. Many of their creations found their way to Europe; George Heye purchased one of these cigar cases in Paris.

These marvelous objects, made for sale to strangers and for uses foreign to Huron life, challenge assumptions regarding Indian art. Surely today we recognize this work—created of indigenous materials, grounded in a culture that values artistic excellence and fine craftsmanship, and employing designs and techniques in use for more than two centuries—as traditionally Huron.[2]

M.J.L.

These three containers, all made by people of the Eastern Woodlands, span the nineteenth century, a time when native people fought for their lands; struggled to maintain beliefs; observed the customs of European-Americans, who had become a powerful, visible presence in their lives; and found new ways to market their skills to survive.

Women of the many Algonquian tribes were, by the seventeenth century, already masters of quillwork decoration for ceremonial clothing and ornament. The production for sale of elaborate quilled mosaics on birchbark—such as the work on this Micmac box—was a step easily taken. Model canoes, letter holders, purses, cigar cases, chair seats, miniature trunks, and lidded boxes—carefully tailored to a foreign market—were resold by ships' captains at ports of call all over the world. Most quilled designs are geometric, some of them personal to a particular family, and the meaning of many of them has been forgotten. This box shows two motifs whose names are known: the *kagwet*, or eight-legged starfish, and the fan-shaped *waegardisk*, or Northern Lights.[1]

During the eighteenth and nineteenth centuries, basket-makers, too, began to market their goods to non-Indians, sometimes selling baskets door to door in towns. We do not know the meaning of the designs painted and stamped on this storage basket.[2] Native commentaries make it clear that the construction and decoration of baskets is accompanied by religious observance and imbued with spiritual belief.[3] Others suggest that designs express group or family identity or resistance to removal from the land.[4]

This wall pocket is one of hundreds of birchbark objects Passamaquoddy artist Tomah Joseph made to sell to tourists from 1880 to 1914. Wealthy visitors at resorts in Maine and New Brunswick sought "Indian work" to decorate their summer houses and carry home as souvenirs. The local Passamaquoddy, Penobscot, and Abnaki people responded by producing "fancy baskets" and birch-bark curios. Joseph tailored his birchbark work to the Victorian market.[5] Unlike other craftspeople of the time, he inscribed his name on his work, and often included the date. Many of his illustrations are traditional home and hunting vignettes—"authentically Indian" subjects, in the eyes of summer visitors, though by the 1880s they were scenes of the past. Joseph also included images from Passamaquoddy legends. Mikamwes, a little man who lives in the woods, is a favorite character, as is the Snowy Owl, who may be Joseph's personal mark.[6] Some of Joseph's early work includes Passamaquoddy phrases; *Kolelemooke* (Good Luck) and *Mik'wid'hamin* (Remember Me) are two he inscribed on this wall pocket. These sentiments do not appear in his work after 1900, perhaps because he realized that people did not understand them.[7]

The people who purchased a basket or a box may have chosen it for its aesthetic appeal. For the men and women who made and decorated these things, however, something of the art of being Indian is forever embedded in them.

M.J.L.

MICMAC BIRCHBARK BOX WITH
QUILLED DECORATION, EARLY TO
MID-19TH C. 28 X 23 X 19 CM (10.96)

CHIPPEWA WOMEN SELLING
BIRCHBARK BOXES, 1928. ONTARIO,
CANADA. PHOTOGRAPH BY
FREDERICK JOHNSON. (14411)

BIRCHBARK WALL POCKET, CA. 1900.
MADE BY TOMAH JOSEPH (1837–1914),
PASSAMAQUODDY. 36 X 37 CM
(10.4353)

TUNXIS OR MOHEGAN WOODSPLINT
STORAGE BASKET, CA. 1840.
25 X 18 X 13 CM (24.2832)

Finely twined Aleut baskets, made to sell to collectors, are world famous for their artistry and their exquisitely fine, clothlike texture. Some baskets have more than a thousand stitches per square inch, and the preparation of materials and the twining itself can take months of a weaver's time.

The most common material is wild rye beach grass gathered at particular times of the year. It is split into thin strands, dried, and tied into small bundles, ready for use.[1] Baskets are woven upside down, hanging from a string or suspended on a stake, and are sometimes made around a mold to preserve the shape; a soup can or lard pail serves as a basket-mold when necessary. The designs on this basket were created by wrapping the weft strands with colored thread, a technique known as false embroidery. The threads on this basket are silk, giving it a soft, glossy sheen. Fragments of early false embroidery, their patterns made with dyed grasses or strips of baleen, have been found in archaeological sites.[2]

Basketry was an ancient craft in the Aleutian Islands, a skill essential for survival. Women fashioned baskets in a variety of twining techniques and used them to store dried fish, edible roots, and berries, as well as to collect sea-bird eggs.[3] Basketry hats, mitts, socks, and capes protected against the weather. Basketry mats, large and small, were used as wall hangings, room dividers, bedding, and for wrapping the dead.

Baskets with lids and knoblike handles, like the one pictured here, are said to have originated on the island of Attu during the nineteenth century, but women of other islands quickly adopted the form, with some regional variations. The classic decoration is a border along the bottom repeated on the edge of the lid, with other motifs around the body of the basket. This basket incorporates flowers, buds, leaves, and stems in exuberant designs that suggest both Russian and European embroidery and patterns from cross-stitch catalogues.

Designs on lidded baskets were passed from one weaver to another, and included such untraditional sources as wallpaper. One gifted weaver, Anfesia T. Shapsnikoff, enjoyed asking visitors to guess the origin of one of her ancient-appearing designs. It was copied from the Whitman's chocolate box she used to keep her sewing supplies.[4]

A souvenir market in grasswork began very early, certainly by the first decade of the nineteenth century. Sailors, merchants, and missionaries carried home examples of baskets, as well as cigar cases, place mats, covered bottles, and other items made for sale to a foreign market. By the time the United States purchased Alaska in 1867, basketry souvenirs had become an important source of income, not only for individuals, but for communities as well. The last church built on Attu was paid for with proceeds from the work of seven Attuan basket-weavers. It took the women an entire year simply to prepare the grass. Today a few Aleut basket-makers are still working, among them Agnes Thompson (born 1947), whose basketry is sold to private collectors and through Alaska Native Arts and Crafts in Anchorage.

M.J.L.

UNANGAN (ALEUT) BASKET AND COVER, LATE 19TH C. HEIGHT 19 CM (9.7038)

ALEUT BASKET-MAKER, LOUISIANA PURCHASE EXPOSITION, ST. LOUIS, MISSOURI, 1904. PHOTOGRAPH BY CHARLES CARPENTER.

"I learned basketry from my mother. . . . She wouldn't slow down and show me. I had to kind of catch on myself. She gave me a small piece and told me to work on it. I'd work on it, and she'd laugh and say it wasn't right, and then I'd undo it and do it all over until I got it right."

—AGNES THOMPSON, ALEUT

ESKIMO WITH FISH NET, CA.
1917–1919. MACKENZIE RIVER
DELTA, NORTHWEST TERRITORIES,
CANADA. PHOTOGRAPH BY DONALD
A. CADZOW. (2018)

INUPIAQ ESKIMO KAYAK, LATE
19TH/EARLY 20TH C. LENGTH 4.5 M
(8.2719)

The people of the Arctic have lived for thousands of years in a region rich in sea life, but harsh and difficult. The clothing, tools, and equipment invented by these Arctic hunters are fashioned with such intelligence and skill that modern technology has been unable to improve on them. Innovations such as the parka, the harpoon, ice creepers, and snow goggles have instead been adopted by others and have traveled far from their place of origin. Among these inventions is the skin-covered boat known as the kayak.

Kayaks are made in a variety of styles, but everywhere, from Siberia to Greenland, their basic construction remains the same. Men build the wooden frame of pieces of driftwood lashed together with rawhide. Women sew the sheathing of seal or walrus skins, closely cut and fitted to size. The kayak must be light enough to be hauled and handled by a single hunter and flexible enough to encounter heavy seas and large waves without breaking. The design of a kayak admirably serves these needs, since the rawhide ties on the frame take up the stress and strain of movement.

In the Bering Sea region, building a kayak was traditionally permeated with ritual. Hunting songs and prayers were recited; the kayak was blessed with offerings of food; charms or amulets were fastened to the deck or sides to bring protection and good fortune. A hunter's kayak was the means by which he could make a living and support a family. Kayaks were used on the open sea

to hunt seals, walrus, and, where available, whales, to net salmon and catch birds, to hunt caribou in the mainland lakes, as well as for general transport.

The hunters of King Island, Alaska, where this boat was made, traveled as far as the shores of Siberia, through the stormy waters of the Bering Strait. King Island kayaks are extremely sturdy, built to survive rough seas while carrying gear or game stowed fore and aft in the interior.

Today, as in the past, a boy is taught to hunt by his father and other men, and usually begins with toy weapons, first a bow and arrow, and then a harpoon or, today, perhaps a .22 rifle. By watching and listening he learns the ways of the animals, the weather, and the water. He is taught the proper ways to respect the spirits of the animals and rituals to ensure good luck in the hunt. He also learns the art of handling a kayak: how to launch in heavy surf, how to recover from capsizing, how to paddle soundlessly when stalking a seal or swiftly when covering long distances.

Today few of the old, traditional skin kayaks survive outside of museum collections. Hunters instead use wooden or fiberglass boats with outboard motors, not as efficient as kayaks, but quicker and easier to obtain. The kayak design lives, however, as sportsmen worldwide have adopted it for racing and recreation.

M.J.L.

And I think over again
My small adventures
When with a shore wind I
drifted out
In my kayak
And thought I was in danger.
My fears,
Those I thought so big,
For all the vital things
I had to get and to reach.

And yet, there is only
One great thing,
The only thing:
To live to see in huts and on
journeys
The great day that dawns,
And the light that fills the world.

—ESKIMO SONG

For Athapaskan men of northwestern Canada and interior Alaska—including those called Slavey[1] and their northeastern neighbors, the Dogrib—beautiful clothing and ornament reflected social standing and wealth, hunting and trading abilities; for women, they represented skill at dressing skins, weaving, and sewing. People had dress clothes to wear at home or to meet visitors and dressed up their dog teams when entering a camp.

Among the most spectacular clothing of both men and women were fringed belts such as this one woven of dyed porcupine quills.[2] This belt displays quill weaving of exquisite fineness, mounted on a moosehide backing trimmed with red and blue trade cloth. The long fringe of smoked hide is characteristic of Slavey work, but the row of bear claws sewn to a fur band is unusual. Quills are woven on a bow-shaped loom strung with strands of sinew separated by a template of birchbark or, today, cardboard. Women weave moistened quills over and under the warp so closely that it is not visible. An 1824 account tells how Slavey men would bring "specimens of their wives' needlework to the [trading] forts and exhibit them with much pride."[3] When, in 1862, B.R. Ross of the Hudson's Bay Company sent belts to what is now the Royal Scottish Museum, he wrote that "the quantity done in a day by a skillful operative is about two and a half inches of belt size—and one of these articles is completed in about a fortnight, when it would be bartered for about eight pounds worth of goods,"[4] a very high price. A few women still produce woven quillwork. They take great pleasure and pride in keeping the art and cultural values of their predecessors alive.

This doll, catalogued in museum records as Eskimo, is in all likelihood a Tanaina depiction of a shaman wearing a "rich man's belt," a symbol of wealth and prestige. It may be one of the small wooden dolls Tanaina shamans used to cure illness. The Tanaina, of Cook Inlet, Alaska, believed that these dolls came alive at night while people slept and stopped moving at the first light of dawn.

The ornaments hanging from the doll's belt reflect the foreign commerce that swept the shores of southern Alaska during the eighteenth and nineteenth centuries. They include not only costly glass beads traded from Russia and China and dentalium shells traded from Vancouver Island, but also a French gaming token of the kind made during the seventeenth and eighteenth centuries, a Russian token from the same period, an American infantry officer's uniform button, and the teeth and jawbone of a baby caribou, prized decorations on Eskimo women's belts. Bits of metal have been fashioned into a miniature saw, a knife with a wooden handle, and a metal plate that may represent a mirror used by Sino-Manchurian shamans to see into the future. Objects from distant places hold a fascination and a kind of power, and often become part of the accoutrements of a shaman. This fascination is not confined to traditional peoples—note the enormous appeal for museum visitors of objects such as moon rocks and meteorites.

M.J.L.

SLAVEY QUILLED BELT, PROBABLY
1860–1870. 91.5 X 61.5 CM (15.1696)

TANAINA WOODEN DOLL, PROBABLY
MID-19TH C. HEIGHT 27.3 CM
(10.6091)

This Bear crest hat, from a Chilkat clan of the Tlingit, was an *at.oow*, or family treasure. The concept of at.oow refers not only to the physical object, but to the ancestral spirit it depicts and the songs and speeches that accompany its display.[1] Each Tlingit lineage possesses a number of at.oow, but the greatest treasure is the crest hat that embodies the history of the clan from the time of its creation to the present. A crest hat is somewhat analogous to a royal crown in European tradition, displayed on important ceremonial occasions and worn by the reigning head of the family.

    This Bear has eyes and ears inlaid with costly abalone shell. They would have glittered in the firelight as the hat was danced during ceremonies accompanying a potlatch. The moveable tongue is made of copper, a symbol of wealth. The head is crowned with eight rings twined of spruce root, another emblem of prestige. When the hat was new, the rings would have swayed back and forth in the dance, like the stalk of wild celery or *kookh* from which these hats derive their name: *shadakookh*.

    The rings are often called "potlatch rings," with the idea that a new ring was added for each potlatch where the hat was displayed. Artist Bill Holm has pointed out, however, that there is no evidence that rings were added in this way; rather the number of rings on a hat is simply part of the crest of a particular lineage.[2] The proverb "It takes eight feasts to make a prince" describes the ideal number of potlatches a rich man could hope to give in his lifetime.

    Wealthy Tlingit house owners stored at.oow in elaborately carved chests sometimes considered treasures in their own right. This is a particularly fine old one, from no later than the early part of the nineteenth century and possibly earlier. It is constructed as a double chest—the top and sides slip over an inner box, to which the bottom is attached, like the sections of a telescope box. The sides of the chest are made from a single plank of cedar, carefully grooved, steamed, and bent at the corners, a technique widely used on the Northwest Coast to make bentwood boxes and containers. The small faces along the top of the lid are bordered with inlaid opercula shells. The front panel is carved to represent the head of an undersea monster named Gonakadet, the guardian of wealth, while the back panel depicts the being's hindquarters.

    A widespread Northwest Coast story tells how Raven brought light to the world by stealing it from a wealthy chief who kept it in a treasure box. G.T. Emmons, who acquired this box in the Tlingit village of Klukwan, recorded that it was made by the neighboring Tsimshian. Tsimshian carvers enjoyed a reputation for their artistry, and a wealthy Tlingit house-owner may well have commissioned this chest from a Tsimshian artist, who would have been well rewarded for his work.

M.J.L.

A rich man is coming—
Keep your thoughts to yourself!

—TLINGIT SONG

TSIMSHIAN DOUBLE CHEST CARVED
OF WOOD, LATE 18TH/EARLY 19TH C.
52 X 81 CM (9.8027)

CHILKAT CHIEF COUDAHWOT (?) IN
THE WHALE HOUSE AT KLUKWAN,
1895. CHILKAT, ALASKA. PHOTO-
GRAPH BY WINTER AND POND.

For the people of the Northwest Coast, potlatches and feasts are significant social and spiritual occasions, and beautifully carved food bowls and serving utensils provide one way in which a host can display wealth, status, and lavish generosity towards his guests. Most bowls, including some of enormous size, are carved of wood, but some of the most beautiful small feast dishes are made from the great spiral horns of the mountain sheep. Sheephorn is a tough, semitranslucent material. Softened with hot water or steam, it can be cut and spread into a bowl form; after it cools, it can be carved into a finished shape and the surface decorated with additional carving. Bill Holm has observed that the art of making a sheephorn bowl is analogous to that of making a canoe, demanding the same ability to visualize changes in form as the sides are spread.[1]

Sheephorn bowls were usually filled with oil or grease rendered from seal and whale blubber or from the highly-prized oolachon (candlefish), still a favorite feast food today. Guests dip chunks of dried salmon, potatoes, and other delicacies into the grease to add richness and flavor.

The Haida carver who made this graceful and elegant little bowl (right) probably lived on the Queen Charlotte Islands and had to obtain the sheephorn on a trading trip to the mainland. The carving depicts two mice, one at either end, in the act of crawling into the bowl. Mice were notorious food thieves and particularly fond of the delicious grease that would have been served in this bowl. The eyes of the mice are inlaid with costly abalone shell, also received in trade. Their bodies are shallowly carved on the outside of the bowl in classic Northwest Coast formline style. Although sheephorn bowls were made all along the Northwest Coast, the artistry of Haida carvers was particularly admired.

The basic techniques for making sheephorn bowls were essentially the same throughout the Coast, but variations in form separate the north and the south. Museum records attribute the second bowl (left) to the Chehalis, but bowls of this style were made by many people of the lower Columbia River of western Washington and traded widely throughout the state. Many of the bowls are family heirlooms, used over several generations and so darkened with age and wear that they are frequently mistaken for wood.

Columbia River bowls are characterized by square-cut raised ends, often slotted, and the use of geometric forms such as triangles, zigzags, and parallel lines as surface decoration. Some bowls, including this one, are also carved with human faces in a distinct style: straight brow, thin nose, stepped-back chin. A few bowls depict what appears to be a skeletal human figure. Many of these designs seem to be very old; some of them are found as decoration on objects excavated at Ozette, a five-hundred-year old village on the Washington coast. We do not know their meanings. We do know that this bowl and the Haida grease bowl are more than food-serving dishes; they carry associations that sustain the aesthetic sense and the spirit.

M.J.L.

HAIDA CARVED SHEEPHORN BOWL,
19TH C. 11.5 X 18 CM (9.8059)

CHEHALIS CARVED SHEEPHORN
BOWL (2 VIEWS), 19TH C. 12.4 X 23
CM (15.4647)

ROBERT DAVIDSON.

Raven Stealing the Moon by Haida artist Robert Davidson refers to the Northwest Coast story of how Raven brought light to the world by playing a trick on the chief who kept the sun, moon, and stars hidden away in three wooden boxes. Raven's head is seen in profile; in his beak he holds the crescent moon depicted as a red figure. The sun, already set free, views the scene from the upper right corner.

A great-grandson of the artist Charles Edenshaw, Davidson has an international reputation for his work in wood, argillite, and silver, as well as for his printmaking. He is part of a remarkable artistic renaissance along the Northwest Coast. Except in a few areas, the traditional arts of the region, based on carving, painting, textiles, and basketmaking, had nearly been forgotten by the middle of the twentieth century. Since the 1950s and 1960s, however, new generations of artists have drawn inspiration from the work of a few remaining master carvers, painters, and weavers. This resurgence of creativity is accompanied by a renewed dedication to traditional ceremonies. For example, in 1969 Davidson carved the first totem pole in living memory to be erected in Masset, British Columbia, his home village.

In addition to carving totem poles and masks, making weavings and button blankets, crafting decorated boxes, and painting house-screens, the artists of the Northwest renaissance are exploring nontraditional media. Silkscreen printing, in particular, is well-suited to the complex and beautiful iconography of the region. Some prints are created as potlatch gifts within native communities, but most are designed and printed for a worldwide, non-native clientele. Sold in galleries and museum shops, given wide distribution through museum exhibitions and publications, and reproduced on note-cards, T-shirts, posters, and program covers, screen prints enable artists to make a living and encourage them to experiment with new colors and new concepts.

In 1982, Davidson graciously presented the museum with one of his own artist's proofs of *Raven Stealing the Moon*. His contributions to the museum, however, go beyond this gift. While studying the Haida collections, Davidson identified a carved feast dish as the work of his great-grandfather. The museum also owns a magnificent chief's seat carved by Edenshaw. Davidson's art is a fine example of innovation grounded in tradition and, with Edenshaw's carvings, tells a wonderful story of how culture is both inherited and created anew by each generation.

M.J.L.

The Raven must have been a
great fellow.
He went down under the sea.
Then they pulled up his nose.
He went through the town for
his nose.
When it was given him he started
to fly out of doors.
He flew out with it.
Why! instead of looking like
himself, he looks as if he ought
to have a drink.
After you have done as he has
done you can wander about
the entire world beach.

—TLINGIT SONG

RAVEN STEALING THE MOON, 1977.
ROBERT DAVIDSON (BORN 1946),
HAIDA. SILKSCREEN ON PAPER,
58.3 X 26.5 CM (25.1150)

This mask was on display for many years at the Museum of the American Indian in an exhibit case entitled "Masterworks of Northwest Coast Art." George Heye purchased it in London in 1914. There is no cultural documentation for the mask beyond the attribution Tsimshian. In Western terms it is an artistic masterpiece, a sensitively carved portrait of a man whose face is painted with mysterious and beautiful designs. His mouth is open as if about to speak or sing; his half-closed eyes may signify faraway thought or impending death. Because the work appears so realistic—masks such as this are often referred to as portrait masks—it transcends time and distance and can be appreciated simply as a beautiful work of art.

For the people who, more than a century ago, saw this mask being danced by firelight to the sound of drums, whistles, and song, and for the artist who carved it, it had a power and a meaning that viewers today cannot fully comprehend. It was in all likelihood a *naxnox* mask, the representation of a supernatural spirit power belonging to a particular family and danced to demonstrate that power.[1] During the ritual initiation of a young person into a secret society, the chief sometimes wore a mask as he endowed the initiate with supernatural power.

The anthropologist Franz Boas called the naxnox the "Helpers of Heaven," mediators between the divine and human.[2] In the Coast Tsimshian language the word for mask also means *mouth*, *edge*, or *rim*,[3] suggesting that the donning of a mask during a ritual performance allows the wearer and the audience to approach the edge or boundary of everyday life and touch the world of the sacred and supernatural. Naxnox objects, including masks, rattles, and mechanical devices, were created by a group of professional artists, the *gitsontk*, who seem to have occupied an important social class in traditional Tsimshian life.[4] Today little is known about them. They worked in secret and were the only people qualified to produce the ritual equipment the chief employed as a visible manifestation of his sacred powers.

While naxnox masks define and elaborate the world of the supernatural, another kind of art, exemplified in this painted hide tunic, refers to the social world of rank. The tunic is painted with a crest design depicting, according to the collection notes, a Bear and a mountain spirit. Crest designs belong to a particular lineage and commemorate mythical ancestors or events in the family's history. This one is painted in the sophisticated, highly stylized form used by artists throughout the northern Northwest Coast: curving, almost calligraphic lines of varying thickness; a visual splitting of images to show two sides of a figure simultaneously; the use of U-form and ovoid motifs as joint marks and space fillers.

We can be sure that the people who made and used these beautiful objects valued them both for their aesthetic qualities and for their ability to express, in visible form, the social and spiritual meaning of their lives.

M.J.L.

TSIMSHIAN PAINTED HIDE TUNIC, EARLY TO MID-19TH C. LENGTH 78 CM (1.8045)

TSIMSHIAN SINGER JOHN LAKNEETS PLAYING DRUM, BRITISH COLUMBIA. (41467)

". . . Your letter of Sept. 18th And the check of $11.00 received. I am very glad the basket & cap reached you in good condition, I was afraid they would get mashed. . . . I am making a large black & white basket at present. It has a pretty large mark And quiet fine. It is for a gentleman who lives in Eureka . . . . I remain as ever, very Truly Yours, Mrs. Luther Hickox"

—ELIZABETH HICKOX TO GRACE NICHOLSON,
6 OCTOBER 1908

LIDDED TRINKET BASKETS,
1910–1930. MADE BY ELIZABETH
HICKOX (1873–1947), KARUK.
HEIGHT 6.5 TO 13.5 CM (18.8227,
22.1927, 24.4103, AND 24.6949)

The daughter of a Wiyot mother and a German father, Elizabeth Conrad Hickox lived for most of her life with her husband, Luther Hickox, in Karuk country along the Klamath River in northwestern California. Karuk translates, roughly, as Upriver. A dignified but reclusive woman, Elizabeth Hickox was known as a fine weaver of lidded trinket baskets such as those illustrated here. She was under contract until 1934 to her patron and friend Grace Nicholson, the Pasadena art dealer, who sold her baskets to museums and collectors across the country.

Trinket baskets, originally used to hold valuables or other objects, were made in many sizes and forms. As exquisite as jewels, Elizabeth Hickox's baskets are twined in the Karuk way and decorated with old patterns—often at the request of buyers who sought "traditional" Indian designs. The shape of her baskets was considered "modern" by other weavers,[1] and the high knobs were her innovation. Klamath River basketry materials include hazel, willow, and myrtle sticks for the foundation, pine roots for the twining elements, and spruce root, bear grass, *Woodwardia* fern, maidenhair fern, and porcupine quills dyed yellow for the overlay elements.[2] Plant fibers used in baskets were once Ikxareeyav, Spirit Beings who invented the languages, ceremonies, and ways of life adopted by humans. To the Karuk, baskets are alive, and they remain important actors in traditional Karuk ceremonies.[3]

The work of Pomo master artists Mary Benson and William Benson, Mary's husband, like the work of Elizabeth Hickox, is also rooted in tradition and was produced largely for sale to Grace Nicholson.[4] This lovely twined basket by Mary Benson is the type traditionally used to cook acorn mush; the materials are sedge, redbud, and willow.[5] These finely incised bone ear ornaments by William Benson are decorated with red woodpecker and quail topknot feathers, clamshell beads, and abalone-shell pendants. Ear pendants of bone or wood were worn by men and women in central California as part of their dance dress. In a letter to Nicholson dated February 6, 1918, William Benson wrote that Quail Woman went to the hawk for a special wedding gift to give to her brother's wife, a beautiful woman who belonged to the goldfinch family: "so he polished up two peciss of bones design them beutfully and gave them to the quial woman. she then got some feathers from her husband the red feathers and made a basket woven the feathers in. and got plumes from her brother and added to the work. and glue them to the long end of the bones. . . . the first of its kind ever seen."[6] Produced for the commercial art market, baskets and objects like these provided needed cash income and encouraged new generations of creative and skilled artisans.

E.H.B.

COOKING BASKET, 1900–1930. MADE BY MARY BENSON (1876-1930), POMO. HEIGHT 24 CM (24.2107)

PAIR OF BONE EAR ORNAMENTS, CA. 1900–1930. MADE BY WILLIAM BENSON (1862–1937), POMO. LENGTH 26.5 CM (16.1176)

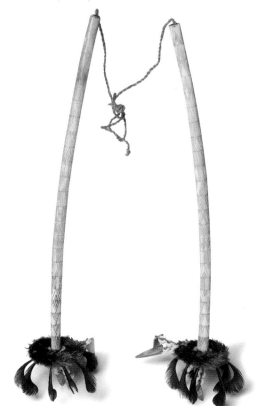

MARY BENSON, POMO. LOUISIANA
PURCHASE CENTENNIAL EXPOSITION,
ST. LOUIS, 1904. (37932)

INDIAN BASKETS, LATE 19TH/EARLY 20TH C.

PIMA BASKET-MAKER, 1921. BLACKWATER,
ARIZONA. PHOTOGRAPH BY EDWARD H.
DAVIS. (25075)

NORTHWEST COAST ARTS AND CRAFTS FOR
SALE. PHOTOGRAPH BY LLOYD WINTER
AND PERCY POND.

CHUMASH BASKET WITH SPANISH COIN
DESIGN, LATE 18TH/EARLY 19TH C.
CALIFORNIA. DIAM. 48 CM (23.132)

THE LEGACY OF BASKETS
RICHARD W. HILL SR.

Barre Toelken, director of folklore and ethnic studies at the University of Oregon, tells a story about a northern California Indian basket-maker, Mrs. Matt, who was hired to teach basketmaking at his university. After three weeks, her students complained that all they had done was sing songs. When, they asked, were they going to learn to make baskets? Mrs. Matt, somewhat startled, replied that they were learning to make baskets, that the process starts with songs that are sung so as not to insult the plants when the materials for the baskets are picked. So they learned the songs and went to pick the grasses and plants to make their baskets.

Upon their return to the classroom, the students were dismayed when Mrs. Matt began to teach them new songs, those that must be sung as you soften the materials in your mouth before you start to weave. The students protested again, but Mrs. Matt patiently explained, "You're missing the point. A basket is a song made visible."

✳

At the beginning of this century, California Indian baskets could be found in "Indian rooms" or "Indian corners" in non-Indian homes all across America. It was, not coincidentally, the era of the Vanishing Indian. Many people collected baskets as curios, "the last industry of a dying race." Yet even then, serious collectors and curators accepted basketry as an art. Many baskets purchased during that era are now in museum collections around the world.

The collecting craze created a demand for literature to explain the making, use, and symbolism of baskets. In fact, Indian baskets became so popular that a quarterly journal called *The Basket: The Journal of the Basket Fraternity or Lovers of Indian Baskets and Other Good Things* was published in California in the early 1900s. The Basket Fraternity lent basket collections, stereopticon slides of basketmaking activities, and models of basket designs to its members. A 1903 advertisement for an Indian basket shop in New York City declared: "The splendid decorative effect produced by the use of Indian baskets in country homes is just beginning to be realized." In 1904, Otis Mason, a curator at the United States National Museum in Washington, published a major study of Indian baskets with more than two hundred illustrations; its central premise was that these baskets were primitive handicrafts. Postcards of Indian basket-makers were printed. By the time the basket frenzy died down around 1910, basketmaking and Indians had become forever linked in the public's mind.

The old basketry catalogues are startling on two accounts. The first is the sheer number of fine baskets that were offered for sale—for a dying art, basketry was putting up a good fight. The second is the prices that were asked for baskets we now recognize as priceless. In 1902, a Tulares bottleneck basket nine inches in diameter and decorated with feather tufts sold for twenty-five dollars. In 1911, Pima baskets were selling for under seven dollars, Hopi "sacred plaques" for only four dollars. Almost anyone could afford to buy Indian basketry; collecting was no longer an interest reserved for the wealthy.

Yet as basket collecting boomed, basketmaking for home use among Indians declined. Basket designs began to change, in reaction to the tastes of non-Indian buyers. Miniature baskets became increasingly popular. Basket-makers adapted their skills to the new-found market.

There were other changes as well. Elsie Allen, a famous Pomo basket-maker, remembers:

> My mother and grandmother worked at basket-weaving when I was a child. When I was older I'd gather sedge roots, willows, bulrushes at the same place they did. . . . However, my grandmother died in 1924, so not only did I lose her help, but most of her examples of baskets as well, because it was customary for an Indian woman to have all her baskets buried with her. . . . Mother told me she did not want that to happen with her, as she wanted me to have her baskets to help when I started up basketweaving again.[1]

Allen's mother was willing to break with one tradition—that her baskets should be buried with her—to preserve another—that her daughter should know the family designs. As long as one basket-weaver still makes these baskets—and as long as the natural materials to make them can be found—Allen's mother's legacy will continue.

Crow Indian,
you must watch your horses.
Often, I am a horse thief.

—LAKOTA SONG

ABSAROKE (CROW) WOMEN ON
HORSEBACK. (P22486)

ABSAROKE (CROW) SWORD
SCABBARD, LATE 19TH C. 134 X 64
CM (8480)

Among the tribes of the northern Great Plains, the Crow gained recognition as the wealthiest in horses as early as the 1830s, and they are still known for the number and quality of their horses. These Indians also created colorful formal clothing and elaborate riding gear so that they would look good on horseback. In 1854, Edwin T. Denig, the trader in charge of Fort Union at the mouth of the Yellowstone River, described the sight of a Crow camp:

> When the camp is on the move in the summer, this tribe presents a gay and lively appearance, more so perhaps than any other. On these occasions both men and women dress in their best clothes. Their numerous horses are decked out with highly ornamented saddles and bridles of their own making, scarlet collars and housings with feathers on their horses' heads and tails. . . . When traveling, the women carry to the horn of the saddle the warrior's medicine bag, and shield. His sword, if he owns one, is tied along the side and hangs down. The man takes charge of his gun and accoutrements in readiness for any attack however sudden. . . . The train is several miles in length, wives are separate from their husbands. . . .[1]

Perhaps at that time the Crow had not yet developed the distinctive sword and lance scabbard for which they were known by the 1880s. This handsome scabbard was collected by the artist Edwin W. Deming, probably during the 1890s. It contains a military saber stamped "U.S. 1864."

The scabbard is made of two pieces of rawhide cut in the form of a long-handled spade. Each piece is forty-five inches long, and the two are sewn together with buckskin cord and edged with red flannel. The narrow (or handle) portion is decorated with tall triangles and transverse bars in a technique rarely found in Plains Indian art. The outlines of the forms were incised with a sharp knife, and the surface of the hide within these outlines was scraped away, leaving lighter decorations. Two beaded pendants of red flannel are tied to the blade cover, while the outer surface of the spade portion is covered with red flannel and elaborately beaded. A border of white beads broken by dark blue stripes surrounds a field of light blue beads and designs in dark blue, yellow, red, and green. The major forms are separated by a line of white, an element that often appears in Crow beadwork.

The museum's collections also contain three scabbards of the same general form and used to house lances. One of these was collected as recently as 1923. During the reservation period (beginning around 1880), mementos of earlier, more warlike times were carried in mounted parades at the annual Crow Fair in August. As in the past, the scabbard was attached to the side of a woman's saddle.

J.C.E.

This rare quilled mask for a horse was acquired from the Northern Cheyenne. It would have been used on parade occasions when both horse and rider were outfitted in their most striking regalia, the mount a visual extension of the man. Horses revolutionized the economy of the Plains in far-reaching ways. They became the ultimate measure of value: objects were priced and payments defined by how many horses they were worth. Horses trained for war were particularly prized, and a man would apply protective paint to his horse as well as himself before going into battle.

Quill embroidery—using porcupine quills or sometimes bird quills or even plant fibers—is an ancient women's art practiced in many parts of North America. Among several tribes of the central Plains there were formal quilling societies. The Cheyenne guild has been most extensively described. A woman seeking to join had to be sponsored and tutored by another member. The guild was concerned only with quillwork using the sacred stripe style, in which the emphasis was not on artistic innovation, so important in other types of work, but on technical perfection.

Sacred quillwork—or later, following the spread of trade, beadwork—was undertaken in fulfillment of a vow. A woman might pledge to quill a robe, a tipi liner, or another traditionally accepted piece as a form of prayer for the welfare of a relative. While a woman was doing sacred quillwork, her behavior was constrained by various rules, and her embroidery was carefully put away from view after each work session. Once she was finished, however, the vow had been fulfilled, and the piece was no longer considered sacred. The product that resulted from the vow was of secondary importance to the process of creation.

J.C.E.

SPOTTED RABBIT, ABSAROKE
(CROW). MONTANA. PHOTOGRAPH
BY WILLIAM WILDSCHUT. (13765)

TSISTSISTAS (NORTHERN
CHEYENNE) QUILLED HORSE MASK,
LATE 19TH C. 55.8 X 30.5 CM (1.4445)

Wakan'tanka,
when I pray to him,
hears me.
Whatever is good,
he grants me.

—SUN DANCE SONG

Native artists' portrayals of their tribes' most significant religious ceremonies are not common. But Black Chicken, a noted Yanktonai religious leader of the Fort Peck Reservation in Montana, sought to picture his tribe's traditional Sun Dance not once, but several times, in paintings on muslin at about the turn of the century.

The upper part of this painting shows the medicine lodge, a circular arbor with a center pole and an entrance to the east, set up in the middle of the tribe's camp circle. Five participants in the ceremony are pictured. Four men stand by, blowing whistles made of eagle wing-bones as they dance in place. The fifth dances suspended from the center pole by two hide cords attached to wooden pins through the skin of his back. Contrary to popular belief, a young man did not undergo this excruciating experience in order to become a brave. He did it to fulfill a vow he had made during a harrowing experience. It was not uncommon for warriors, just before battle, to vow to be tortured in the next Sun Dance if they came through the fight safely.

Although the notes accompanying this painting state that the six warriors on horseback depicted in the lower portion of the muslin "represent visions received [by participants] during the ceremony," we cannot be sure of that. Perhaps they show a young warrior's desire for victory over his enemies in one-on-one combat, which would rank as a noteworthy achievement or coup on his war record.

Muslin sheeting was a part of the annuity goods promised to reservation Indians under treaties with the U.S. government. Indian artists began to paint war records, winter counts (calendars in which each year is represented by an image of a single significant event), and other subjects on muslin even before the buffalo—whose hides had been their traditional canvases—were exterminated on the northern Plains during the early 1880s. Many of these paintings were made for sale to non-Indians.

Black Chicken, a recognized shaman among his people toward the end of the nineteenth century, painted several drums as well as muslins now in museum collections in this country and abroad. Some of his paintings are erroneously identified as Shoshone, as this one was in original museum records. It was collected by Emil W. Lenders, a German-American artist who visited the Sioux and many other western tribes at the turn of the century.

J.C.E.

BLACK CHICKEN (RIGHT) AND ONE BULL, YANKTONAI, EARLY 20TH C. WASHINGTON, D.C.

GRAPHIC INTERPRETATION OF THE SUN DANCE, LATE 19TH C. BLACK CHICKEN, YANKTONAI. PAINTED MUSLIN, 190.6 X 91.5 CM (2.3304)

READING LEDGER ART
RICHARD W. HILL SR.

Our museum's collections include a ledger book that has taught me a great deal. It contains the sketches of the late-nineteenth-century Lakota artist Red Dog. The first part of the book consists of many beautiful drawings of men on horseback, with the subjects frozen at the moment of the charge into battle. Images such as these are the source of much contemporary art by Indians, as well as of the stereotypes served up by Hollywood. Yet here is the real thing—the Plains Indian warrior portrayed by that warrior. These are scenes from his life.

The most revealing drawings, however, are the unfinished pictures toward the back of the book. Red Dog started each page with an outline of a horse, drawn as large as he could make it on the page: the tail extends to the left side margin, the head to the top right corner, the hoofs to the other edges. Next, he added a rider, often drawing over the outline of the horse; the contour lines of the horse's body show through the rider's leggings. More important, by drawing the horse first and to the edges of the page, Red Dog left disproportionate space for the rider. The rider's head must always be at the same level as the horse's, which means in turn that his body must be too small. Red Dog was concerned with filling the page with the horse—the most important design element. Everything else followed from that.

If you know how Plains Indians feel about horses, this makes perfect sense. The horse is as much a part of their identity as the shirt, the pipe, and the tipi. I went riding once with an Arapaho friend of mine on the rolling hills of the Wind River Reservation in Wyoming. It was the first time I had ever been on a horse. As we rode and stopped along the way, he told me his people's stories about the horse. All of a sudden, our horses began to get restless, and it felt like they wanted to run. A shiny black stallion appeared on the horizon, his mane and long tail flowing in the wind. He would run toward us, then back away. My friend explained that we had entered that horse's turf on the open range. Our horses wanted to run free. Who wouldn't? But we rode on.

We came to a small hill, and as we rode over the top of it I could see a slender column of smoke rising. A single tipi came into view at the bottom of the hill. The white canvas of the tipi stood out against the golden grass. Inside, people were making their annual pledge to the sacred pipe of the Arapahos. My friend's uncle was inside as the pipe carrier. Out of respect for the power of the pipe, I declined an invitation to enter. My friend understood.

Riding back to his house, I thought about all we had seen—the ancient petroglyphs to the north, the eagle-shaped mountain to the west, the sacred Bear's Heart

Butte to the east, and the buffalo herds to the south. All these and much more are sacred to my friend. The horses we rode are sacred as well, powerful creatures that had given his people greater ability to follow buffalo on the Plains, reach sites that are sacred to the Arapahos, and defend their sacred world.

That black stallion, proud and strong, made me think of the warriors of the past who were honored in ledger art. Plains Indians on horseback, chasing buffalo or fighting soldiers, are still dominant themes in contemporary Indian art. While some critics see warriors as clichés from a romanticized past, they are real to people like my friend. Dances are held in their honor. When old-time honoring songs are sung at powwows, you can see the older women rise and stand in tribute to the men who fought. There are songs about ancient fights, the First and Second World Wars, Korea, and Vietnam. I'm sure there are songs about the Gulf War, as well. Younger women wear designs and insignia on their shawls to show that their relatives serve in the armed forces. Ledger art—and, later, painting and sculpture—is a way of honoring those warriors. Researchers who study such things have found that Indians who went to Vietnam suffered fewer cases of delayed stress syndrome if their communities stepped forward and honored them for their service. If dances were held, feathers bestowed, and gratitude shown, Indian veterans made the transition back home more easily.

Viewed in this light, making images of warriors can be seen as part of a continuing effort to understand war and the effect it has on soldiers. This art is an acknowledgment that people who fight and shed blood see life differently. The point is not to argue over the morality of acts of war, but to deal realistically and compassionately with the fact of war. Painting images of battle on shirts, tipis, tipi liners, ledger books, and canvases is one way that Plains Indian men have always achieved that goal.

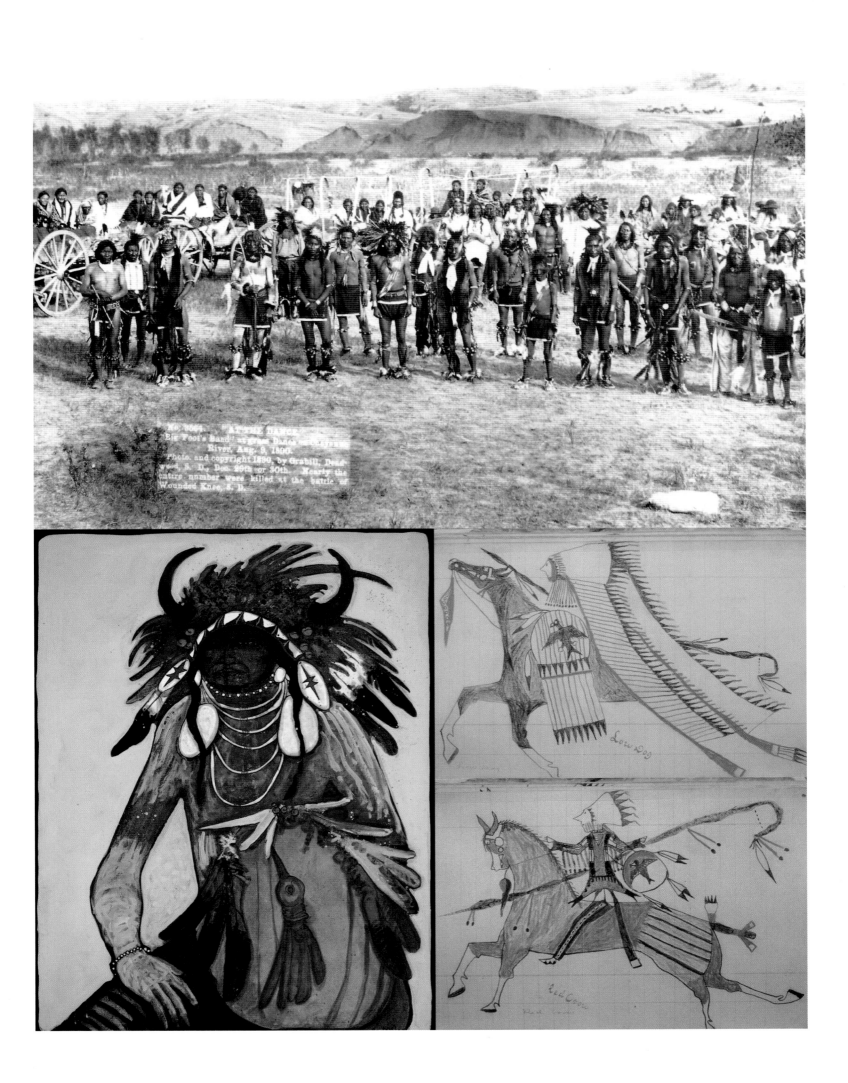

No. 3064. "AT THE DANCE"
"Big Foot's Band" at grass Dance on Cheyenne
River, Aug. 9, 1890.
Photo. and copyright 1890 by Grabill, Dead-
wood, S. D., Dec. 29th or 30th. Nearly the
entire number were killed at the battle of
Wounded Knee, S. D.

LLEWELLYN LOUD AT LOVELOCK
CAVE, 1924. NEVADA. PHOTOGRAPH
BY M.R. HARRINGTON, 1924. (9453)

DAVIN GEORGE (CA. 1960–1991),
PAIUTE-WASHOE.

These two duck decoys, found in 1924 in Lovelock Cave, in what is now western Nevada, are part of a cache of decoys about two thousand years old.[1] They are the oldest known decoys in the world. They were stored in a pit dug into the floor of the cave and arranged to appear empty. Several large stones had been placed over a layer of rush matting and basketry fragments, beneath which lay the bundle of decoys wrapped in more matting. Perhaps they had been hidden in readiness for the next season.

Other objects recovered from Lovelock Cave to date—among them tule bags, fiber nets, baskets, cordage, wooden fishhooks, twig snares, bone awls, ornaments, and stone tools—indicate that the cave served as storage and may have been occupied seasonally for more than four thousand years, until the middle of the nineteenth century.[2] Before the encroachment of white settlers and the subsequent introduction of wage work, survival in the western Great Basin depended on an intimate knowledge of the land and its plant and animal resources. Lovelock Cave, located at the base of a limestone outcropping overlooking the marshes of the Humboldt Sink, is just the kind of local habitat that could have been exploited most productively. The marshlands yielded fish, several species of waterfowl, and tule and cattail plants, the building materials for boats and numerous other articles. Hunters, armed with bows and arrows or nets and hidden in the tall reeds that grew along the marshes, lured waterfowl with decoys floated on the water.

Archaeologists M.R. Harrington and Llewellyn L. Loud, who discovered the Lovelock Cave decoys, identified two types: painted and stuffed. These decoys—one painted and feathered, the other plain—are ingeniously constructed of tule reeds shaped in a strikingly realistic pose. The feathered decoy has a painted head, breast, and tail; its resemblance to a canvasback drake is unmistakable. The plain decoy may represent a female.[3] Stuffed decoys imitated not only ducks, but geese and other waterfowl. They were easier to construct: the head of a real bird was positioned on a rush stub projecting from a reed body; skin, feathers, and beak were left intact and drawn over the frame of the decoy.

Stuffed decoys were still being made in the 1920s by Northern Paiutes living in the adjacent Stillwater area.[4] By the middle of this century, however, many of the old ways had been lost or were remembered only by elders. Wuzzie Dick George and her husband Jimmy taught their children many traditional skills, including decoy making. According to Wuzzie George, the best kind of duck skin for a decoy was the canvasback, although the decoys attracted mudhens and other birds as well. "On warm sunny days," she said, "ducks just sit in one place and be lazy, like people."[5] Working from photographs, her grandson Davin George adapted what his family had passed on to him to re-create the more complex construction of painted and feathered decoys. His replicas are masterpieces in their own right.[6] By this time, however, the decoys were made for personal satisfaction or sale, not for regular use.

E.H.B.

PAINTED AND FEATHERED DUCK
DECOY AND PLAIN DUCK DECOY,
CA. A.D. 200. FOUND IN LOVELOCK
CAVE, HUMBOLDT COUNTY,
NEVADA. LENGTH 26.5 AND 27 CM
(13.4512D AND 13.4513)

That the pictorial arts have been a living tradition among the Pueblo peoples and their ancestors is evident in their painted ceramics, cloth, shields, altars, and kiva murals. Easel painting, however, was a European concept, introduced to the Southwest at the turn of the century. For Fred Kabotie, Awa Tsireh (Alfonso Roybal), and other southwestern artists, the new medium provided a way to preserve traditions and promote understanding and respect for native cultures among non-Indians. Yet paintings produced for sale did not serve Pueblo needs, and individual artists, including Kabotie, often met with resistance in their own communities.

Born in the Hopi village of Shungopavi, on Second Mesa in Arizona, Fred Kabotie began drawing as a child, scratching katsina figures on rocks and making paintings with earth pigments. "That was just play," he later remembered, "but I loved to draw."[1] Kabotie was sent to compulsory boarding school at the Santa Fe Indian School. "I've been brought up and raised right out here, in Hopi," he later said. "And then they sent me way out in the foreign country and told me to forget it, forget it. How could you forget it, when it is all imprinted in your mind?"[2]

In Santa Fe, Elizabeth Willis DeHuff, the wife of the superintendent of the school, invited Kabotie and other students to her home on Saturday mornings to paint. She encouraged them to paint scenes from their home lives. It was a stance in direct conflict with federal policy, which favored the assimilation of Indian children. In the spring of 1919, Edgar Lee Hewett, director of the Museum of New Mexico, arranged for an exhibition by the group. Mabel Dodge Sterne, a patron of the arts, bought the exhibition and showed it in New York.

Between about 1920 and 1923, Hewett employed Kabotie and Awa Tsireh, from San Ildefonso Pueblo, at the School of American Research in Santa Fe and gave them time and space to paint. Kabotie probably created *Snake Dance* in the early 1920s.[3] In 1927, convinced that the old ways were being lost and that he had a responsibility to record them, Kabotie agreed to produce a series of paintings of important Pueblo ceremonies for the Museum of the American Indian–Heye Foundation. By this time he had moved back to Hopi.

Throughout Kabotie's career, his work was recognized by numerous exhibitions, commissions, and awards in both the United States and Europe. In 1941, Rene d'Harnoncourt opened an exhibition of American Indian art at the Museum of Modern Art in New York that included reproductions by Kabotie of some of the kiva murals of Awatobi, an ancient Hopi village. The catalogue states, "The close relationship between aesthetic and technical perfection gives the work of most Indian artists a basic unity rarely found in the products of an urban civilization." It was an important step in the effort of museum professionals, art patrons, and collectors to define native arts as "fine arts," an issue still debated today.[4]

E.H.B.

SNAKE DANCE, CA. 1921. FRED
KABOTIE (CA. 1900–1986), HOPI.
WATERCOLOR AND GRAPHITE ON
PAPER, 48.0 X 57.5 CM (22.8647)

KOSHARE KACHINA, CA. 1930. AWA
TSIREH (ALFONSO ROYBAL,
1898–1955), SAN ILDEFONSO
PUEBLO. INK ON PAPER, 28.2 X 18.2
CM (22.7874)

This finely woven sarape poncho, with terraced zigzag stripes and diamonds in indigo blue and white handspun yarns on a brilliant crimson ground, was made between 1825 and 1860, the Classic period in Navajo weaving. Balanced pattern, the play of positive and negative spaces, and superb workmanship are qualities characteristic of Navajo textiles, whether early wearing blankets or contemporary tapestries. But these weavings are more than art objects: they speak of continuity and invention, adaptation to changing worlds, and the role of women in Navajo society.

Scholars believe that the Navajos or Dine'é (the People), who traveled to the American Southwest from the far north, probably took up weaving during the second half of the seventeenth century. They are believed to have adopted the wide upright loom of their Pueblo neighbors, although, unlike the Pueblos, they came to regard weaving as primarily a women's art. *Churro* sheep wool, indigo dye, and the sarape, a blanket made longer than it is wide, came from Spanish settlers; red yarn was made by raveling worsted trade cloth. Navajo weavers first created terraced designs similar to indigenous basketry patterns, then adapted complex serrate designs derived from Mexico.

Spanish documents indicate that by 1706, the Navajos had their own flocks of sheep.[1] Weavers made two-piece dresses, shoulder blankets, and wide Pueblo-style mantas or shawls for themselves, as well as surplus blankets for a trade network that reached as far as the Great Plains.[2]

The Classic period of Navajo weaving ended in 1863, when the U.S. government, determined to end hostilities against settlers, forcibly marched thousands of Navajos to remote Bosque Redondo in eastern New Mexico.[3] The Long Walk is still remembered with pain. In 1868, the Navajos returned to a reservation within their old homelands—and to an altered economic base. Their sheep herds destroyed, more and more Navajo women adopted European-American styles of dress, and weavers increasingly experimented with factory-processed yarns and chemical dyes. These yarns and dyes had been among the annuity goods issued by the government at Bosque Redondo; later, they were carried by trading posts. Weavers collaborated with traders well into the twentieth century to develop regional-style rugs for sale to travelers and for an Eastern market.

This tapestry by Evelyn Curly of Ganado, Arizona, illustrates how old designs are reinterpreted. Navajo women say they weave not only out of economic incentive, but because they enjoy the challenge and because their mothers and grandmothers weave. Women still balance weaving with keeping house, caring for children, and tending sheep; today, they often hold professional positions and attend classes as well. Above all, weavers cherish their autonomy and respect that of others.[4] These values—adaptability, experimentation, and individualism—have ensured the vitality of Navajo weaving for hundreds of years.

E.H.B.

NAVAJO SARAPE PONCHO, 1825–1860.
176 X 133.4 CM (9.1912)

TAPESTRY, CA. 1980. WOVEN BY
EVELYN CURLY (BORN 1930), NAVAJO.
177 X 145 CM (25.638)

Ruins at Casas Grandes, in northwestern Chihuahua, Mexico, reveal a city of ball courts, temple platforms, enclosed public plazas, multistory apartment houses, and an elaborate canal system. Paquimé, the heart of Casas Grandes and possibly a religious center, played a pivotal role in Mesoamerican trade with the North American Southwest. Imported raw materials filled its storehouses, and macaw parrots, shells, and other exotic goods were sent north, possibly in exchange for turquoise.

Ceramists at Casas Grandes produced exquisite painted effigy jars (left) modeled after humans, birds, and other animals. Used in religious contexts, as well as for cooking and serving food, these pottery vessels were traded as far away as the Pueblo of Mesa Verde in Colorado. In time, Casas Grandes collapsed, but, judging from the evidence, not before its rich ceramic tradition had taken root in the north.

As early as A.D. 400, the ancestors of the Rio Grande Pueblo peoples made small, unfired clay figurines, most of them of women in a frontal pose. By 900, potters were creating figurative jars with painted designs that strongly suggest Mesoamerican influence. Both sixteenth-century Spanish priests and later Anglo-American missionaries considered Pueblo figurative pottery idolatrous and made every effort to stamp out its production, with the result that few examples survive from this period.[1]

The figurative tradition was not abandoned, however. Pueblo effigy vessels and figurines made in the nineteenth century at Cochiti on the west bank of the Rio Grande in north central New Mexico are especially reminiscent of ancient Casas Grandes ceramics. Between about 1880 and 1900, Cochiti potters produced large, standing male figures with black painted designs, like this Pueblo man, for sale to tourists in Santa Fe. Earlier efforts to market smaller animal and bird figurines, as well as effigy vessels decorated with traditional motifs such as clouds and corn plants, had failed. In response, Cochiti potters created large human forms decorated not only with traditional Pueblo pottery designs, but with Anglo clothing, such as fringed vests and boots. Soon, potters were producing portraits of cowboys, priests, tourists, and other visitors to the Southwest.

Until recently, museums dismissed Cochiti figures as curiosities or tourist art. Today, they are collector's items, highly valued for their humor and keen social commentary. The figurative tradition continues to thrive at Cochiti, passed on in the famous Storyteller dolls of Helen Cordero and in the work of other potters.

E.H.B.

COCHITI POTTERY FIGURE OF A
MAN, CA. 1880. HEIGHT 46.7 CM
(19.6726)

POTTERY FIGURES, CA. 1882.
COCHITI, NEW MEXICO.
PHOTOGRAPH BY BEN WITTICK.

Though jade it may be, it breaks;
Though gold it may be, it is
* crushed. . . .*
Not forever on earth, only a little
* while.*

—KING NEZAHUALCÓYTL, AZTEC

TRIPOD VESSEL WITH LID, A.D.
400–550. ATTRIBUTED TO
TEOTIHUACAN, MEXICO. HEIGHT
25.2 CM (24.7490 A,B)

OLD GOD EFFIGY, A.D. 200–750.
ATTRIBUTED TO TOLUCA, MEXICO.
HEIGHT 30.6 CM (16.6067)

Teotihuacan (150 B.C. to A.D. 750) was the first great civilization in central Mexico. By A.D. 600, the city of Teotihuacan—in the center of the Teotihuacan Valley, northeast of present-day Mexico City—was the sixth largest urban center in the world, with an estimated population of 125,000.[1] Today, it is one of the most spectacular archaeological sites in the Western Hemisphere, famous for its massive pyramids dedicated to the Sun and the Moon, Street of the Dead, and Temple of the Feathered Serpent. The Aztecs, who came to the Valley of Mexico hundreds of years after Teotihuacan was destroyed and abandoned, revered the old city. Teotihuacan is the name they gave it: the Place Where Men Become Gods.[2]

Teotihuacan fostered great economic and intellectual activity and produced splendid art. One type of ceramics distinctive to Teotihuacan is called Thin Orange ware. Thin Orange ware objects have been found in settings of household use, dedicatory offering, and burial.[3]

We do not know the purpose of Thin Orange effigy vessels; few seem to represent Teotihuacan symbols or beings. Perhaps they are simply beautiful and evocative funerary offerings. This effigy vessel, however, may refer to the Old God figure depicted on Teotihuacan stone braziers.[4] There, the Old God appears as a hunched man with a wrinkled face who carries a round vessel on his head; his legs are crossed in front of him, and he wears nothing but ear spools. The old man depicted on this vessel fits this description except that he wears a loincloth. Scholars have pointed out that the Teotihuacan Old God is similar to later, equally mysterious old gods found in offerings at the Aztec Templo Mayor. Perhaps the old age of this figure signifies ancestor worship. We cannot say which—if any—of these theories is correct.[5]

Manufacturing sites for the extraordinary clay used to make Thin Orange ware have been found in only one area, southeast of Teotihuacan in southern Puebla, which suggests that the pottery may have been a luxury item. Thin Orange was an important trade-ware, as well as the pottery most prized by Teotihuacanos.[6]

Teotihuacanos also seem to have admired simple and elegant pottery forms like this polished brown tripod vessel. This form—a cylindrical vessel with a lid and three rectangular supports—appears to have been the primary design for ceremonial vessels at Teotihuacan, but, again, we know little about the form's meaning or the vessels' ritual use.[7]

N.R.

The ceramic sculptures of Colima, near the Pacific coast of central Mexico, have long been admired for their beauty, naturalism, and expressiveness. Colima vessels are generally monochrome, with red or brown burnished slips and spots of black patina. Pieces are also heavily modeled and sometimes incised with decorations.[1] Of the three western Mexican ceramic styles—Colima, Jalisco, and Nayarit—Colima is the most homogeneous, and it differs markedly from the others. In its realistic modeling of subject matter, Colima pottery may have been influenced by Chorrera ceramics from Ecuador. Some scholars have gone so far as to describe Colima as the northern outpost of a South American effigy vessel tradition that encompasses the Cupisnique (coastal Chavín) and Moche cultures in Peru, as well as Chorrera.[2]

Colima is particularly famous for its strikingly realistic redware dog effigies. This piece, an adorable puppy with wrinkled skin, is hollow; perhaps liquid was poured through the hole in the left ear as an offering. Colima dogs may represent the *tepescuintli*, a hairless dog that was bred for food. But these animals also seem to have had special mythological significance for the Colimans.[3]

The beliefs and customs of the present-day Huichol and Cora, who are likely to be descendants of the ancient western Mexicans, offer additional insights into the possible meanings of Colima animal symbolism. In Cora and Huichol creation myths—which, like many native beliefs and rituals, have survived centuries of Christianization—the dog represents a powerful being associated with both the underworld and the creation of mankind.[4] According to a Cora origin myth:

> The people followed the tail of a dog, leading to a high mountain, in order to escape from drowning in a rising flood. Meanwhile, the dog beat a drum, the sound of which caused the water to swell up in waves, whereupon the people climbed to the summit. Most of them died of starvation while waiting for the water to recede. Those few who survived are believed to be the ancestors of mankind. The dog disappeared into a large lake, where the wandering souls visit it on their way to their final resting place.[5]

Perhaps dogs had a similar significance for the ancient people of Colima. Colima artists sometimes depicted dogs wearing human masks, further support for the theory that dogs played a supernatural role.[6]

Another animal depicted in Colima art is the parrot, shown here supporting a voluptuous gadrooned vessel. Many jars of this shape, often called pumpkin pots, were made and, like the dog effigies, used for offerings. The parrot is still a sacred bird among the Cora. It symbolizes the sprouting corn plant and represents the Morning Star.[7]

N.R.

"There is a water over there, where the soul of one who has died must pass. And there is a dog there, a little black dog with a white spot on its throat. And one must ask permission from that dog to pass, so that one may travel on, to reach that other level, where those who have died are waiting, where those ancient relatives are living in their rancho."

—RAMÓN MEDINA, HUICHOL

GADROONED VESSEL WITH PARROT TRIPOD SUPPORTS, 400 B.C.–A.D. 300. COLIMA, MEXICO. HEIGHT 21.6 CM (24.7346)

EFFIGY VESSEL IN THE FORM OF A DOG, 400 B.C.–A.D. 300. COLIMA, MEXICO. HEIGHT 33.6 CM (24.452)

Famous for its exquisite designs and fineness of weave, the Saltillo sarape was the unlikely product of two very different conventions—the textile industry established by Spanish administrators in the "New World" and an ancient, native weaving tradition. Saltillo sarapes were woven by Indians, in Spanish sheep wool, on European treadle looms. Named for the town of Saltillo, an important textile center, these blankets were actually made all across northern Mexico.

Little is known of the origins of the sarape, but the model may have been the native manta, a woven rectangular blanket sometimes made with a vertical slit for the head and worn as a poncho with open sides. No similar garment existed in Spain.[1]

Production of the Saltillo sarape began with Spanish efforts to settle the rugged northern frontier, an area rich in silver ore but hostile to foreign incursions. Tlaxcalan Indians, allies of the Spanish who had fought with Cortés against the Aztec Empire, were recruited as colonists. In August 1591, eighty Tlaxcalan families from central Mexico arrived in Saltillo, in the state of Coahuila. They were granted a special barrio, San Esteban de Nuevo Tlaxcala, with water rights and other privileges. More Spanish settlements followed, with communities of Tlaxcalans settled nearby.

Skilled weavers, Tlaxcalan Indians were producing wool blankets in colonial workshops long before they traveled north.[2] Under the Spanish system, the men were the weavers; women continued to weave traditional garments for their families on native looms.

It took a master craftsman to create a Saltillo sarape, usually woven in two matching, vertical panels, then seamed together. Traditional native textile patterns may have been design sources. The classic design system, established by the eighteenth century, includes a central concentric diamond outlined in bands of tiny serrate motifs, a figured background, and a decorated border. Sarapes with round, scalloped medallions, such as the piece illustrated here, may have been woven in San Miguel de Allende; the floral vine motif suggests European influence. Until the introduction of chemical dyes in the nineteenth century, colors were natural and included many shades of red derived from cochineal dye, as well as indigo blue.

Valuable trade items, the blankets were marketed at Mexico's trade fairs, commercial hubs for luxury goods flowing between Mexico and Europe and the Orient, as well as north into the southwestern United States. After 1821, when Mexico won independence, the sarape became a preeminent nationalist symbol. To this day, Mexico is equated in the popular imagination with her horsemen, resplendent in their sombreros and leather chaps, with colorful sarapes flung over their shoulders.

Production of Saltillo sarapes had ceased by the early twentieth century. Saltillo sarape patterns survive, however, in textiles woven throughout Mexico and by both Hispanic and Navajo weavers of the American Southwest.

E.H.B.

During the Classic period (A.D. 200 to 900), the Gulf Coast of Mexico—and in particular the Veracruz area—produced fascinating and diverse works of art. Especially notable are ceramic figurines with grinning faces and skillfully carved stone objects associated with the ball game, a ritualistic sport played on stone courts throughout Mesoamerica.[1]

Initially, scholars labeled all Veracruz smiling figures Remojadas, after the name of an archaeological site. But later excavations in central Veracruz revealed a very different style of smiling figures, now called Nopiloa.[2] Some Nopiloa figurines have articulated arms and legs, like the one shown below. The head and body of this figurine are mold-made, while the arms and legs are separate hand-modeled pieces that were probably joined to the body with cord or sinew. The figurine wears a simple headdress, earspools, and a pendant of a deity's face.

The function of these figurines is not known. Some scholars associate them with Xochipilli, the Aztec god of dance, music, and joy;[3] others believe that some of the figurines represent specific deities. The goggle-eyes and prominent lip volutes shown in low-relief on the body of this figurine suggest the central Mexican rainwater god. Perhaps the figurines were displayed in shrines and presented with offerings.[4] The articulated form may have made the figurines more animated and lifelike. Or perhaps, rather than representing gods themselves, they are images of men and women who portrayed deities during monthly festivals. Some scholars believe that these stand-ins were given a euphoria-inducing drink before they were sacrificed—hence the grinning faces of the figurines.[5]

In the north central region of Veracruz, a tradition of stone sculpture developed around the ball-game ritual and the production of game paraphernalia such as yokes, *hachas*, and *palmas*.[6] Hachas— "axes"—like most ball-game objects, are misnamed. Originally described by scholars as votive axes, they are now believed to be stone trophy heads that were attached to yokelike belts used in ball-game ritualism;[7] hachas have been found in archaeological sites with yokes, and both are depicted on ceramic figurines and stone sculptures. Some scholars have suggested that stone yokes, hachas, and palmas are replicas of objects originally made of perishable materials.[8] Other hachas—thinner, often perforated, and with distinct bases—may have been placed in the walls of sanctuaries or ball courts. This hacha, an example of the second type, depicts a human head with a deeply furrowed face and wide open eyes that may have been inlaid with bone or stone.[9]

N.R.

MAYA RUINS AT PALENQUE.
CHIAPAS, MEXICO. (P16999)

MAYA CERAMIC WHISTLES, A.D.
550–850 (LATE CLASSIC). JAINA
ISLAND, MEXICO. LENGTH 13.5 CM
AND 11.8 CM (24.451)

MAYA POLYCHROME CERAMIC VASE,
A.D. 550–850 (LATE CLASSIC).
CAMPECHE, MEXICO. HEIGHT 16.4
CM (24.8750)

The Classic Maya of Mexico, Guatemala, and Belize mastered slip painting on low-fired pottery to create one of the world's great painting traditions. The high gloss and exquisite control of their slip work have not been equaled by ceramic artists of any other culture.

Maya burials and tombs often contain painted pottery, although it is also found in everyday trash deposits at Maya sites, including middens near palaces and other buildings associated with the ruling elite. The texts on Maya painted pottery also argue against its having had a single funerary function.[1] Beautiful hieroglyphics, only recently translated, bless the vessels for their ritual uses and record their contents, including a beverage made from *cacao* (the Mayan word for chocolate), a corn-based gruel called *sa'* (atole), and *wah* (tamales).[2] The glyphs end with the name of the owner or patron of the piece and, occasionally, the name of the artist who painted it, making these some of the very few signed works of art from the pre-Columbian era.

The painting on this vase depicts one of the rituals that were the duties of Maya rulers and the foundation of their power: a lord or *ahaw*, seated on a throne in a palace or ritual building, is engaged in a vision-quest rite that replicates the original vision and sacrifice by the gods who created the universe.[3] The ahaw performs this ritual to transcend human existence and commune with the deities on behalf of his people.[4] He smokes a tobacco cigarette to facilitate his transformation. A ritual mirror, angled toward the throne and propped against a roll of knotted cloth, is the portal through which he enters the supernatural realm. He holds a bloodletter, and red splotches on the stiff cloth strips tied to it show that he has already undergone the requisite autosacrifice.

Dance was an integral part of Maya public rituals. It was performed on the broad stairways that characterize Classic Maya civic architecture.[5] Judging from the instruments depicted in Maya art, including wood and ceramic drums and *raspadores* made from gourds and turtle shells, the music was primarily percussive.[6] However, the Maya also made ceramic whistles. Whistles and their musical cousins, multinote ocarinas, were usually made in molds in rounded forms that could be cradled in one hand and played by people as they danced.

These two ceramic whistles—hand-modeled in the shape of long, delicate, five-petaled flowers—are unusual. They may have been played by professional musicians who did not dance. Their bright "Maya blue" paint—applied after they were fired—is unique to the Classic Maya and frequently embellishes whistles and figurines from Jaina Island, Mexico, in the Bay of Campeche.[7] Emerging from the flowers are an old man—who may be the deity Pauahtún—and his beautiful, young female consort. They comprise a special theme in Maya art originating in Maya religious beliefs, although we do not fully understand their meaning.

D.R.-B.

Only a few Classic Maya wood sculptures have survived, but they are evidence of a magnificent tradition. This exquisite pottery bowl (right), found sometime before 1917 on the Montagua River in southern Guatemala, closely resembles carving in wood. The artist conceived images on multiple overlapping planes to create a three-dimensional picture, then carved the forms from thin slabs of malleable clay and applied them to the surface of the bowl in successive layers. Details were incised into each layer.

The imagery is a complicated representation of Classic Maya cosmology. The Sun God sits crossed-legged, cradling two undulating, feathered Vision Serpents, carved in mirror image. The figures surrounding the Vision Serpents imply that this is a representation of the Maya universe at the moment of creation. The Sun God's pose was also used by Classic Maya kings, establishing a relationship between the deity and Maya rulers.[1] This unique imagery has led some scholars to believe the bowl is a forgery.[2] Yet in the past five hundred years no one has created a masterpiece of such skill or cosmological knowledge.

Although the people who inhabited the Ulúa Valley in northwestern Honduras were non-Maya speakers, they were in close contact with the Maya of Belize and Guatemala throughout the era of Maya ascendancy (A.D. 300 to 1000 or the Classic period). Beginning around A.D. 500, the valley was an important trade route linking Maya areas with the Nicoya–Guanacaste region of present-day Costa Rica. Toward the end of the Classic period, when Maya sites were in decline, Ulúa sculptors working in local marble created distinctive vessels that became luxury items from northern Guatemala to northwestern Costa Rica.[3]

Perhaps one-hundred-and-fifty complete Ulúa marble vessels exist today. Most are cylindrical, and half of these are set on ring-shaped bases pierced with string-sawed designs. Their sides are decorated with carved panels, usually framed above and below by bands of overlapping rectangular or semicircular plaques. These overlapping designs may have been influenced by the jade plaques worn on the headbands of Maya royalty. The reliefs are dominated by regular rows and columns of scrolls, often imbedded with the faces of deities and serpent heads in profile. The handles depict various animals—such as felines, crested animals, monkey heads, bats, serpents, and birds—and, in one instance, a human being.

The shape and design of the Ulúa vessels were influenced by earlier ceramics, created with the same fondness for regularity, symmetry, and exact repetition. This aesthetic contrasts with that of the Maya, who preferred irregularity, asymmetry, and constant variety in their art. The shift from Ulúa pottery to stonework, however, was probably inspired by the strong tradition of stone carving in the Nicoya–Guanacaste region. The small number of vessels found and their well-defined style and iconography suggest to some scholars that the vases were manufactured in a few workshops over only two or three generations.

D.R.-B. and N.R.

CARVED MARBLE VESSEL, A.D. 800–1000. ULÚA VALLEY, HONDURAS. HEIGHT 13.3 CM (4.3956)

MAYA SCULPTED AND CARVED CERAMIC BOWL, CA. A.D. 400–550 (EARLY CLASSIC). SAN AGUSTÍN ACASAGUASTLÁN, GUATEMALA. HEIGHT 20.2 CM (20.7626)

Gold, jade, precious raiment,
quetzal feathers,
everything once of value
has become nothing.

—AZTEC POET

The Indians of Mesoamerica considered jade to be more valuable than gold. Jade had a deep symbolic meaning. Green is the color of water, the life-giving liquid, and of the maize crop, also associated with life.

No carved jade more elaborate than beads has been found from the first centuries of the Olmec culture, the earliest great civilization in Mesoamerica. But between 900 and 400 B.C., Olmec stone carvers used jade on a scale matched only by the Maya five hundred to a thousand years later. The Olmecs, who lived along the Gulf of Mexico in present-day Tabasco and Veracruz, were expert craftsmen, creating beautiful carvings—in basalt and serpentine, as well as jade—that were traded as far away as the Guatemalan highlands. Exquisitely carved jade objects have been found in burials of the Olmec elite. One important figure portrayed in Olmec art is an anthropomorphic jaguar depicted in at least three different forms: mythical, supernatural, and human. Olmec shamans may have used jade spoons to administer hallucinogenic snuff.

Jade was traded on a large scale from the Guatemalan highlands to the Mexican lowlands. At one time, scholars believed Olmec jade came from Guerrero, but a deposit of fine, blue-green jade has been found in the Olmec region itself, at Arroyo Pesquero.

The scarcity of jade in some areas made it an even more precious commodity. More than two thousand years ago, the Zapotec Indians of Oaxaca imported large quantities of jade from the Guatemalan highlands to make ritual garments worn by their priests and chieftains.

Among the Maya, jade was as valuable as the green feathers of the quetzal bird, and both symbolized life. The Maya often placed a small piece of jade in the mouth of the dead to ensure the spirit's survival. Jade was also an important sacrificial object; large numbers of jade and gold offerings have been found in the sacred *cenotes* or pools of Chichén Itzá, a city in Yucatán inhabited by the Maya and their successors from the seventh to the sixteenth centuries A.D. Jade objects were kept in families for generations as charms that brought strength and good health. One Olmec jade piece carved around 800 B.C. was discovered in a royal Maya tomb where it had been buried sixteen hundred years after the carver made it.[1]

R.M.

GOLD CROWN, 800–200 B.C. CHAVÍN
CULTURE, PERU. HEIGHT 24 X DIAM.
15.9 CM (16.1972B)

GOLD STAFF HEAD, A.D. 1000–1600.
SINÚ CULTURE, COLOMBIA.
LENGTH 20.3 CM (10.507)

The earliest evidence of metalworking in South America is gold found in Peru and dating to 1500 B.C. Several centuries later, goldsmiths of the Chavín civilization of central Peru (800 to 200 B.C.) hammered thin gold sheets over stone matrices carved with images of the natural and spiritual worlds to create beautiful repoussé designs like those on this crown.

Chavín was the first South American civilization to bring communities together in a social and political system based on shared religion. It is named after the temple at Chavín de Huantar, a remarkably cosmopolitan complex reflecting interaction between the highlands and the lowlands. The most important Chavín deities are anthropomorphic beings that archaeologists call the Staff God—seen on this crown—and the Snarling God. Both deities have attributes of the jaguar, eagle, and serpent. Priests mediated between the spiritual and natural worlds by transforming themselves into these supernatural animals during shamanistic rituals. Imagery representing these beliefs appears in Chavín stone sculpture, ceramics, and textiles, as well as on objects of bone, shell, silver, and gold. These pieces may have been made as offerings to the deities.

From Peru, metalworking spread north to Ecuador, Colombia, and Mesoamerica. When the Spanish arrived in Colombia at the beginning of the sixteenth century, the culture of the lowlands around the Sinú River in the northwest was rich in gold. Artists there had developed a realistic style of representing the natural world around them, as we can see by this lost-wax casting, an elegant staff head with five lively birds.

The people of Sinú lived in large, communal houses around a temple that held wooden idols covered with gold sheet. Also around the temple were the burial mounds of chieftains, each mound topped with a tree whose branches were decorated with golden bells.

In a passage that, on first reading, seems to echo the native beliefs described by Cieza de Léon above, Christopher Columbus wrote: "Gold is the most exquisite of all things. . . . Whoever possesses gold can acquire all that he desires in the world. Truly, for gold he can gain entrance for his soul into paradise." Yet gold, a spiritual symbol to the natives, had an entirely different meaning for the Spanish conquistadors: European thirst for gold money destroyed many of the most beautiful pieces of art of the South American cultures. Ironically, Spain spent most of the gold of the New World to pay for wars.

R.M.

SPOUT VESSEL, A.D. 200–600. NAZCA
CULTURE, PERU. HEIGHT 18.4 CM
(21.6914)

GOLD MASK WITH SERPENTS, A.D.
200–600. NAZCA CULTURE, PERU.
24 X 19 CM (16.9827)

In South America gold was valued for its shining color and esteemed as a sacred metal, often associated with sun cults. Many Andean societies regarded their chieftains as living representatives of the gods and adorned them with gold breastplates, necklaces, bracelets, earspools, nose ornaments, crowns, and other treasures. Important leaders were buried with their possessions, like this striking Nazca mask, with its crest of serpents. Snakes, like gold, had religious meaning for Andean peoples, linked to fertility and water cults. Water has many qualities, including the power to capture and reflect the light of the sun so that ordinary mortals may look at it. Gold, sun, water, serpents—a complex cosmology is revealed in this mask.

The highly stratified Nazca culture flourished on the coast of southern Peru from A.D. 200 to 600. There, gold and silver objects were used exclusively by priests and chieftains, and were produced by highly skilled specialists.

The principal Nazca deities were associated with springs and mountains. One of the most important gods was Carhuarazo, associated with a snow peak located in the distant cordillera. The Nazca River was believed to flow from his veins or tears. In Peru today, some Quechua people observe a water-cult ritual in which they take offerings of shells and water from the sea to the mountaintops. Participants wear masks similar to this one during their ceremonies.

This stirrup-spout vessel in Classic Nazca style depicts an anthropomorphic bird wearing a nose ornament that is similar to the serpent mask. The vessel may represent a shaman who has entered a trance in which he has the ability to fly. Many Nazca ceramic vessels were made exclusively for ritual use.

R.M.

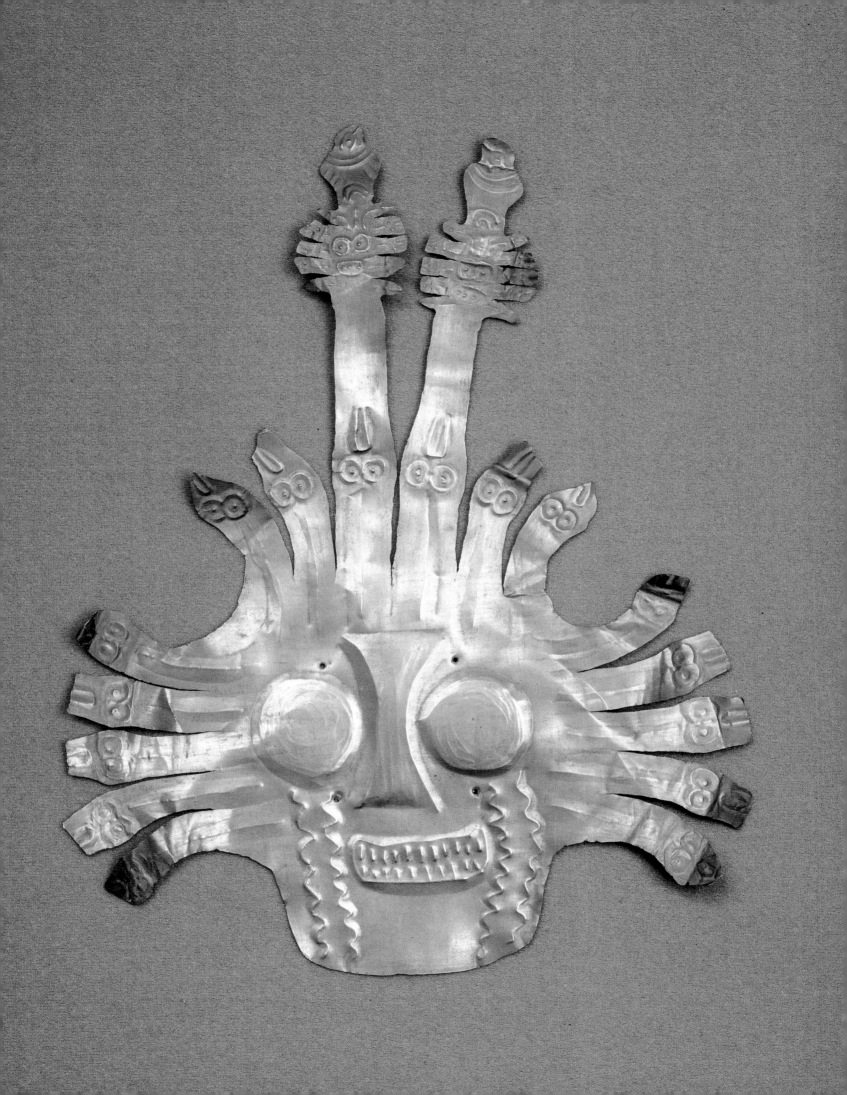

The Piro live in the mountainous tropical forests of southeastern Peru. Unlike their better-known neighbors the Shipibo and Conibo, who speak a Panoan language, the Piro speak an Arawakan language. The three groups do share many cultural characteristics, however, including clothing styles.

The traditional outfit for a Piro man—rarely worn since the introduction of Western clothes—is a large, poncho-shaped garment called an *ikanopi* (right). The neck opening runs from front to back, and the sides of the garment are sewn together from the armholes to the ankles. Such a long garment provides warmth and protection from mosquitos. Piro women usually wear a below-the-knee-length skirt (*emkatceri*), woven in one piece, then seamed along one side (left). A woman slips the skirt on, then folds the top edge down to make a waistband. With the emkatceri, she wears a cloak over her shoulders. The cloth for these garments is woven of wild cotton by women working on backstrap looms.[1]

Women decorate textiles with beautifully painted geometric designs. Some scholars have suggested that the images express the mythological universe of the Piro. For example, the road is a central theme in Piro designs, suggesting the passage that every person must take in life. Patterns are shared among the Piro, and there is a common understanding of each design's mythological significance and role in maintaining a spiritual balance among nature, individuals, and the community. These designs may therefore be viewed as aesthetic manifestations of the Piro world view.[2]

Other scholars have suggested that Piro designs are derived from those used on Shipibo and Conibo pottery and textiles.[3] This is quite possible: the Piro have always been great river travelers and successful traders.[4] Perhaps the Piro women who decorated these two textiles were inspired by the bold, block patterns on Shipibo–Conibo pottery. Shipibo–Conibo textiles, on the other hand, are decorated with thinner, more graceful lines. This Piro man's shirt, for example, is decorated with a Shipibo–Conibo X-motif, but does not have any of the lighter filler lines that are so characteristic of Shipibo–Conibo painted textiles. Among the Shipibo and Conibo, the X-motif is associated with the Great World Boa, Ronin, the mythical donor of all designs. The woman's skirt appears to be a sampler of three different Shipibo–Conibo motifs: the cross, wing/hand, and X. Like the shirt, the skirt does not have any filler work, but some of the spaces have been filled in with black (*sageri*) and yellow (*apina*) dyes to make a bolder, more dynamic pattern.[5]

These Piro textiles may borrow Shipibo–Conibo motifs, but they use them in an innovative way. Whether the images reflect the spiritual world of the Piro or are creative extensions of Shipibo–Conibo art forms, the resulting designs are beautiful and unique.

N.R.

PIRO IKANOPI (MAN'S SHIRT), EARLY
20TH C. LENGTH 120 CM (19.5858)

PIRO EMKATCERI (WOMAN'S SKIRT),
LATE19TH/EARLY 20TH C. LENGTH
66 CM (15.3456)

"PIRO CHIEF AND CHILD-WIFE. RÍO
PICHIS, PERU." PHOTOGRAPH BY
KRÖHLE AND HÜBNER (?).

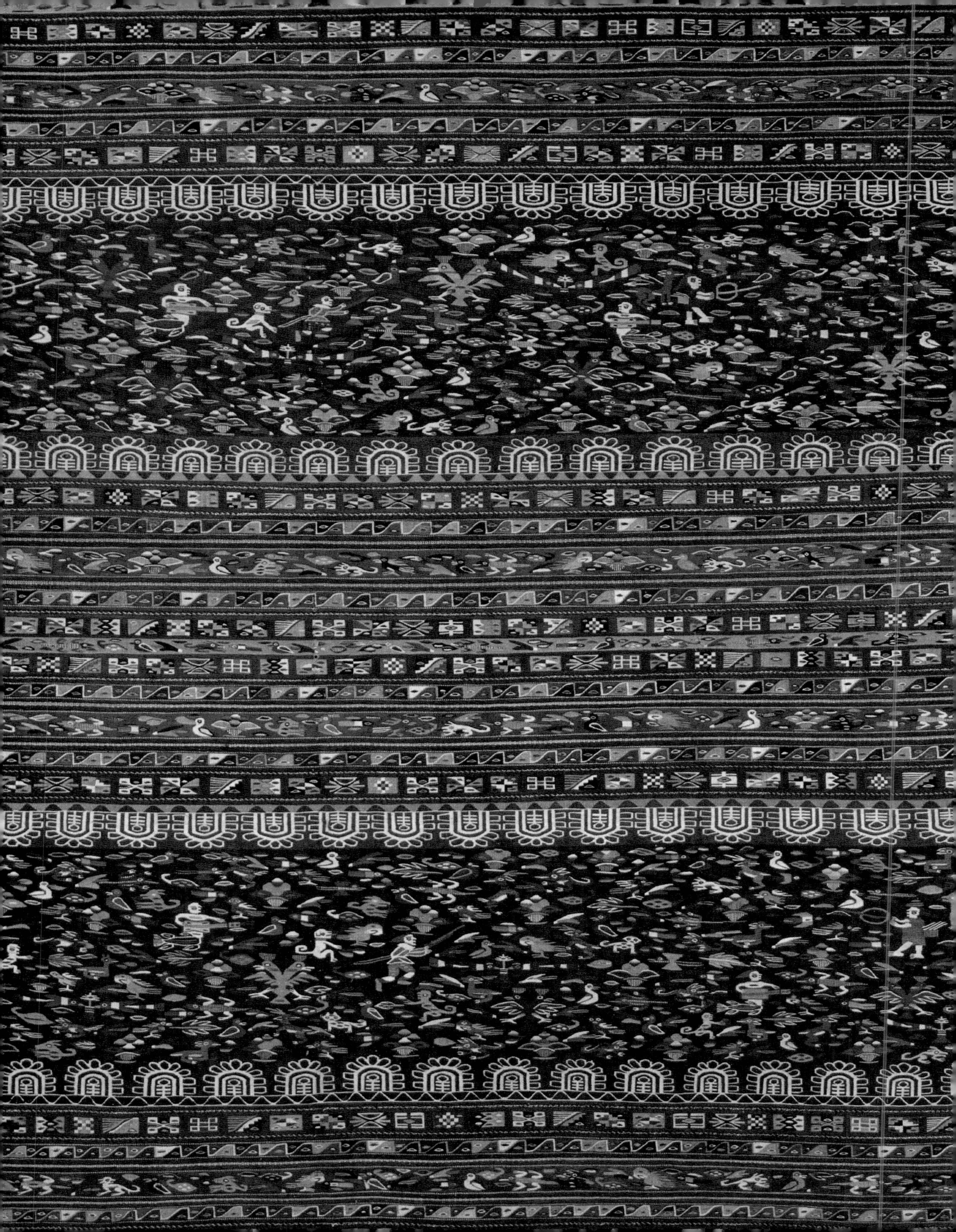

This extraordinary manta, probably made at the end of the eighteenth century in a village on the high plains of the Lake Titicaca basin, is a native weaver's impression of the Noah's ark story. Although the story comes from the Christian Bible, the weaver chose to tell it with animals from the Andean region and surrounding ecological zones: the parrot and monkey from the tropical forests, the vicuña and vizcacha (similar to the chinchilla) from the altiplano, the hummingbird and owl from the valleys, and fish and birds from the coast. They are arranged in lines between rows of arches that may signify doorways into the ark. The weaver used animals closely associated with human beings and depicted most of them in lively and characteristic poses: the parrot picks at a fruit, the monkey eats with its hands, the dog barks and jumps. The vicuña, however, is shown wounded by the arrows of a hunter. There are also mermaids, playing guitars; we do not know whether they were inspired by Western stories or by a local myth about a village at the bottom of Lake Titicaca where mermaids sing and play *charangos,* or native guitars. Surrounding the animals are traditional designs taken from *tucapus,* large mantas decorated with Inka symbols.

From their earliest days in South America, European soldiers, administrators, and priests condemned and tried to destroy native beliefs and traditions. Yet despite the trauma of conquest and more than three hundred years of colonial rule and oppression, the Indians preserved many aspects of their spiritual world. They secretly observed ancient ceremonies and concealed their reverence for the old spirits within the symbolism of Spanish culture and the Catholic faith. *Amaru* (the sacred serpent), for example, was transformed into the Spanish bull, and powerful *wamani* (mountain spirits) were converted into the Catholic figure Santiago (Saint James).

Too large to have been worn as a shawl, this manta may have been used during a native ritual, perhaps as an offering to the Temple of the Sun on one of the islands in Lake Titicaca. But the story of cultural strength that it tells goes beyond the syncretism of native and Christian beliefs. The people of the region, famous for their skill as weavers when this striking piece was made, still produce beautiful multicolored textiles decorated with native symbols. Through centuries of change, ancient arts and ways of life have endured, as have old beliefs.

R.M.

INKA MANTA, PROBABLY LATE 18TH C. 118.9 X 109.5 CM (5.5773)

"INKA PRINCESS IN NATIONAL DRESS." ILLUSTRATION FROM COUNT FRANCIS DE CASTELNAU, EXPÉDITION DANS LES PARTIES CENTRALES DE L'AMERIQUE DU SUD, 3EME PARTIE, ANTIQUITÉS DES INCAS (PL. 58), 1854.

"They killed the Inka and also our wakas [holy spirits of nature] . . . and now they search for our camaquenes, which are our goddesses. . . . The Christian God is only for the white people, and the camaquenes are for the Indians."

—FRANCISCO DE AVILA, 1608

Expédition de F. de Castelnau (Amérique du Sud).   3ᵉ Partie. Antiquités des Incas PL. 58.

Llanta lith.   P. Bertrand, éditeur, rue St André des Arcs 53.   Imp. Lemercier, Paris.

PRINCESSE INCAS EN COSTUME NATIONAL, d'après un tableau conservé à Cuzco.

ACROSS THE GENERATIONS

TOM HILL AND RICHARD W. HILL SR.

Henry David Thoreau once described an Indian arrowhead as a "fossil thought." He believed that ancient Indians had something to teach through the objects they made and that we could understand their thoughts by studying those objects.

What knowledge from our ancestors is reflected in the treasures and everyday objects now housed in museums? Each of us can read different things into these creations. But they express underlying principles that have great meaning to many Native Americans. These principles are a legacy that we take to heart and are grateful to receive.

The first gift from our ancestors is our deep connection to the land. The second gift is the power and spirit that animals share with our people. The third is the spirit forces, who are our living relatives and who communicate with us through the images we make of them. The fourth is the sense of who we are, which is expressed and sustained through our tribal traditions. The last gift is the creative process—our beliefs made real through the transformation of natural materials into objects of faith and pride.

✳

How does our knowledge as natives square with what archaeology teaches about the people who lived here before Europeans came? Is there, for example, a connection between archaeological findings and native oral histories about tribal origins? Most native peoples traditionally believe that they were created from the earth itself, from the waters, or from the stars. Archaeologists, on the other hand, have a theory of a great land bridge across the Bering Strait, over which Asians migrated to the Americas; these Asians, the theory

POTTERY SEALS, A.D. 1000–1500.
GUERRERO, MEXICO. HEIGHT 4.1 TO
11.5 CM (24.6534, 24.6512, 24.6531,
24.6520, 24.6541, 24.6515, 24.3170,
24.6527, 24.6530 AND 24.6536)

maintains, were the ancestors of the native peoples of the Western Hemisphere.

Until 1926 and the discovery of nineteen stone Folsom points in New Mexico, scientists generally thought Indians arrived in North America about three thousand years ago. The Folsom find suggested that the date might be closer to ten thousand years ago—that Indians were here at the close of the last Ice Age. In 1932, the famed Clovis point, also found in New Mexico, pushed that date back another sixteen hundred to four thousand years.

It is interesting to note that the first object that could be cited as proof of the Bering Strait theory was found in 1966, less than thirty years ago: a notched caribou bone—evidence of human tool-making—discovered near Old Crow in the Yukon. Conflicting tests have shown that the tool is either twenty-seven thousand years old or less than fourteen hundred years old.

A controversial site in Calico, California, under excavation since 1964, has been reported to show human habitation as far back as two hundred thousand years ago, which would change everything once presumed to be true about the origins of Native Americans. The oldest architectural remains in South America date to fourteen thousand years ago. Petroglyphs in Brazil may be older than the renowned cave paintings of Lascaux, France. The debate continues, fueled most recently by genetic research that argues for humankind's arrival in Central America no later than twenty-two thousand—and more likely twenty-nine thousand—years ago.

What is most troublesome about the archaeological approach to native history is that it defines cultures by technological, agricultural, and artistic movements, based upon the notion that simple cultures advance over time into complex civilizations. The more closely native societies resemble European models, the more advanced archaeology considers them to be. "We can trace the growth of pottery, agriculture, weaving, towns, and ceremonialism from crude beginnings to an advanced stage of development," wrote archaeologists from Chicago's Field Museum in 1947. Archaeology regards the Inuit as a primitive society, but sees the Maya, with their architecture and ruling classes, as an advanced civilization.

Scholars have marked off periods and cultures based upon their interpretations of artifacts and architectural remains. And they have usually labeled these periods and cultures with Greek words or named them after archaeologists or towns, rivers, and landforms near sites. As a result, Indians of the past are not defined by their tribal identities. Indeed, scholars have often been unwilling to recognize any connection between ancient and contemporary natives. We are left with the impression that cultures come and go, with thousands of people disappearing in the process. The link to our past is broken. Indians, however, see a direct connection, a tie through spirit.

In 1927, archaeologists adopted the Pecos classification, identifying four distinct cultures among early Southwestern Indians:

the Mogollon culture, whose people lived in pit houses, grew corn, and developed painted pottery in the style known as Mimbres; the Hohokam culture, whose people lived in above-ground houses in the desert, developed an irrigation system, and made clay figurines of animals and human beings; the Patayan (Hakataya) culture, whose people lived in brush houses, developed agriculture, and had their own style of ceramics; and the Anasazi culture, whose people lived on high plateaus and grew corn in river valleys. Scholars have further divided the Anasazi into five Pueblo and three Basketmaker periods.

These classifications—based on technologies and objects—create the impression that vast groups of people disappeared in "prehistory." They discredit any sense of cultural continuity from our ancestors, through the natives the explorers and colonists first met, to ourselves. Yet when we look at the ancient cultures of the Southwest through Indian eyes, we see a spiritual legacy.

Archaeologists believe that pottery was introduced to North America by way of Mexico about two thousand years ago. The Pueblos believe that pottery was part of the world at the time of Creation. Their ancient world view included the concept of the earth as a living entity. Clay, which Pueblo potters use to make bowls, jars, plates, vessels, and figures, is still considered to be the flesh of the living earth, which potters transform into objects of great beauty.

The Pueblos believe this gift from Mother Earth must be handled with care and sincerity. While they collect clay, they offer prayers of thanksgiving. Songs may be sung while potters work. The process of making pottery entails many traditions—learning the meaning of the designs, collecting the clay, finding the right polishing stone, constructing the pot, firing the pot, and gathering, mixing, and using paint to decorate the piece. It also involves learning how to feel the connection to the Earth spirit through the clay itself. In 1886, the anthropologist Frank Hamilton Cushing, working among the Zuni, reported that "when a woman has made a vessel, dried, polished, and painted it, she will tell you with an air of relief that it is a 'Made Being.'"[1] The process of creation is the same even for utilitarian pots. Making pottery as they have been taught to do for generations keeps the Pueblo people in touch, literally, with their beliefs and those of their forebears.

※

There is a sense of urgency when native people gather these days: our communities are losing their cultural leaders. The elders are dying, and with them a bit of knowledge seems to pass away. Native Alaskan Willie Hensley puts this into perspective. As a principal proponent of the Alaska Native Claims Settlement Act of 1971 and president of the Alaska Federation of Natives, Hensley has long reflected on the future of native peoples. He has seen that in the past Indians were asked to give up their native identities. Funding provided by the Settlement Act was supposed to prevent this. But Hensley reminds us all that the tools of economics and politics, although important, cannot save our cultural heritage. Instead, he

"GLIMPSE OF ZUNI FROM THE BRIDGE," CA. 1895. ZUNI PUEBLO, NEW MEXICO. PHOTOGRAPH BY BEN WITTICK.

says: "The fact of the matter is that unless we, individually and collectively, make up our minds that we are going to pass on the spirit of our people in the language that expresses that spirit, and our traditions, and our culture, we are simply not going to survive."[2]

Becoming an elder represents a point in a person's life where leadership and teaching are his or her primary responsibilities. The elders serve as stabilizing forces within the community. They maintain its sense of continuity. We have tried in this book to show how culture is a dynamic force, a problem-solving mechanism that has preserved native societies during times of hardship and radical change. Yet people need guidance to understand how their culture addresses their concerns. Elders provide this guidance.

Children are the reason we seek information, share it, and pass it on. They are the focus of the transfer of knowledge from the elders, completing the cycle of life's journey. In the past, grandparents played a major part in raising native children. (In many families, this is still true.) They shared stories of their experiences as Indians in a very different world. Personal stories have always been as important to native education as histories and myths.

MARIA MARTINEZ (LEFT) WITH HER SISTER AND ANOTHER POTTER, 1917. SAN ILDEFONSO PUEBLO, NEW MEXICO. PHOTOGRAPH BY T.H. PARKHURST. (9609)

BLACK-ON-BLACK POTTERY PLATE, CA. 1930. MADE BY MARIA MARTINEZ (CA. 1887–1980) AND JULIAN MARTINEZ (1885–1945), SAN ILDEFONSO PUEBLO. DIAM. 37 CM (24.7564)

When the reservation system was established in the latter half of the nineteenth century, churches were chosen to undertake the re-education of native children. The idea was to replace the native world view with Christian morality, Western thinking, and the spirit of capitalism. Educators saw their task as killing the Indian and saving the human being. Native children were taken from their families and communities and sent to boarding schools, sometimes great distances away. The setting was usually military. Indian boys' long hair was cut; girls' braids were pinned into buns. Native clothes were replaced with uniforms. Children were forbidden to speak their own languages or practice traditional skills, as these were considered pagan, backward, and too reminiscent of their former lives.

Carl Sweezy, an Arapaho born around 1880 who went on to become an outstanding painter, recalled his boarding school days this way:

> We had everything to learn about the white man's road. We had come to a country that was new to us, where wind and rain and rivers and heat and cold and even the plants and animals were different from what we had always known. We had to learn to live by farming instead of by hunting and trading. . . . We had to learn to cut our hair short, and to wear close-fitting clothing made from dull-colored cloth, and to live in houses, though we knew that our long braids of hair and embroidered robes and moccasins and tall, round lodges were more beautiful.[3]

What many Indians see as beautiful, other people may find boring, or inauthentic. What many Indians find powerful, others may see as superstitious. The ways in which many Indians define the universe, others may think of as myths.

The objects in this book can be read in many different ways. They mean different things to each of us. But one of their realities lies in how their makers intended them to be perceived. For many things, we may never know what that intention was. Yet, if we can look beyond art, anthropology, archaeology, and museology, we can see in some things the beliefs of the individuals who made and used them.

Native cultures are not preserved in books, films, or museums. They are preserved when native children learn the traditions of their people and express them in new ways. Objects live when they are used as their makers intended. Then it no longer matters whether these things are called art, artifacts, or sacred objects. What matters is that young people know the dances, songs, speeches, rituals, and arts that surround them.

By the way, the boarding schools are still operating, missionaries still visit the reservations, trading posts are still major forces in native life. Scholars still argue over what it all means, and governments still wrestle with native cultural rights. Most important, we are still here. We still walk on this land. We still dance in ceremonies of thanksgiving. And we still depend on art to express what it is like to live on our side of the world.

PEDESTAL DISH, A.D. 600–800.
COCLE CULTURE, VERAGUAS,
PANAMA. HEIGHT 21.5 CM (22.9512)

TOTA, HOPI, WITH HIS ZUNI WIFE
AND FAMILY. ZUNI PUEBLO,
NEW MEXICO.

One of the most outstanding examples of prehistoric North American art in existence, this bowl, perhaps representing a crested male wood duck, is carved from a single piece of diorite. Using only stone tools, the artist created a perfectly proportioned and symmetrical masterpiece. Its maker clearly had a well-conceived design and the skill to execute it, including some means of calibration. Excavated near Moundville, in Hale County, Alabama, the bowl dates to between A.D. 1250 and 1500, the archaeological period known as Middle Mississippian.

By the mid-thirteenth century A.D., raw materials and finished goods associated with status and religion were in great demand in the chiefdoms of what is now the southeastern United States. The apparent popularity of certain themes and motifs and the wide area in which they have been found suggest a shared belief system throughout the region, which may have helped support political alliances as well. Southeastern Indians in general recognized a cosmos consisting of the upper world, this world, and the lower world. The upper world was above the sky arch and associated with the sun and fire; animals of the upper world comprised most creatures of flight, including birds. Reptiles, creatures living in water, and water itself were ascribed to the lower world.

Circular shell gorgets (throat armor or ornaments) appear as early as the Late Archaic period (3000 to 2000 B.C.). Made from *Busycon perversum*, a type of conch commonly found along the Gulf of Mexico, and excavated from sites in Tennessee, the examples here illustrate the extent to which trade networks existed in eastern North America before European Contact. Gorgets may have been emblems of authority, status, or religious adherence.

The gorget above, at right, is one of the best known examples of North American shell art. It was apparently worn not with the human figure kneeling, as implied by many published photographs, but with the legs and torso facing down and the head turned upward, suggesting a free fall or possibly an imaginary journey through time or space.

The second gorget shows four redheaded woodpeckers attached to the outermost of four concentric squares with scrolled corners. For most southeastern Indians, the number four was sacred. Adherents to the traditional Cherokee religion in Oklahoma arrange four logs pointing in each of the cardinal directions at the center of the sacred fire. Cherokee medicinal remedies generally include four plant components, and their healing formulas are recited four times. The woodpecker may have represented civil or religious, rather than military, power.

D.K.

WOOD-DUCK EFFIGY BOWL, A.D. 1250–1500. MIDDLE MISSISSIPPIAN, ALABAMA. 29 X 40 CM (16.5232)

GORGET WITH HUMAN FIGURE, CA. A.D. 1250–1300. MIDDLE MISSISSIPPI-AN, TENNESSEE. 10 X 9.5 CM (15.853)

GORGET WITH WOODPECKERS, CA. 1250–1300. MIDDLE MISSISSIPPIAN, TENNESSEE. DIAM. 8 CM (15.855)

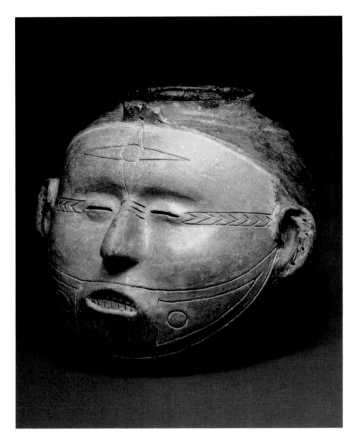

TROPHY HEAD VESSEL, A.D.
1300–1500. NODENA PHASE, MIDDLE
MISSISSIPPIAN. 15.6 X 18.5 CM
(23.980)

JAR, A.D. 1300–1700. LATE MISSISSIP-
PIAN (CADDOAN). HEIGHT 14 CM
(17.3248)

This unusual Nodena Red-and-white vessel was found near Paducah, in McCracken County, Kentucky, and dates to about A.D. 1300 to 1500. The red pigment was produced by applying a thin slip of red ocher or iron oxide to the surface of the pot before firing. The holes in the ears were probably for the suspension of ornaments. The incised lines on the face seem to represent tattoos. Most effigy vessels of this type show slits for eyes and a stretched mouth exposing clenched teeth in what is generally interpreted as a death pose. Severed heads are common in Mississippian military iconography and apparently represent undisputed proof of triumph over the enemy. Whether the ceramic effigies commemorate war trophies or the veneration of ancestors or other honored dead is not certain. Garcilaso de la Vega, who wrote about the de Soto expedition through the Southeast from 1539 to 1543, gave the following account of the Spanish sack of Capaha: "Many of the heads of Casquin Indians, which the men in Capaha had placed on the points of lances at the doors of the temple as a symbol of victory and triumph, they now removed, substituting for them the heads of citizens of the town whom they themselves had decapitated on that very day." Capaha—or Pacaha, as the name appears in the primary reports of the expedition—was located near Wapanocca Lake in present-day Crittenden County, Arkansas. The Casqui chiefdom was probably centered at the Parkin site on the St. Francis River west of Capaha.

This water bottle with four points at the base is a classic example of pre-Contact pottery by the Caddoan-speaking people who lived in hunting and farming villages along the lower Red River. It dates to between A.D. 1300 and 1700 and was found in Ouachita Parish, Louisiana. The spiral/scroll incised design has a large number of possible symbolic associations. One theory is that it represents water, either directly or through association with rain or the rainbow; another, that the interlocking scrolls are animals locked in combat. The nested arcs may represent the rising or setting sun, with the elaborative designs representing the sun's rays or rain clouds.

The curvilinear motifs may also reflect ritual movement. Southeastern Indian stomp dances, in addition to circular movements around the sacred fire, are characterized by "snakelike" winding patterns. In 1729, a Frenchman named Antoine le Page du Pratz observed the funeral procession of the Tattooed Serpent, a Natchez chief. The Natchez, cultural descendants of the Mississippians, followed a looping course as they carried the body of their leader from his house to the temple.

D.K.

Two hundred years ago near one of the Great Lakes of North America, a young British officer acquired a remarkable collection of Indian objects. This feather headdress is perhaps the rarest of all, for although early illustrations depict similar headdresses being worn, few others, if any, have survived from the eighteenth century. This one is remarkable, too, because we can document its collection history. The collector, Lt. Andrew Foster of the 24th Foot Regiment, served from 1792 to 1795 at Fort Miami, near Detroit, and at Fort Michilimackinac in northern Michigan, a staging center for the fur trade routes from eastern Canada to the western Plains. Oral history in the Foster family is that Lt. Foster became an "honorary chief" during his stay in North America, and the headdress may have been made and presented on that occasion.[1] Trading in furs and other commodities, seen by Europeans as a commercial transaction, was viewed by Indians as embedded in a web of personal and kin relationships and obligations, requiring gifts as tokens of friendship and alliance.[2]

Despite this history, we cannot identify the cultural affiliation of the headdress's maker except in the most general way.[3] The late eighteenth century was a time of great change and movement for the Indians of the Great Lakes area, and "tribes" as the political entities we know today were still being formed. Settlements around Fort Michilimackinac included people called Ottawa and Huron, each comprising several separate groups; frequent visitors there and at Fort Miami were reported to be (in the terminology of the twentieth century) Potawatomi, Miami, Sauk and Fox, Chippewa, Menominee, and Mohawk, as well as Métis traders whose heritage was both Indian and French. Foster's regiment returned to England in 1800, and he probably brought his collection home to Warwickshire.[4] His family carefully preserved the headdress until 1936, when it was transferred to a museum in England. It was acquired by the Heye Foundation in 1967.

The cultural meaning of this beautiful headdress has undergone several transformations since it was passed from the hands of its maker. For Andrew Foster's family the headdress became a memento of his life. For the museum it is part of a rare, documented early collection. And for the viewer it survives as a window onto the world of the eighteenth-century Great Lakes people and the North American fur trade.

This pair of beaded leggings, made of buckskin blackened with dye or by smoking, is in all likelihood from the same period as the feather bonnet. Black buckskin seems to have been popular in the Eastern Woodlands and the Great Lakes area in the eighteenth century and perhaps before. These leggings, decorated with white trade beads and dyed quillwork, suggest the splendid appearance of a man in full dress. Early accounts of the Iroquoian peoples and peoples of the eastern Great Lakes refer to the rich and "gaudy"[5] clothes and ornaments they wore, particularly during feasts and on ceremonial occasions.

M.J.L.

"Just before the Shawnees have a war-dance, the dancers hold a ceremony out some distance from the dance-ground, in which they have the sacred bundle open and dance around near it, just after they have painted themselves and dressed for the dance. At this time they talk to the bundle, and then they can get good luck in war. . . . No woman is allowed in this ceremony. Then they get on their horses and ride around before they dance."

—EARNEST SPYBUCK

Although *Procession before War Dance* depicts the ceremony described by painter Earnest Spybuck, Spybuck chose not to show the sacred bundle. "The Shawnees," he explained, "did not like to have the picture of this bundle painted."[1]

Spybuck was born in 1883 on the Potawatomi/Shawnee reservation near Tecumseh, Oklahoma. He was raised among the various Native American groups who—like his own Absentee Shawnee—had been removed from their historic homelands to Indian Territory. Entirely self-taught, Spybuck developed a talent for capturing scenes of daily life—mostly cattle ranching—in vivid and realistic watercolor paintings. One day in 1910, Spybuck was introduced to Mark Raymond Harrington, an ethnologist and field collector for the Museum of the American Indian–Heye Foundation, by Harrington's field assistant. Spybuck had some of his watercolor paintings with him, and his keen attention to detail caught Harrington's ethnographic eye. Harrington commissioned Spybuck "to record in watercolors the ceremonies, games, and customs of his own people and those of other tribes in the vicinity."[2]

Over the next eleven years, Spybuck produced thirty-three works, mostly watercolors, for Harrington. While Spybuck did paint among his Sauk and Fox, Kickapoo, and Delaware neighbors, almost all the paintings he produced for Harrington were of Shawnee ceremonies or social gatherings. Joe Billy, a Shawnee ceremonial leader with whom Harrington also worked, described the opening of these ceremonies: the Shawnee, he said, "would come to the dance ground on the appointed evening and lay tobacco on the earth for an offering and one of the party would say to the Creator, 'I have offered tobacco as I was taught to do. Now we will have our dances.'"[3]

At the time Spybuck was painting them, the Shawnee dressed, for the most part, like non-Indian farmers and ranchers. But according to Harrington, they also wore cotton coats with ruffled collars and cuffs. Typically, these distinctive coats were made of two thicknesses of cloth, so that the inside of the jacket was fully lined with a different calico pattern.

C.R.G.

PROCESSION BEFORE WAR DANCE, CA. 1910. EARNEST L. SPYBUCK (1883–1949), ABSENTEE SHAWNEE. WATERCOLOR ON PAPERBOARD, 44.2 X 63.9 CM (2.5735)

SHAWNEE CLOTH COAT, LATE 19TH C. LENGTH 84.5 CM (2.356)

EARNEST L. SPYBUCK, 1910. PHOTO-GRAPH BY M.R. HARRINGTON. (2865)

Most written histories of the American West describe the Cheyenne as they appeared in the mid-nineteenth century—rich in horses, dressed in beaded clothing and feather headdresses, moving their tipis over the grasslands of the central Plains in pursuit of the bison. Here Southern Cheyenne artist W. Richard West Sr. draws on oral histories of a much earlier time, when the Cheyenne were an agricultural people of the Eastern Woodlands, living in domed lodges built of reed mats and tilling fields of corn, beans, and squash. The Cheyenne have seen many changes since that time, but the old stories are still told.

In this painting, a mythical hero is a guest at a dance of the Little People. Stories of a race of tiny beings who lived in the ancient past are known to many Indian nations; miniature arrowheads and other ancient artifacts—seldom found within living memory—provide evidence of their existence. West has chosen to paint a night scene. The Cheyenne see the hours of light and the hours of darkness as two parts of the day's cycle, balanced yet in opposition to each other. Each is the proper time for certain activities. The Dark Dance was an activity of the nighttime, as is storytelling, through which tales of the Little People have been preserved.

Oral literature is a highly developed art form in native North America. The storyteller is a specialist, well respected within a community. In the past in some cultures, important stories were owned by individuals and could not be retold by other people without special training. In this way the accurate transmittal of important traditions was ensured. The graphic arts have often been used to supplement oral tales and histories, serving as both illustrations and guides to memory. West's paintings carry on this long tradition. Like earlier images painted on bison hides or engraved on sheets of bark, they tell the stories of his people.

West, whose Cheyenne name is Wah-pah-nah-yah, or Lightfoot, was born in Oklahoma in 1912. He studied art at Bacone College, graduating in 1938, and subsequently attended the University of Oklahoma, where he earned a Master of Fine Arts. As director of the art department at Bacone from 1947 until 1970, West had a profound influence on a generation of Indian painters. Early fine arts programs at the University of Oklahoma and the Studio at the Santa Fe Indian School had provided important opportunities for Indian artists to develop their talents. Bacone offered them the chance to study under Indian professors. West believed that native students must be free to explore a variety of styles derived from many traditions, but he encouraged them to draw on stories from their own tribes for inspiration and subject matter.

J.C.E.

DARK DANCE OF THE LITTLE
PEOPLE, 1948. W. RICHARD WEST SR.
(WAH-PAH-NAH-YAH, BORN 1912),
TSISTSISTAS (SOUTHERN
CHEYENNE). OPAQUE WATERCOLOR
ON PAPER, 30.5 X 45.8 CM (23.8382)

W. RICHARD WEST SR.

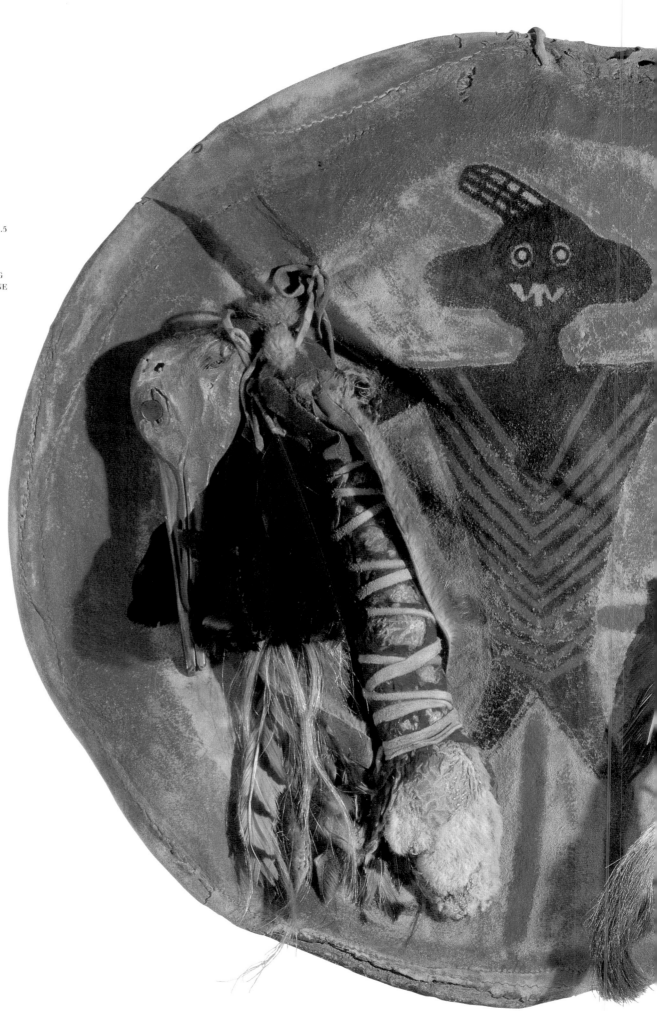

SHIELD, BEFORE 1830. MADE BY
ARAPOOSH (SORE BELLY, DIED
1834), ABSAROKE (CROW). DIAM. 61.5
CM (11.7680)

PETROGLYPHS OF SHIELD-BEARING
WARRIORS, 1931. WRITING-ON-STONE
PROVINCIAL PARK, ALBERTA.
PHOTOGRAPH BY
GENERAL HUGH L. SCOTT.

A common motif in the prehistoric rock art of the northwestern Great Plains is the shield-bearing warrior, a man with a circular, featureless head and linear lower legs who is covered from his neck to below his knees by a round shield. Archaeologists have traced this image back as far as nine hundred years among the tribes living in present-day Wyoming, Montana, and Alberta, and shield-bearing warriors can be seen painted or incised on rock walls at scattered sites in that region.

During the 1740s, at a time when their Shoshone enemies possessed horses but they did not, the Blackfeet still carried rawhide shields large enough to stand behind. By the nineteenth century smaller shields for use by warriors on horseback had replaced the old design. These shields covered only the vital parts from about the waist up.

Among the tribes of the area, the Crow were recognized as the best shield makers. And the most famous Crow shield was one that belonged to Arapoosh or Sore Belly, head chief of the River Crow in the early 1800s. This shield consists of an outer cover of undecorated buckskin, an elaborately decorated inner cover, and a circular rawhide base twenty-four inches in diameter and one-quarter inch thick, painted solid red. The figure painted on the inner cover, shown here, is said to represent the moon, who appeared to Sore Belly in a vision and gave him this shield. Attached to the painted cover is the head and body of a stork, a bird normally found along the Gulf coast, although occasionally seen as far north as Maine and British Columbia. Also tied to the cover are a single eagle feather, on the upper right, and a deer's tail, at the lower right, partially covered with red flannel.

This shield possessed magical powers of prophesy. Once, before leading a large war party against the Cheyenne, Sore Belly rolled the shield, promising that if it fell painted side down he would not proceed. It stopped painted side up, and Sore Belly led his people to a great victory on the Arkansas River. In 1834, he led an unsuccessful siege of Fort McKenzie, the American Fur Company post on the Missouri River, which was furnishing guns and ammunition to the Crow's enemies, the Blackfeet. He was killed in action against the Blackfeet later that year.

J.C.E.

PERFORATED BUCKSKIN SHIRT,
LATE 19TH C. BLACKFEET. LENGTH
72 CM (14.3567)

LOUIS BEAR CHILD, BLACKFEET,
OFFICER OF ALL THE BRAVE DOGS
SOCIETY, 1941. PHOTO BY DONALD
SCHMIDT.

This elaborately decorated buckskin war shirt, like many Blackfeet shirts, bears colorful beaded strips over the shoulders and the sleeve seams, and long pendant strips of weasel fur. It is noteworthy, however, because its entire surface is painted half red and half yellow, while the skin is full of a great many small, deliberately cut holes.

There is evidence that perforated hide shirts were worn by men on both sides of the Rockies in the upper valleys of the Missouri and Columbia Rivers during the nineteenth century—west of the mountains among the Flathead and Spokane Indians, east among the Blackfeet and Assiniboine.

East of the mountains, some of the men who wore them were members of the powerful Bear cult and obtained powers from the most dangerous and awesome of the region's animals, the grizzly bear. Others acquired special powers in dreams or visions.

The most famous war shirt among the Blackfeet was bestowed upon Big Plume in a dream when he was separated from

his colleagues during a horse raid. The shirt, remade several times, was worn in combat by more than one generation of Blackfeet warriors. Its wearer always survived unharmed. One of several known versions of Big Plume's shirt is still in the possession of a family on the Blackfeet Reservation in Montana.

Farther east, among the Assiniboine, members of the Bear cult wore perforated shirts, bear-claw necklaces, and striking red face-paint raked as though by a bear's claws. They might own bear-painted shields and tipis and carry into battle two-edged knives with bear-jaw handles. They used their Bear power as war medicine and to heal the sick.

Among the Blackfeet, members of several men's societies wore Bear cult symbols. As recently as 1941, Louis Bear Child, a member of the last Piegan Blackfeet men's society, All the Brave Dogs, was photographed wearing his painted and perforated buckskin shirt.

J.C.E.

Painted coats and leggings were worn by Innu hunters of the Quebec–Labrador Peninsula to honor the spirit of the caribou and thereby bring success in the hunt. The Innu revere the spirits of their prey, the caribou above all others because it is the mainstay of life.[1] Thus for the Innu, and their Algonquian neighbors the Cree, hunting is a holy occupation based on establishing a relationship of respect and reciprocity with the spirits of animals.

The designs painted on an Innu coat came to the hunter in a dream and expressed both spiritual power and the desire to please the caribou, who would then allow themselves to be captured. The hunter described to his wife the designs in his dream. It was her responsibility to incorporate them into a coat. The basic forms, including circles, crosshatching, double curves, and leaf shapes, belong to an ancient and widespread northern tradition, but each coat is unique, a combination of the hunter's dream and his wife's interpretation of it.[2] A man needed two coats every year, for the summer and winter hunting seasons. It is reported that each coat was discarded or traded away at the end of the season, its power spent.[3] If true, this may be the source of the Innu coats, spanning the period from about 1700 to 1930, in private collections and museums throughout the world.

Remarkable skill and labor were needed to make painted coats and leggings. Each coat required three finely tanned caribou skins, shaped to the body and sewn with sinew thread. The coats were, to some degree, modeled after European fashions of the eighteenth and nineteenth centuries, but earlier northern Athapaskan coats were prototypes as well. One feature of Innu coats is unique: a triangular gusset inserted at the center back or, in twentieth century coats, painted on. It seems to have no practical use; it does not make the coat roomier. It may represent the mountain home of the Lord of the Caribou and be the symbolic center of the coat's power. Painting was done not with a brush, but with pronged tools dipped in paint and drawn across the hide.[4]

That these beautiful coats were created by nomadic hunting people living in a sparsely populated northern environment makes them especially remarkable. The rich elaboration of designs must have represented an enormous outlay of time, energy, and artistry, and may reflect the fact that caribou hunting is both essential to Innu life and fraught with uncertainty. Even today, Innu hunters tell of people who starved to death—in the recent, as well as distant, past.[5] A hunter wearing such a beautiful garment showed respect for his quarry and hope for success.

This coat exemplifies many objects whose meanings have changed with their use. Conceived in a dream, worn with reverence, then discarded, it is now a rare museum piece, admired for its beauty by people far removed from its creation, who can only imagine its original significance.

M.J.L.

INNU HUNTER, MICHIKAMAU BAND, 1924. SEVEN ISLANDS, QUEBEC. PHOTOGRAPH BY FRANK G. SPECK. (12077)

INNU (NASKAPI–MONTAGNAIS) CARIBOU-SKIN COAT AND LEGGINGS, PROBABLY 1800–1820 AND BEFORE 1845. LENGTH 109 CM AND 46 CM (15.3165 AND 3.2899)

YUP'IK DANCE MASK, LATE 19TH C.
LENGTH 99 CM (9.3417)

MAN WEARING YUP'IK MASKETTE,
CA. 1927. NUNIVAK ISLAND, ALASKA.
PHOTOGRAPH BY EDWARD S.
CURTIS.

The surrealist artists of the 1920s were among the first outsiders to perceive Eskimo masks as "primitive art" and use them as inspiration for their own work. For the Yup'ik people of western Alaska who made and danced with these masks, however, they were profoundly religious instruments, symbols of the unity and dignity of all forms of life. They were worn in dance festivals to please the spirits of animals, bring success in hunting, and maintain an orderly universe. Each mask was the product of an individual vision, to be worn once and then discarded, its spiritual energy consumed. Belief was eternal, but the mask itself was ephemeral: making the mask and dancing with it were meaningful acts; keeping it for display was not.

In the past, and to some degree today, the daily lives of the Yup'ik depended on seals, beluga whales, sea lions, fish, land mammals, and waterfowl. In the Yup'ik world, both animals and humans have immortal souls—*yuas* or *inuas*—born and reborn in an endless cycle. Animals give themselves to hunters in response to the respect the hunters show them. A hunter never brags about his accomplishments and always takes care to apologize to his prey.

The inua of an animal appeared in Yup'ik dance masks in the form of a small human face, here shown on the belly of the crane. The only information we have about this mask is what the collector was told—that it depicts "a crane that carries a sick medicine man to his home." We also know that Eskimo medicine men, or shamans, were closely associated with birds and were believed to have the power of magical flight. Some shamans could fly to the moon; some to the land of the dead. Some could fly under the ocean, appearing to die, only to come to life again. This mask depicts one shaman's vision at one particular time.[1]

Festivals and religious ceremonies took place in the *qasgig*, or men's house, the social and ceremonial center of the village. The Bladder Festival, held at the time of the winter solstice, honored the spirits of the animals hunted during the year and reflected the Yup'ik belief that every living being will die, but, in time, will be born again. Animal bladders, collected through the year, were inflated and brought into the men's house, treated as honored guests, entertained with masked dances, and returned to the sea with a request that they be reborn the following season. At other ceremonies, too, members of the spirit world, animal and human alike, were invited into the community, formally hosted, and returned to their own domain.[2]

This mask is one of a large collection of Yup'ik masks George Heye acquired in 1919 from a trader named A.H. Twitchell. Twitchell may have been on the scene at the conclusion of a ceremony, when the masks had served their purpose. In the 1940s, Heye sold about half the masks from the Twitchell collection to a group of surrealists, including Max Ernst and André Breton.

M.J.L.

Although rattles can be thought of as musical instruments to accompany song and dance, or as beautiful works of art, to the peoples of the Northwest Coast they have a deeper and more profound meaning. The sound of a rattle can signify the presence of the supernatural or assist in curing spiritual or physical illness; the form and decoration of a rattle are the material embodiment of centuries-old spiritual beliefs, passed on through songs and stories, and often hidden from outsiders.

All along the Northwest Coast, globular wooden rattles made of two halves carefully fitted together are associated with shamans or with ceremonial practices that refer to the powers of shamans. It was said that a skilled shaman could handle a rattle so that it would twirl, seemingly by itself.[1] Some of the most exquisitely carved rattles were made by Nisga'a and Gitksan artists of British Columbia. Members of an elite group, these artists were trained from childhood, not only in the technical skills of carving, but also in the ritual observances required during the process of creation. A Nisga'a carver, for example, would fast for two days when he had finished a work, to prevent disaster to the carving or to the dancer who would use it.[2] The collector of this rattle (right) recorded the designs as a beaver and a frog. The beaver's tail encloses a small human face; the frog appears on the opposite side. Frogs, amphibious creatures who change shape as they mature, are often associated with shamans. However, because the designs on the rattle probably derive from personal supernatural powers, their full meaning was known only to the original owner.

The Cowichan and other Central Coast Salish peoples used sheephorn rattles (left) as instruments for ritual cleansing during potlatches and winter dances. The rattles are constructed from a sheet of horn bent over and sewn along the edges to form a bulging triangle.[3] Strands of mountain goat wool are attached to the sides, and the end of the wooden handle is usually carved. The surface is usually carved with incised designs or, as here, a face surrounded with zigzag rays. This rattle is also adorned with two flat metal strips cut out with stars. It is likely that the meaning of these designs was confined to the person who made and used the rattle, and that it signified his or her special powers. This tradition continues today.

Rattles depicting birds are made throughout the Northwest Coast, although this rattle—a fat, bright-eyed grouse—is distinct to the Makah people of the Olympic Peninsula and their Vancouver Island neighbors, the Nuu-chah-nulth. Carved of a hard wood, probably alder, the unpainted surface retains the marks of the carver's knife. Sections of wood cut out along the bird's neck lighten the rattle and increase the resonance as it is shaken.[4] George Heye purchased this rattle around 1920 and provided no information on its use, but a virtually identical rattle in the Burke Museum in Seattle was identified by a traditional elder as Kokhmin—Makes Noise—used for all kinds of dancing.[5]

M.J.L.

GITKSAN WOODEN RATTLE, LATE 19TH/EARLY 20TH C. LENGTH 35 CM (9.7998)

COWICHAN SALISH SHEEPHORN RATTLE, 19TH C. LENGTH 47.5 CM (16.2079)

MAKAH WOODEN RATTLE IN THE FORM OF A BIRD, 19TH C. LENGTH 32 CM (9.9907)

"The ts'ika is a kind of prayer that things will go well and nothing will go wrong. . . . It is always done with a rattle, never a drum."

—HELMA WARD, MAKAH

Some time around a hundred years ago in a Nuxalk village, in the darkness of a winter night, a group of uninitiated people would have witnessed this carved head of an Eagle appearing in a strange and frightening series of events. A Cannibal dancer, possessed by a craving for human or other flesh, was seen to run amok, biting people, making loud, unhuman cries, and having to be physically restrained. The Cannibal was a member of the Kusiut, a secret society of those who had acquired special names related to supernatural ancestors; his dreadful hunger was incited by a cannibalistic spirit, in the form of an Eagle, which had entered his body.[1] His madness could be driven out by rhythmic beating on a sounding board. As the sound of drumming filled the house, the head of the Eagle spirit, its eyes glistening, suddenly appeared next to the Cannibal, as if it had left his body. The Eagle opened its mouth and vomited pieces of meat into a box, from which steam rose. The Eagle's head was then concealed, and the audience was told that it had returned to the supernatural world. At the same time, the Cannibal became calm and quiet, resuming his human behavior.

This powerful event was accomplished through a fairly simple artifice. Meat was fed into the back of the Eagle's head and dropped from the mouth onto hot stones; the steam created the appearance of having been disgorged by a living creature. This is only one of a number of theatrical devices created by specialists in the arts of illusion and drama. In Western terms these carvers, called "carpenters" by the Nuxalk, made what appear to be theatrical props intended to fool the uninitiated. In the cultural context of the Nuxalk, however, the role of carpenters was to make visible the supernatural world that exists alongside the world of the everyday. The illusions they created were more than simple tricks; rather, they were reenactments of powerful relationships with supernatural beings who occupied a complex universe.[2]

A Kusiut performance lasted for four days and nights and preparations included the composing and practicing of new songs, as well as the carving of special masks. The work was done in great secrecy; old stories tell of uninitiated persons encountering the preparations and being killed or, sometimes, forcibly initiated and sworn to uphold the Kusiut mysteries.

By the 1920s, many of the old songs and ceremonies had been forgotten. But some of them remained alive in the memories of elders, and in 1922 they were recorded on wax cylinders. By the 1960s, the Nuxalk people themselves were preserving their songs on tape. They began a program to relearn them, together with the dances, and today Nuxalk singers and dancers perform on public occasions. This kind of performance itself has a long tradition: in 1885 and 1886, nine Nuxalk (then known as Bella Coola) singers performing in Germany excited the interest of the young anthropologist Franz Boas, who went on to make the cultures of the Northwest Coast the subject of lifelong study.

M.J.L.

NUXALK (BELLA COOLA) CARVED WOODEN EAGLE SPIRIT, LATE 19TH/EARLY 20TH C. 46 X 27 X 20 CM (23.8521)

GEORGE GUSTAV HEYE (LEFT), MRS. R.C. DRANEY, AND E.S. ROBINSON, WITH NUXALK CARVINGS. VANCOUVER, BRITISH COLUMBIA. PHOTOGRAPH BY T.P.O. MENZIES. (36887)

From Prince William Sound in the Gulf of Alaska to the Columbia River Valley, the people living along the coast wear hats, twined or woven in a variety of styles and materials, for both everyday and ceremonial uses. Some hats protect from rain or sun; some are painted with family or clan crest designs and displayed proudly at potlatches and other important occasions; some were worn by native doctors as evidence of special powers. Perhaps the most distinctive of all basketry hats were the so-called Whaler hats worn by members of chiefly families from the west coast of Vancouver Island. They caught the attention of a number of eighteenth-century artists who produced portraits of specific individuals wearing them.

This conical hat with an onion-shaped crown is actually two hats, one within the other. The inner hat, fitted to the head, is composed of woven cedar bark joined to the outer shell at the rim. The outer hat is twined with split spruce root, black-dyed cedar bark, and surf grass to create a design that consists primarily of scenes of hunters in canoes pursuing a whale.

John Jewitt, an English ship's blacksmith who was the prisoner of the powerful chief Maquinna at Nootka Sound from 1803 to 1805, reported that these hats were worn exclusively by chiefs. They were without doubt associated with the dangerous art of whale hunting, a venture pursued only by the Nuu-chah-nulth and their neighbors, the Makah of the Olympic Peninsula.[1] Whale hunting required leadership, the wealth to acquire a craft and a crew, skill, courage, and a considerable element of luck. The hunting of a whale was surrounded with ritual and religious observation, and a successful whaler commanded the highest possible prestige within a community.

Only a few of these old hats exist today. Several of them, including this one, were collected in 1792 by a Boston sea captain named James Magee, who traveled the West Coast waters during the years of the trade in sea-otter furs. The hat style has recently been revived. It is referred to as a Maquinna hat, not only for the eighteenth-century chief, but for his descendants, who still bear the name and position today.

M.J.L.

I have come to see how your house is.
Is it prepared for large crowds?

—MAKAH WHALE SONG

"FASTENING THE HARPOON POINT," 1915. PHOTOGRAPH BY EDWARD S. CURTIS. (P4491)

NUU-CHAH-NULTH (NOOTKA) BASKETRY HAT, 18TH C. HEIGHT 21 CM (16.4130)

"Everybody of any wealth and importance had a belt. People married with them. The man gave it. Men wore it in the War Dance. This was the only way they used it. It was a woman's belt."

—MARY AZBILL, MAIDU

This Shasta dance apron and belt (right) offer mute testimony to a vibrant way of life shattered by war, foreign diseases, and famine. On special occasions, Shasta women wore pine-nut, seed, or grass aprons over fringed hide back-skirts. Belts similar to this one of finely braided horsehair may originally have been made from human hair cut off in mourning by widows, widowers, or parents who had lost a child.[1] This belt, held in place with hide thongs, is studded with large brass buttons, but decorations vary, and similar belts in the museum's collection incorporate glass beads, mother-of-pearl buttons, clamshell disk beads, and even thimbles.

By the early twentieth century, only a small number of Shastan people remained scattered throughout their homelands in the valleys and heavily forested mountains of northern California and Oregon, survivors of a population that once numbered in the thousands.[2] Old men among the Shasta at the turn of the century remembered stories about the first European-American fur trappers to enter the region in the 1820s and 1830s.[3] After gold was discovered in the region in 1850, miners came and bustling towns sprang up. In the scramble for land, Indian villages were attacked; native homes were burned and the inhabitants shot. An 1851 treaty establishing a reservation for the California Shasta was never ratified. Today, leaders of the Shasta Nation are working to restore their political and cultural heritage and to receive federal recognition for a coalition of seventeen tribes.

Important ceremonial dress made by the Maidu of central California includes shimmering and brilliantly colored feathered ornaments. Maidu tales recount how, long ago, two doctors arrived from the north wearing elaborate clothing decorated with scarlet woodpecker scalp feathers.[4] This spectacular belt (below, left) was made by the Konkow, or Northwestern Maidu. It is woven of native fiber cord with scarlet acorn-woodpecker scalp feathers, iridescent green mallard duck feathers, and large white glass beads; the layout of the design panels may have been unique to particular Maidu groups.[5] Stewart Culin, who collected it, was told that it "was made on a loom. . . . The knot on this belt, where the threads came together at one end, was called the navel."[6] Woven feather belts might measure six or seven feet in length. They were worn by dancers wrapped twice around the waist or over one shoulder as sashes.[7]

Mary Azbill, a leader among the Maidu at Chico, told Culin that the last master belt-maker was an old man named To-no-ko, and that when he passed away, production of these great belts ceased. Although belts might be given as gifts or traded, they were rarely sold to, or even seen by, non-Indians. Culin collected this feather belt in 1907 from a Pomo family at Upper Lake who had acquired it from the Chico Maidu many years earlier.

E.H.B.

SHASTA HAIR BELT WITH METAL
ORNAMENTS, SECOND HALF OF THE
19TH C. 70 X 9.5 CM (6.1043)

SHASTA PINE-NUT DANCE APRON,
SECOND HALF OF THE 19TH C.
LENGTH 67.5 CM (12.2912)

Mosaic work is very old in the American Southwest. Ancestors of today's Pueblo peoples crafted exquisite pendants, rings, bracelets, necklaces of beads, and other jewelry from shell, bone, turquoise, jet, and other stones. These ornaments might be carved, incised, covered with inlay, or left plain; sometimes, a whole shell was decorated with mosaic, such as the pendant illustrated here.

Few intact examples of ancient mosaic shell work are known today. This *Spondylus* shell pendant decorated with turquoise and jet was collected from the great Anasazi ruin of Pueblo Bonito, in Chaco Canyon, in northwest New Mexico. It dates to A.D. 900 to 1250. Marine shells had been imported into the region from the Pacific Coast or the Gulf of California for a few thousand years before this time. Turquoise was probably mined in the nearby Cerillos area.[1] Jet, a soft stone that can be polished to a deep lustrous black, was obtained from local coal beds.

The Chaco Canyon region of the eleventh and twelfth centuries is traditionally defined by its massive multistoried towns, Great Kivas, and complex network of roads leading to outlying Chacoan communities. Pueblo Bonito, an extraordinary five-storied masonry ruin of more than six hundred rooms, was the largest town. Today, scholars argue that there was a larger Chaco regional system, extending perhaps even beyond the San Juan Basin.[2] Chaco Canyon itself was probably a great ceremonial and trading center and possibly a pilgrimage site, but whether or not it played a political role in the larger system is a matter of debate.[3]

The ear pendants and combs shown here are from Hawikku, an ancestral Zuni town in what is now western New Mexico. These beautiful and extremely rare ornaments are made of pieces of wood set with turquoise and jet; the adhesive is probably pinyon pitch.[4] Like the people of Pueblo Bonito, the Zunis obtained turquoise from the Cerillos area, probably through trade, and they mined the precious stone in the Zuni Mountains.

Hawikku was one of the two largest towns occupied by the Zunis at the time of the Spanish entry into the American Southwest. A great battle took place here on July 7, 1540, between the Zunis and Spanish conquistadors traveling north from Mexico under Francisco Vásquez de Coronado. Hawikku was abandoned after the Pueblo Revolt of 1680; later, the people moved to Halona:wa, the site of present-day Zuni Pueblo.

Today, jewelry making at Zuni is an important and highly successful enterprise. Artists work with turquoise, jet, coral, and shell, as well as modern stones such as amber, opal, and lapis. Distinctive Zuni techniques include mosaic work, channel inlay, and cluster work, the latter characterized by large blue stones set in flowerlike motifs; needlepoint, an offshoot of cluster work, consists of arrangements of tiny, pointed pieces of stone set in individual silver bezels. Lapidary work has roots deep in Zuni history and is a source of great pride for the people of the pueblo.

E.H.B.

EAR PENDANTS WITH TURQUOISE MOSAIC AND COMBS WITH TURQUOISE AND JET MOSAIC, CA. 1400–1680. HAWIKKU, NEW MEXICO. LENGTH 3 TO 12.8 CM (6.8642, 8.6573, 6.8643, 6.8644, AND 8.6568)

SHELL PENDANT WITH MOSAIC OF TURQUOISE AND JET, CA. 900–1250. PUEBLO BONITO, CHACO CANYON, NEW MEXICO. LENGTH 7.7 CM (7.1615)

KECHIPAWAN POLYCHROME BOWL, CA. 1375–1475. HAWIKKU, NEW MEXICO. HEIGHT 11.5 CM (8.6832)

ZUNI POLYCHROME WATER JAR, CA. 1875. ZUNI PUEBLO, NEW MEXICO. HEIGHT 28 CM (22.7879)

TRANSITIONAL ASHIWI/EARLY ZUNI POLYCHROME WATER JAR, CA. 1750–1800. OJO CALIENTE, NEW MEXICO. HEIGHT 23.5 CM (9.3773)

ZUNI PUEBLO, 1879. NEW MEXICO. PHOTOGRAPH BY J.K. HILLERS.

By the time that museums and collectors began their wholesale acquisition of Southwest ceramics in the late nineteenth century, Pueblo peoples and their ancestors had been producing handmade pottery vessels for centuries. Until the introduction of metal containers and European-American cooking ware, generations of Zuni potters from the area around Halona:wa or present-day Zuni Pueblo made an enormous variety of clay storage jars, jars for carrying and storing water, bowls for cooking and serving food, cups, canteens, ladles, and figurines, both for their own use and to trade. Old vessels are vital links to the past. For example, Zuni artist and ceramist Randy Nahohai readapts painted designs from pottery recovered from Hawikku, an abandoned Zuni village, and speaks of his work as a collaboration with his ancestors; he considers this bowl (center) important to Zuni because the parrot design represents a clan that is still around today. "To have one in your home," he says, "especially if you were from that clan, would make you feel real proud."[1]

Zuni ceramic production has always encompassed invention and change, one reason, perhaps, why the tradition survives. Potters have experimented with designs, revived old pottery styles, and combined traditional elements in creative ways. The two water jars shown here represent an evolution of new forms and design systems, yet they remain distinctively Zuni.

The older of the two (far right), made between about 1750 and 1800 and collected in the farming village of Ojo Caliente, is a transitional piece. The diagonal opposed elements are characteristic of Ashiwi Polychrome pottery (1700 to 1750), but the design incorporates an early example of the stylized Rain Bird motif found on Zuni Polychrome vessels of the early nineteenth century. It lacks, however, the decorative hatching and pronounced shoulder of early-nineteenth-century vessels, and its red base and interior rim

are eighteenth-century attributes.[2] The Rain Bird design as it appears on the body of the other water jar was developed in the early 1800s and is still a favorite design among Zuni potters.

For most of the twentieth century, Zuni pottery continued to be made primarily for local use, not the art market, and it remained basically unchanged.[3] Clay, considered a gift from Mother Earth and Clay Woman, is still collected from sites around Zuni. Large bowls and jars are traditionally constructed by coiling and then scraping; small items, by hand modeling. Plant and mineral pigments are applied with trimmed, narrow yucca-leaf brushes, as well as modern brushes, and pots are still fired outdoors, although potters also use commercial kilns. Young girls learn pottery making from relatives or in the schools; boys learn in schools, too. Primarily a women's art, pottery is also made by some men—today as in the past.

Zuni ceramics are a vehicle for symbolic imagery. Stepped or terraced designs filled with hachure represent clouds filled with rain, a central element in Zuni religion; Zuni prayers encompass the perpetuation of all life. Feather motifs occur in many forms and have been interpreted as prayer sticks: "Women do not prepare prayer sticks," one potter explained in 1924, "and that is why we always put feathers on the jars."[4] Terraced cornmeal bowls represent the world. Today they are commissioned for use in rituals, and gifts of pottery are exchanged between kin on special occasions. Zunis value old vessels for their age and traditional uses; water tastes better from a pottery jar, it is said.[5] Ceramics are also family heirlooms, displayed in wood-and-glass cabinets placed in prominent spots in many Zuni homes.

E.H.B.

A century ago, when ceramic production had almost ceased in some of the eastern pueblos of the American Southwest, excavations at ancestral village sites began yielding pottery fragments that would provide the models for new generations of ceramic artists. Encouraged by collectors, dealers, and scholars, including Edgar Lee Hewett and Kenneth M. Chapman, potters began recreating the ancient designs and signing their works. Their success on the art market helped sustain the pottery tradition in many pueblos.

Maria Montoya Martinez is renowned for the perfect symmetry of her pieces and for their flawless, highly polished surfaces. She was born about 1887 in San Ildefonso, New Mexico, and learned how to make pottery as a child. "I watched my aunt, Nicolasa, my mother's sister who had married my father's brother, so we are all in the family," she once said.[1] In 1919, Maria and her husband, Julian, developed the famous Black-on-black style equated ever since with the Martinez family. Their pots were built by the traditional method of coiling and scraping and were smoked black; matte designs were painted on the polished surfaces before firing.[2]

Maria began signing her work in 1923, but pottery-making was always a family enterprise. Julian decorated Maria's pots, modifying painted designs, including the stylized feather motifs shown here (center), from Mimbres pots and other ancient painted wares. After his death in 1943, Maria's daughter-in-law, Santana, did the painting. By 1956, her son, Popovi Da, was a full partner. Popovi Da revived the traditional polychrome style of the pueblo and developed the black-and-sienna style; his son, Tony Da, experimented with carved designs and inlaid stones.

Lucy Martin Lewis, from Acoma, also reworked motifs from ancient ceramics. The lightning design on this Black-on-white jar (left) derives from Anasazi Chacoan pottery. In 1958, Kenneth Chapman showed her the Mimbres collection at the Laboratory of Anthropology in Santa Fe. Today, Mimbres designs are the hallmark of both Acoma and San Ildefonso ceramics. Lucy's daughters—among them, Emma Lewis Mitchell, Delores Lewis Garcia, and Mary Lewis Garcia—are also exceptional potters. Emma speaks of the spirituality and playfulness that surround their work: "There's a prayer that goes into digging the clay, there's a prayer that goes into refining it. There's a prayer for making the pots, and maybe two prayers for bringing them to the dealer."[3]

Rachel Namingha Nampeyo was the granddaughter of Nampeyo, the legendary Hopi–Tewa potter from Hano, on First Mesa in Arizona, who is credited with the revival of Hopi pottery. Nampeyo drew inspiration from pieces of pottery she collected with her husband, Lesou, at Sikyatki and other Hopi ruins. Rachel believed in traditional designs and re-created many of Nampeyo's patterns, including the beautiful fine-line or migration design on this jar (right). Rachel's daughter, Dextra Qutoskuyva, still remembers many of her mother's patterns, sketched on newsprint. According to Dextra, Rachel explained the lines of the migration design as people going out over the whole world, a reference to Hopi legend.[4] The design is contained within two black framing bands at the top and bottom of the jar, another characteristic of Hopi pottery. Although Rachel was a conservative potter, her large jars exhibit a superb mastery of form and line that is her own.

E.H.B.

The great Aztec civilization established in the Valley of Mexico in 1345 reached its zenith by the late fifteenth century. At that time, the Aztec military empire extended to the Gulf and Pacific coasts and controlled ten to twenty million people. The capital, Tenochtitlán, located on the site of present-day Mexico City, was one of the world's largest cities, with 75,000 to 150,000 inhabitants.[1]

Religion governed everything the Aztecs did. Xipe Totec (Our Lord, the Flayed One), shown here, was the god of springtime and the patron of goldworkers.[2]

Xipe's main festival, called Tlacaxipehualiztli (Flaying of Men) took place from about March 6 to March 25. This springtime festival, which involved tens of thousands of participants, had a strong military character. In addition to agricultural dances, gladiatorial sacrifices were staged in which captives were slain by knights wearing jaguar and eagle costumes. The victims were

skinned and their skins worn by priests who became Xipe imper-
sonators, wandering the streets for twenty days, begging for food
and gifts and blessing people. At the end of that time, the reeking
skins were thrown into a ceremonial pit.[3]

This sculpture, carved of volcanic stone, depicts a Xipe
impersonator dressed in the skin of a sacrifice. The skin, its hands
dangling, is tied together at the back. The line of sutures on the
chest shows where the victim's heart was taken from his body.[4]

Aztec ceremonies and feasts were accompanied by music,
dances, and elaborate costumes. One of the musical instruments
was the *teponaztli*, a drum fashioned from a hollowed-out log with
an H-shaped cut creating two slats in the top. By striking the wooden
slats with rubber-tipped drumsticks, the drummer could play two
tones.[5] This teponaztli is particularly remarkable because its side
is carved with a glyph that signifies the year 1493.

N.R.

*"It is through
The sacred spirits
That all live . . .
They give us
Our daily fare
And all that we drink,
All that we eat."*

—AZTEC PRIEST

AZTEC TEPONAZTLI (WOODEN
DRUM) WITH 1493 GLYPH. AXZOTLA,
MEXICO. LENGTH 43.8 CM (16.3373)

AZTEC FIGURE OF XIPE TOTEC, A.D.
1450–1521. TLALPAN, MEXICO.
HEIGHT 78.8 CM (16.3621)

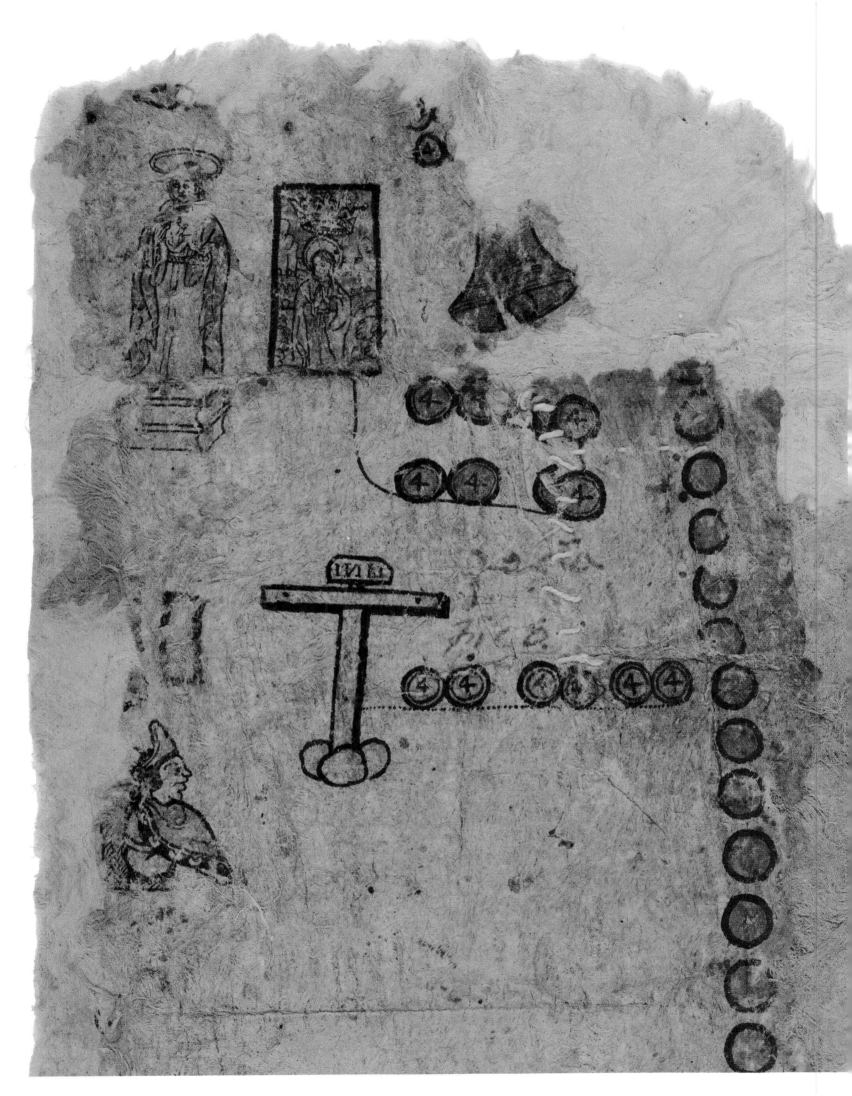

This codex—a Latin word used to describe ancient books and scrolls—made with ink and dyes on a roll of native paper, was begun sometime during the middle of the fifteenth century and completed around 1557. It records significant events in the history of the Aztecs from the time they arrived in the Valley of Mexico. The top portion of the manuscript describes the Spanish Conquest. The large cross at the year 1526 represents the coming of the Franciscans, who erected such a cross at their mission.[1]

Above the cross, associated with the year 1531, is an image of the Virgin Mary. In December of that year, a Christianized Indian named Juan Diego encountered a woman on the top of Tepeyac Hill. Speaking Nahuatl, she identified herself as Cenquizca Ichpochtzintli—Santa Maria de Guadalupe. The Virgin commanded Juan Diego to go to the archbishop of Mexico and inform him of her desire to see a sanctuary built in her honor at that site. Twice the archbishop refused to believe Juan Diego. So the Virgin appeared to Juan Diego again and told him to pick roses in an area where roses never grow, wrap them in a cloak, and present them to the archbishop. When Juan Diego unfolded the cloak before the archbishop, it miraculously bore the image of the Virgin. The archbishop acknowledged the miracle and ordered that a shrine be built where the Virgin had first appeared to Juan Diego. The cloak, with its miraculous image of Our Lady of Guadalupe, was hung in the sanctuary, and a popular devotion to the Virgin developed among the native and mestizo peoples of central Mexico.[2]

It has been suggested that this story is a myth to explain the conversion of the natives of Mexico to Christianity, but it is not that simple. Rather, it reflects the syncretism of native and Hispanic beliefs. Before Contact, Tepeyac Hill was the site of a temple dedicated to Tonantzin—Our Mother—the Nahuatl goddess of earth and fertility. The natives who first venerated Our Lady of Guadalupe drew inspiration from their worship of Tonantzin. Certainly their continued references to the Virgin of Guadalupe as Tonantzin greatly disturbed the Spanish missionaries.[3]

Native people accepted the Virgin of Guadalupe on their own terms. She became a symbol of hope and survival in the ruins of conquest and colonial oppression. Today, Nuestra Señora de Guadalupe still expresses the personal and cultural identity of many natives in Mexico and throughout the Americas.[4]

N.R.

CODEX TETLAPALCO (DETAIL), CA. 1450–1557. VALLEY OF MEXICO. 145.5 X 13.5 CM (13.6913)

FOLK IMAGE OF OUR LADY OF GUADALUPE, 1994. PERU.

MÍSKITO PURA-YAPTI (DANCE
MASK), LATE 19TH/EARLY 20TH C.
HEIGHT 70 CM (13.2502)

YAQUI DEER DANCER, 1924. SONORA,
MEXICO. PHOTOGRAPH BY EDWARD
H. DAVIS. (24434)

YAQUI PAHKO'OLA MAHKA (PASCOLA
DANCE MASK, RIGHT), EARLY 20TH
C. HEIGHT 29 CM (10.2075)

The Yaqui, who live in southern Sonora and northern Sinaloa,
Mexico, and, more recently, in southern Arizona, California, and
other parts of the southwestern United States, have maintained
their cultural identity primarily in two ways: they continue to
speak Cáhitan, their native language, and to observe a rich ceremonial heritage. This heritage includes a cycle of fiestas throughout the year during which the Yaqui pray, feast, sing, and take part
in processions and dances. One performer whose presence is essential at all fiestas is the *pascola* dancer.[1]

The pascola dancer—the name is a Spanish spelling of
pahko'ola, the old man of the fiesta—opens and closes the festival.
In addition, he must amuse the crowd with jokes and stories,
distribute cigarettes and water, and dance. He performs two types
of dances. In one, he wears a mask like this one (right) and dances
to the music of a drum and whistle, pre-Hispanic instruments. In the
other, he pushes the mask to the side of his face and dances to the
music of the Mexican harp and violin, European-style instruments.[2]

The pahko'ola *mahka* (mask) is usually carved of cotton-
wood and depicts a human or goat face. The base color is generally
black, and additional decorations may include incised or painted
floral, geometric, and animal designs. There is almost always a
cross in the middle of the forehead, and frequently on the chin, as
protection for the dancer. The pascola dancer gets his power from
the *yo'ania* (world of the woods) and the animals associated with
it. The snake and goat in particular are important animals and
appear to boys in dreams, prompting them to become involved in
the fiesta arts. Triangles representing goats' teeth are usually
painted around the perimeter of the mask, and the mask has a
long beard of white horsehair, like a goat's beard. It is said that
the special ability to dance the pascola comes from the mountain
goat spirit, *yochiba'ato*.[3]

This Mískito mask, *pura-yapti*, may have been worn during
the *sikro*, the commemorative festival for the dead. Sikro masks
are known by the general name of *yapti* (mother), although they
are used in pairs, one male and one female. Mounted on a bark
headpiece is a wooden carving of an animal, person, or object.
This bark mask is mounted with an elegant female figure carved
of balsa wood, wearing a strip of blue cloth around her neck, her
arms extending from her sides. The bark headpiece is surrounded
by dried vegetal fibers to simulate hair. We do not know the meaning of the female figure, because the sikro is no longer performed.
According to earlier descriptions, masks were worn briefly during
the festival by masqueraders who would emerge from the forest,
circle the house of the deceased a few times, then return the way
they came. Perhaps their dance represented the journey from this
world to the next.[4]

N.R.

The people who inhabited most of the islands of the West Indies in 1492 and greeted Columbus when he struck land had no single name for themselves, although they shared the same language and culture. Rather, they identified themselves by the places in which they lived, such as Borinquen (Puerto Rico) or Lucayo (small islands). The name Taíno, which means good or noble, was recorded by the Spanish when several natives used it to refer to themselves.[1]

Much of what we know about Taíno religion and customs comes from a report prepared for Columbus circa 1498 by Fray Ramón Pané. According to Pané, the Taínos worshipped deities called *zemis*. In addition to two main gods, Yúcahu (the lord of cassava and the sea) and Atabey (the goddess of fresh water and human fertility), these deities included ancestor spirits and spirits who lived in trees, rocks, and other natural features.[2]

Images that represented Taíno deities were also called zemis. Made of wood, bone, shell, stone, pottery, and cotton, they were placed in niches and on tables in homes or kept in separate structures. Zemis have been discovered in caves as well, as this one was, perhaps hidden from the Spaniards, who sought to destroy them.[3]

Zemis occupied a central place in rituals of fertility, healing, divination, and ancestor worship. As intermediaries to the supernatural world, they safeguarded the Taíno people.[4]

This zemi, a human figure with a turtle on its back, represents Deminán Caracarakol, one of four brothers central to the Taíno creation story. Deminán asked his grandfather to teach him how to use fire. The old man was so angered by this request that he spit *cohoba*, a narcotic powder, on his grandson's back, causing it to swell painfully. When Deminán's brothers cut the inflammation open, a turtle emerged. The brothers lived with the turtle in a house called a *bohío*, and the turtle became the mother of the Taíno people. Despite his ordeal, Deminán learned the secret of fire from his grandfather and passed it on to his descendants, who used it to clear the forests, bake cassava bread, and smoke tobacco.[5]

A zemi also appears on this carved wooden seat, or *duho*. Duhos were used by chiefs, priests, and other important individuals, while their attendants stood, crouched, or reclined in hammocks. These stools are carved from a single piece of wood or, occasionally, stone and are often decorated with geometric designs and the heads of zemis.[6]

N.R.

DESCENDANTS OF THE TAÍNOS, 1918. ARECIBO, PUERTO RICO. PHOTO-GRAPH BY SAMUEL K. LOTHROP. (19473)

TAÍNO DUHO (WOODEN SEAT), A.D. 1200–1492. TURKS OR CAICOS ISLANDS. LENGTH 88 CM (5.9385)

TAÍNO ZEMI OF DEMINÁN CARACARAKOL, A.D. 1200–1492. DOMINICAN REPUBLIC. HEIGHT 40.5 CM (5.3755)

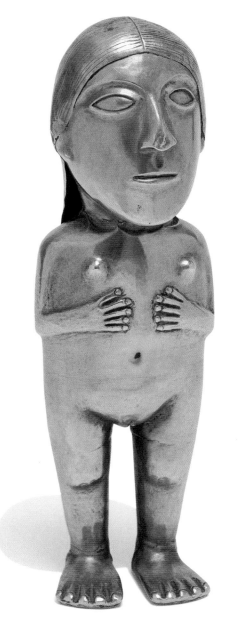

The world is a complex place in which to live. The gods and spirits of the mountains—including Wamanraso, a peak in the central highlands of Peru—have dominion over all life. You must obey them and give them offerings to ensure that you and your family remain in good health, that your fields yield a plentiful harvest, and that your animals multiply. You also have to take care not to offend any of these powerful beings.

The Inka made a variety of offerings to their gods, which included coca leaves, potatoes, maize, and other food crops, grease, and figurines made of wood, clay, metal, and stone. Grease, primarily rendered from llama and alpaca fat, was placed in or on offerings or mixed with foodstuffs such as powdered maize and quinoa, a grainlike seed. Offerings were sometimes burned with coca leaves and used by soothsayers to see into the future.

By the fifteenth century, the Inka, whose language is still spoken by Quechua people throughout the Andes, had an official state religion dedicated to the sun god, Inti, although many other gods and spirits demanded offerings as well. Offerings similar to those discovered in the Inka temple on the Island of the Sun in Lake Titicaca have been found within glaciers on the majestic mountain peaks of the Andean cordillera. During the maize planting in October, one hundred brown llamas and one thousand guinea pigs were sacrificed in the Inka capital of Cuzco to protect the new crop from frost and drought. The harvest in May was accompanied by the sacrifice of a hundred llamas of all colors. Other offerings were made at special ceremonies celebrated when a ruler died and his successor took the throne. Sacrificial objects thrown into rivers during the month of September drove away illness.

In accordance with their rank, rulers presented the gods with precious gifts like this gold figurine. Human figurines in silver as well as gold were dressed in beautifully woven textiles and elegant *Spondylus* shell necklaces. These figurines frequently carried little woven bags filled with coca leaves. Gold and silver figurines and stone effigies are generally found in pairs. The symbolism of duality—day and night, sun and moon, male and female, and so on—was an important part of Andean religious belief.

R.M.

INKA GOLD FIGURINE, A.D. 1470–1552. PERU. HEIGHT 25 CM (5.4120)

INKA BLACK STONE ALPACA EFFIGY, A.D. 1470–1552. PERU. HEIGHT 9.5 CM (14.3676)

INKA SMALL STONE VESSEL, A.D. 1470–1552. PERU. HEIGHT 4.3 CM (21.2262)

NATIVE GOLD, SPANISH GOLD
RICHARD W. HILL SR.

Columbus sought gold above all else, for he believed that, with gold, a man could buy even the salvation of his soul. The desire for gold led Cortés, Pizarro, de Soto, and Coronado deep into the native world. Between 1500 and 1660, more than two hundred tons of gold and nearly twenty thousand tons of silver were taken from the Americas to Spain. This sudden wealth caused severe inflation within Spain and almost bankrupted the Crown. In 1603, one Spanish writer commented: "The New World, conquered by Spain, has conquered Spain in turn."[1]

In 1520, after visiting a European exhibition of treasures amassed by Cortés in Mexico, Albrecht Dürer wrote in his diary:

I saw the things which have been brought to the King from the new land of gold—a sun all of gold a whole fathom broad, and a moon all of silver of the same size, also two rooms full of the armor of the people there, and all manner of wondrous weapons of theirs, harnesses and darts, very strange clothing, beds and all kinds of wonderful objects of human use. . . . All the days of my life I have seen nothing that rejoiced my heart so much as these things, for I saw amongst them wonderful works of art, and I marveled at the subtle ingenuity of people in foreign lands.[2]

Dürer is the only Renaissance artist known to have written about the art of the New World, and it is difficult to say how many Europeans shared his reaction to these treasures. Certainly, many churchmen took a different view. In 1532, Francisco de Vitoria, a Dominican philosopher at the University of Salamanca in Spain, wrote of Indians: "They are without any literature or arts, not only the liberal arts, but the mechanical arts also; they have no careful agriculture and no artisans; and they lack many other conveniences, yea necessaries, of human life."[3]

In 1550, great debates raged in Valladolid, Spain, over whether Indians were human beings or not. Juan Ginés de Sepúlveda, a theologian who argued for the enslavement of natives, gave this justification for appropriating the gold of the New World:

The bringing of iron alone compensates for all the gold and silver taken from America. To the immensely valuable iron may be added other Spanish contributions such as wheat, barley, other cereals and vegetables, horses, mules, asses, oxen, sheep, goats, pigs, and an infinite variety of trees.

Any of these greatly exceeds the usefulness the barbarians derived from gold and silver taken by the Spanish. All these blessings are in addition to writing, books, culture, excellent laws, and that one supreme benefit which is worth more than all the others combined: the Christian religion.[4]

Removing gold idols became a religious, as well as an economic and political, objective of the Conquest of the Americas. Indians were forced to work in the foundries where their treasures were melted down. Not one native-made gold object acquired in the first decades of Spanish colonization survives today.

✳

Yet the popular belief that only Europeans coveted gold is false. After Contact, many Indians buried their gold, hoping to save it from the invaders' greed. These beautiful things, many now in museum collections, make clear that gold was precious in native societies, as well. Firsthand accounts by chroniclers who accompanied the conquistadors provide confirmation. Gold objects taken by the Spanish from South America have been found in burial mounds in south Florida; shipwrecked or abandoned booty was apparently salvaged by the local Indians, who must also have prized gold.

To Renaissance Europeans, gold had value as currency, as well as a glorious tradition in the royal arts. What was the source of its great worth to the natives of the Western Hemisphere, who began no later than 1500 B.C. to fashion gold into images of their world and icons of their beliefs?

In 1553, Pedro de Cieza de Léon, a Spanish historian who traveled widely in the Andes and interviewed Spanish and native veterans of the Conquest, observed: "The Indians were buried with as much wealth as possible . . . believing that the more metal they carried away with them the more esteemed they would be in the places to which they imagined their souls would go."[5] Did Indians believe, as Columbus did, that the possession of gold would assure them a happy afterlife? Why did they put forth such effort to create and safeguard objects of gold?

Gold served as tribute in pre-Contact Aztec culture, where annual levies were paid to rulers in gold, all recorded on tribute rolls. The Aztecs called gold *teocuitlatl*—translated literally, excrement of the gods. Scholars have suggested that the Inka revered gold as a gift from the gods, representing the benevolent rays of the sun. Some of the stone walls of Inka temples were sheathed in gold. Silver was associated with the moon.

The specific meaning of many gold objects has

"ON THE SUBJECT OF IDOLS": THE INKA KING (TÚPAC INKA) MAKES OFFERINGS TO THE ANDEAN DEITIES (WACAS) (LEFT). "OFFICE OF THE ROYAL REPRESENTATIVE": SPANISH OFFICIALS COUNT INDIAN TRIBUTE IN GOLD AND SILVER.

DRAWINGS BY FELIPE GUAMAN POMA DE AYALA (WAMAN PUMA), FROM EL PRIMER NUEVA CORÓNICA Y BIEN GOBIERNO, CA. 1615.

been lost to time. Yet Inka gold figurines remain hauntingly beautiful. Most of these figurines have their hands on their chests, recalling a burial position. Many have been found in the Andes with mummified bodies of children. In other native societies, similar figurines are buried with children as spiritual stand-ins for their parents; they protect the dead on the way to the next world.

Scholars maintain that the Inka believed in the spiritual power of the dead and honored them with gifts—including beautiful textiles, stone carvings, and other treasures, as well as gold and silver. To remove these gifts is to steal from the dead, a theft that surely must have

consequences. Inka figurines taken from tombs appear naked and lost. Yet they also convey the feeling that they are waiting to rejoin their rightful owners.

Today, we are coming to understand that the true significance of many ancient treasures lies beyond our need for visual pleasure. Their meaning rests instead in the belief that the dead are not dead, but have merely continued their journey. And this time around—five hundred years after the looting of the New World began—native peoples will take part in the debate over who may claim a right to these travelers' possessions.

Chicha, a fermented beverage, has played an important role in Andean society for many centuries. It can be made from several products, including the red seeds from the Peruvian *molle* tree, quinoa, potato, manioc, peanuts, and especially maize.

At the time of the Inka Empire (A.D. 1470 to 1532), chicha was an essential component of all religious rituals and public activities. The Inka celebrated great feasts in their administrative centers; these feasts were part of the traditional Andean system of mutual obligation between the government and the people. During the early colonial period, the Spanish tried to restrict the use of chicha, believing that it hindered their control over the native population. A native official from Jequetepeque on the north coast of Peru complained, however, that the restriction was "a great inconvenience, since the main reason that the people obey their leaders here is through the custom that [the leaders] have to give the people drink . . . and if they do not oblige to give the people drink, neither will the people plant their crops for them."[1]

During religious ceremonies, chicha was drunk from *q'iru*, or wooden goblets, named for the tree from which they were carved. Q'iru were always made in pairs, reflecting the significance of dualities in Andean thought. The goblets shown here represent the heads of great cats, sacred animals in the Andean pantheon. They are painted in the spotted pattern of a feline called *otorongo* by the people of the Andes, *jaguá* by the Guaraní to the southeast—the jaguar.

Under the centralized Inka system, the production of q'iru was an important art. The goblets continued to be made after the Spanish Conquest, especially in the highlands of Bolivia and southern Peru during the seventeenth and eighteenth centuries. The shape of q'iru remained largely the same after the fall of the Inka Empire, but over time their pre-Hispanic geometric decorations were replaced by Western pictorial art. Many later q'iru show Spanish people and European customs.

This colonial imagery is an art of both self-negation and survival. In the confluence of pre-Columbian form and meaning with Western subject matter and modes of expression, we can see at the same time the Indians' resistance against European domination and their resignation to the destruction of their culture. What emerges is a new native identity, both Andean and European, created in response to a complex and shifting world.

R.M.

FORTRESS ENTRANCE AT OLLANTAYTAMBO. CUZCO, PERU. PHOTOGRAPH BY E. G. SQUIER. (19120)

INKA JAGUAR Q'IRU (GOBLETS), MID-SIXTEENTH C. PERU. HEIGHT 22 CM (10.5860 AND 15.2413)

PANPIPE PLAYER, A.D. 100–600.
MOCHE CULTURE, PERU.
HEIGHT 17 CM (18.589)

AYMARA DANCERS. BOLIVIA.
(P18847)

TAIRONA CERAMIC OCARINA, A.D.
1200–1600. COLOMBIA.
HEIGHT 10 CM (18.1891)

Traditional South American music was made with percussion and wind instruments of wood, reeds, pottery, bone, shell, or metal: drums and tambourines (*tinya* in Quechua), rattles (*ullucha*), trumpets (*kiwa puku*), panflutes (*mataquena*—two or three flutes of the same length but different widths), panpipes (*zampoña* or *siku*—five to seven flutes of different lengths and widths), flutes (*quena*), conch shells (*pututu*), and ocarinas. Music accompanied religious ceremonies and funeral and military processions; it was integral to the celebration of certain rituals. Among some ancient societies, musical instruments were sacred; they could be played only by certain people and were hidden away when not in use.

Ocarinas are wind instruments with multiple holes to vary pitch and tone; they can sound like birds, human whistling, and echoes. Andean native musicians usually play two instruments simultaneously, an ocarina and a drum, to accompany social gatherings or ritual ceremonies. Every social activity has its own music. In general, men play instruments and women sing.

Most Colombian ocarinas are whistles with human or serpent heads or small anthropomorphic effigies shaped to fit in the

player's hand, like this Tairona bird effigy with a human face. Tairona culture (A.D. 1200 to 1600) was one of the most advanced societies in pre-Hispanic Colombia. Spanish chroniclers described Tairona ocarina music as unusually beautiful. The Kogi—descendants of the Tairona—have preserved many of their ancestors' traditions, including their love of ocarina music. Kogi priests still use Tairona ceremonial objects, including ocarinas. Kogi ocarinas are modeled in the forms of animals and human beings.

In the altiplano region of Lake Titicaca, the music of panpipes and panflutes has always been particularly beautiful and well-loved; today, the Quechua and Aymara preserve this musical heritage.

The antiquity of these instruments is reflected in the art of the Moche culture (A.D. 100 to 600) along the coast of northern Peru, where people produced some of the earliest representations of panpipes in the Andes. Objects of gold and silver, like this lovely silver figurine of a panpipe player, may have been made as offerings to the gods or to the dead.

R.M.

In the Andean world, mountains are the most important part of the earth. They are gods and spirits or the homes of gods and spirits and should be treated with respect and honor. Spirits called *wamani*, divinities of the mountains and protectors of the natural world, live in the Andes and interact in complex relationships that only the priests understand. Large offerings and special rituals are made to the mountains to promote the fertility of the earth.

Both mountains and gods have their own hierarchies in the native pantheon. The inaccessible peaks of the Andean cordillera constitute the most powerful gods. These peaks can also be pathways to the gods, perhaps to Father Sun and Mother Moon. According to native belief, Andean priests called Apus Willacuma climbed the mountains to meet the gods and receive divine power and strength.

The highest mountains are the *pacarina*, or place of origin, of mankind and all other forms of life. Every village, too, has a pacarina where its guardian spirit lives. Pacaritampu, the cave where the Inkas were born, lies in the Inka capital Cuzco.[1]

This modeled and painted stirrup-spout vessel was made by a ceramist of the Moche culture of the coast of northern Peru and dates to around A.D. 100 to 600. Like many Moche ceramic vessels, it is made in the shape of a mountain with many peaks, the center being the summit. These vessels sometimes show a scene of human sacrifice in which a figure with flowing hair sprawls on the highest peak, a metaphor for the origin of the rivers.

Here, Aiapeak, the Moche warrior–priest, represents the summit. He prays over four lower peaks. To his right, on the second highest peak, a shaman sits with his religious articles. Opposite him there is a naked prisoner with his hands tied and a rope around his neck. The shaman, who has the power to cure illness, represents life; the prisoner represents death. Life and death, good and evil spirits—these are important dualities in Andean belief.[2]

Because they also resemble the contours of human hands, mountain vessels have another meaning. Each peak or finger stands for a different ecological zone: the fifth finger signifies the lower valleys, and the thumb, the glacial peaks of the cordillera. The tallest finger, in the center, symbolizes the sacred connection between the lowlands and highlands. This finger promotes the harmony and equilibrium of the two regions and the physical and spiritual health of the Andean people.

R.M.

"Suddenly the clouds spread out and the highest peaks of the mountains could be seen. A condor glided along the deep slope. The power of Apu Salccantay embraced the whole world."

—QUECHUA FOLKLORE

STIRRUP-SPOUT MOUNTAIN VESSEL, A.D. 100–600. MOCHE CULTURE, PERU. HEIGHT 30 CM (23.4865).

PISAQ, INKA SACRED VALLEY. CUZCO, PERU.

Many native groups who live in the tropical forests of South America are known for their spectacular featherwork. Brightly colored tropical feathers are obvious material for personal adornment. Valuable and difficult to obtain, they are often used to make ornaments and decorate clothing reserved for ceremonial and special occasions.[1]

In many cultures, however, feathers have a significance beyond their beauty and rarity. The Karajá, for example, who live on and around the island of Bananal in the states of Goiás and Mato Grosso, Brazil, relate the spiritual world closely to the sky world of birds. The soul of a Karajá shaman can take the form of a bird and fly to the sacred place from which he derives his power.[2]

The Karajá use feathers in a variety of ways, from gluing featherdown to their skin with tree resin to making large, elaborate pieces like this strikingly beautiful *lurina*, a man's headdress. The lurina consists of a radiating pattern of scarlet-macaw and red-and-green-macaw feathers held in place by a double layer of U-shaped reed splints and palm-leaf spines bound with brown and white cotton cords. It is worn on the back of the head, tied to the hair and secured by a band across the forehead. Macaw feathers are ideal for headdresses because they are beautiful on both sides.[3]

Karajá men wear headdresses like this for ceremonies that mark important events in life, such as rites of passage; success in war, fishing, and hunting; and visits from members of neighboring villages. Only men make feather ornaments, and boys begin to learn the art of featherworking when they reach puberty and move into the men's hut. Each Karajá man is responsible for creating his ornaments and those of his children.[4]

Among the Waiwái, who live along the frontier of Guyana and Brazil, basketmaking is also done only by men. The *pakára*, a rectangular, feather-decorated basket, is one of the most outstanding examples of Waiwái basketry. It consists of two rectangular boxes of plaited plant fibers, one inside the other. In the case of this basket, the interior box serves as the cover for the exterior one and slides open on two fiber strings that double as shoulder straps. A man would use this basket for personal items such as gourds of red and black body-paint, feathers, comb, scissors, mirror, knife, and a variety of natural materials that make up an ornament repair kit.[5]

The beautiful, geometric designs on Waiwái baskets, made by plaiting scraped and unscraped strips of plant fiber, symbolize animals, including squirrels, frogs, caterpillars, honeybees, scorpions, and fish. The small black crosses represent opossum teeth. These basketry designs are material manifestations of Waiwái spiritual beliefs in which animals play an important role.[6]

The survival of these art forms is threatened by the destruction of tropical forests that have in the past provided the Waiwái, Karajá, and other native groups with the materials needed to create their beautiful baskets and ornaments.

N.R.

The use of stimulants and narcotics has been associated with magic and religious rites among native peoples for thousands of years. Archaeological evidence for the ancient use of hallucinogenic and stimulant plants is extensive and dates from 1000 B.C. The feline motif on this tray dates to 500 B.C., when the motif was associated with Chavín religious art in Peru. Although most ancient wooden objects have long since disintegrated, these trays and spoons were found in northern Argentina or, in the case of some of the spoons, Chile, regions whose inhabitants were in contact with groups from the altiplano of Bolivia, the highlands of Peru, and the eastern lowlands of South America. Similar objects have been found in the dry coastal desert of Peru and, accompanied by dried plants, in a tomb at Tiwanaku in Bolivia.

Today South American shamans and traditional healers use hallucinogens or stimulants to contact the supernatural world and cure illnesses. Native rituals and treatments involve smoking, inhaling, eating, chewing, drinking, or licking preparations made from plants like the hallucinogens San Pedro cactus and *ayahuasca* or the stimulant coca. From central Bolivia to the Argentine pampas, the leaves of the *cebil* and *coro* bushes are dried and powdered to make a hallucinogen. Tobacco may be combined with other substances or used by itself.

In a ritual context, a shaman may inhale snuff while other participants drink a mixture of snuff and tobacco or other plants. Or one man may blow snuff into the nose of another through a single or double tube. The Witoto in Peru and the Yanomami in Brazil and Venezuela continue this practice. Any man may partake if he wishes. Among some groups, powdered snuff is smoked in large pipes made of clay, bone, or wood.

Carved snuff trays reflect the cultural and religious beliefs of the people who used them. They often depict important deities in human and animal forms. Snuff trays and spoons are still used among the Quechua of Callahualla in eastern Bolivia and by native groups in Catamarca and Humahuaca in Argentina.[1]

R.M.

SNUFF TRAY, A.D. 600–1000.
TIWANAKU INFLUENCE,
COLLECTED IN ARGENTINA.
LENGTH 19.7 CM (15.1489)

CARVED BONE SNUFF SPOONS, A.D.
600–1000. TIWANAKU INFLUENCE,
COLLECTED IN ARGENTINA AND
CHILE. LENGTH 22.1 TO 25.4 CM
(17.6779, 17.6780, 17.6781, AND
17.6783)

"Sneezing and strange sounds came from the interior of the hut. A group of people sat on the floor looking at the shaman, from whom the strange sounds came, as he inhaled tobacco snuff."

—SHIPIBO FOLKLORE

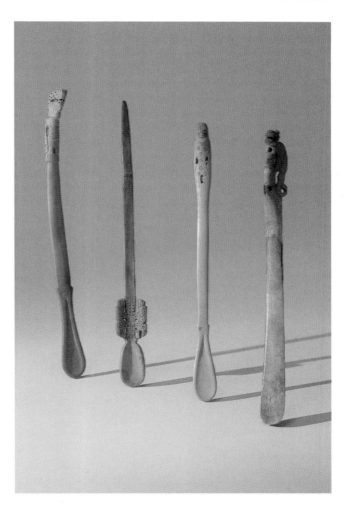

The Yamana culture is, unfortunately, extinct. The Yamana, more commonly called the Yahgan, inhabited the south shore of the island of Tierra del Fuego and many smaller islands at the southern tip of South America. They have often been referred to as canoe people, because each family's existence revolved around its bark canoe. They were hunters and gatherers and derived their livelihood almost entirely from the sea and its beaches, hunting seals, porpoises, whales, fish, and birds, as well as gathering a variety of shellfish.[1]

These two bark masks (*hílix*) were used for the *kína* ritual, which was based on one of the Yamana origin myths. According to this myth, a long time ago women were leaders and dominated men, who performed all the domestic chores. In order to maintain their supremacy, women invented the secret kína ceremony. During the ceremony, they emerged from a special hut, wearing large masks and covered with paint, and pretended to be various kína spirits.

YAMANA FAMILIES, EARLY 20TH C. TIERRA DEL FUEGO. (P7758)

YAMANA HÍLIX (BARK MASKS), EARLY 20TH C. HEIGHT 72 AND 67.5 CM (14.2258 AND 14.2259)

The masks and the performance terrified the men into subjugation. One day, a man discovered the deception and told the other men. Furious, they attacked the kína hut; all the women there were either killed or transformed into animals, birds, and fish. After that day, Yamana society was patriarchal, and men ruled the kína hut.[2]

Only Yamana men who passed through a strict initiation ceremony called *ciéxaus* could participate in the kína ritual. Women were not allowed to approach the large, conical hut without permission, much less to join in the meeting. The masked, painted men emerged from the tent singing, dancing, and threatening the women in the same tradition and manner as women were said to have done in the past.[3]

Although the kína ceremony had fallen into disuse as early as the 1880s, the last surviving Yamana revived it in 1922 so it could be recorded by two missionaries. Their accounts are all we know about Yamana religion.[4]

These bark masks were sewn together with whale gut. The pigments used by the Yamana were not waterproof, and a mask could be washed and repainted to represent a variety of spirits. The mask on the near right represents the rainbow, distinguished by its broad red, white, and black bands. The other mask, with alternating red and white stripes, represents a smeltlike fish.[5]

N.R.

GORGET WITH RATTLESNAKE, CA.
A.D. 1500–1600. DALLAS CULTURE,
TENNESSEE. 11.5 X 13.3 CM (21.1374)

O-O-BE, KIOWA, 1895. FORT SILL,
OKLAHOMA. (P13149)

ASHÁNINKA HUNTER, 1910. RÍO
PERENÉ, UPPER UCAYALI RIVER,
PERU. PHOTOGRAPH BY C.L.
CHESTER.

EPILOGUE
ART THROUGH INDIAN EYES
RICHARD W. HILL SR.

The image of the artist in Western society is that of an isolated genius, distanced from other people by rare insight and talent. True creative vision is of the individual's own making and often apart from the aesthetic of society. Some artists labor without recognition in their own times, as van Gogh did; others live as Picasso did, in self-imposed exile, erecting wholly personal realities through their art. In the modern Western conception, artists are visionary loners, endlessly searching for hidden truths—an enlightened few.

Native societies tend to think of artists differently. The ability to make things by hand is considered a gift given by the Creator, to be used for the welfare of the community. Every person has received such a gift, according to native beliefs. It may be the talent to tell stories, sing songs, weave baskets, carve stone, sew quills or beads, paint skins or canvases, or use photography as an art form. Discovering our gifts, developing them, and using them for the benefit of our communities are major goals in our journey through life as Indians.

Such gifts are tied to tradition. By making things of beauty and belief, native artists keep their people's values, ethics, and ways of thinking alive. Art teaches about ancient world views, as well as modern realities. It bridges differences. And the artist is the bridge-builder.

My father spent thirty-five years as a different kind of bridge-builder. Like many Iroquois men of his generation, he left his family's farm to become an ironworker, building tall buildings and long bridges with steel. He was a hard-working man. All my young life, I never thought of him as an artist.

When my older brother, who was also a builder, fell, my father was forced to face the fact that Indians are not genetically superior ironworkers. In fact, he had seen many men die on the job. But after the death of my second brother, my father began to search for deeper meanings to his life.

At the age of fifty-five, when most people start thinking of retiring, he became an artist. He started to carve deer and moose antler, just as his ancestors had done centuries before. No one else was carving, really; it was considered a lost art. My father carved turtles, because that is his clan and he identifies with them. He carved deer, bears, and eagles, animals that have a cultural legacy among the Iroquois, but also animals he had come to know himself. He carved images of the spirit of corn. He was not raised as a traditional Indian, attending ceremonies for corn and animals. But he grew corn, and he intuitively understood why the old-timers gave thanks for it.

When I ask him about his carving, he speaks of a force within him, within the antler, and within the world that comes together when he carves. In fact, he believes he doesn't carve at all, he simply frees the form that rests within the material. He also feels, after serious reflection on life, that it is the Creator who helps guide his hand. If you could have witnessed the change in my father over these last twenty years, since he has been carving, you would see what he means. Somewhere, all his life, the artist waited to emerge. I still marvel at that fact every time I see his latest carving. His gift has become my reason to believe in the power of the living spirit that connects us to the land, the animals, the plants, the celestial beings, and all our relatives.

✳

For many native people, there is a living spirit in nature that permeates our lives. We know that spirit and communicate with it. One of the most important motives of our art is to show our understanding of that spirit and of our relationship to the world. It is nearly impossible to separate this spirituality from aesthetic principles, or from community ethics. Words such as art, culture, and religion are missing from most native languages because they are unnecessary: the values they represent are ever-present in the daily lives of traditional native peoples.

The separation of life into different components just doesn't work with native societies. That is a problem for publications like this one, which must present objects in some sort of interpretive categories: by use (clothing, utensils, religion, personal adornment, toys), region (Woodlands, Plains, Southwest), time (pre-Columbian, post-Contact, reservation period, contemporary), medium (painting, weaving, pottery, basketry), or tribe (Navajo, Pueblo, Sioux). Here, we have chosen instead to provide a context in which objects may be seen as they were seen by the people who made them, based upon our own experiences as native artists and curators. We have been looking at works like these for many years and have listened to native artists, elders, educators, and community scholars tell about the beliefs behind them. We live our culture firsthand, at

home and in native rituals and social gatherings across North America, and we create art that reflects our experience. Our ideas about these objects are clearly very subjective; we can only hope you appreciate our sharing with you the intensity of our feelings.

There is a belief among many native communities that objects need people in order to be useful. They were meant for use, not necessarily to last forever. We feel a sense of loss, of disconnection, knowing that there are more such objects in museums than in native homes and institutions. But there is an artistic resurgence taking place in native communities, where people are committing themselves to making objects to replace those that have disappeared. These new objects rekindle pride and ancient beliefs. Still, we will always have a deep reverence for old things, objects that gain power from the many generations that used them. In this way, these works have a special spiritual tie to many Indians today. They make us think about what was important in the past. Our ancestors took the time and effort to produce these beautiful objects for us, and we are moved by their faith that we would understand and appreciate them. These works are evidence of the desire of Indians to remain Indians throughout all time. We are still here.

✳

There is an intense dialogue among native groups about culture, art, and spiritual beliefs. There is an equally intense, but very different debate between practitioners and scholars about what objects mean. At times, even native scholars have difficulty accepting the views of Indians who maintain the traditions behind these works, most of which reflect religious beliefs. Without those beliefs, these things can be seen only as specimens, artifacts, or art; history and aesthetics become more important than religious expression. This schism between people who study Indian arts and those who believe in them is why there is still so much suspicion about museums and scholars in the native world.

Nowhere is this schism deeper than in the consideration of burial objects. In working on this book, we spoke to many people about the propriety of showing articles found in graves. One colleague argued that their presentation in a book would not be disrespectful—that readers, perhaps unlike exhibition visitors, would have the time and quiet to reflect on the objects' deep significance for the people who made and treasured them. Besides, she said, some ancient cultures believed that another life would follow this one, and they buried their dead with all their possessions in anticipation of that next life. So, many grave objects may not be sacred, at least not in the same way that objects of worship are sacred.

Perhaps not. But without these things they believed they would need, how are the dead managing in the next life?

To see these objects through Indian eyes requires an imaginative and empathic mind, an openness to the philosophies behind the objects' creation, and a willingness to live with open-ended interpretations of them. You do not have to be Indian to appreciate

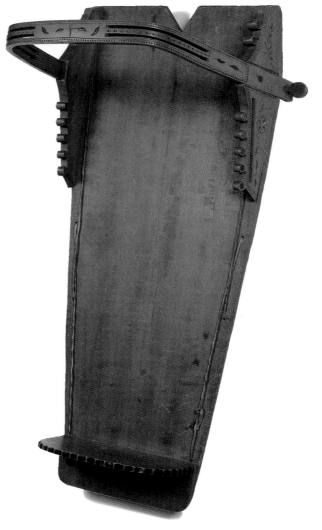

SENECA CRADLEBOARD, INSCRIBED "J.J. MARCH 25, 1861." LENGTH 72.4 CM (2.9542)

ESKIMO MAN WITH MODEL UMIAK. POINT BARROW, ALASKA. (P7863)

JOHN WHITE FEATHER AND HIS
WIFE, CHIPPEWA. LAC DU
FLAMBEAU, WISCONSIN. (36529)

CHIPPEWA WEAVER MAKING RUSH
MAT, BEFORE 1929. PHOTOGRAPH BY
FRANCES DENSMORE.

CHOCTAW ESKOFATSHI (BEADED
BANDOLIER), CA. 1907 LENGTH 111
CM (1.8864)

native objects as their makers and users did. You do, however, have to be open to belief in unseen forces. You have to understand the spirit world of the artist in order to see how an object reflects that world. Elders and practitioners who have spiritual knowledge understand these objects in ways anthropologists and art connoisseurs do not. The Shroud of Turin looks different to a believer; whatever scientists and scholars may think, believers will always see in it the image of Christ.

✳

To the eyes of a native artist, art is less an object, an artwork, than a process by which ideas and materials are transformed into statements of belief. The creative process, by its innovative nature, devises new means of expression to accommodate changing intellectual worlds. In the words of Haida artist Robert Davidson: "The only way tradition can be carried on is to keep inventing new things."[1] How artists use symbols and metaphors from the past, how they reformulate intellectual and spiritual traditions and restate community aesthetics—all these are important aspects of the creative process. Artworks become extensions of shared beliefs and milestones of personal spiritual insight.

The transformation of natural materials through this creative process is itself a sacred transition. Wood, stone, antler, bark, leather, feathers, cornhusks, shells, porcupine quills, metals, and natural pigments are parts of the living universe; each has a spiritual essence. The artist and the object harness the spirits of these materials, increasing their power. The artistic process is therefore a creative ritual whereby the artist makes the metaphysical, physical. The ability to enact such a transformation is a gift. The artist expresses gratitude for that gift through a commitment to outstanding craftsmanship, emotional involvement, and originality.

Many native societies recognize a universal power in all things. The Iroquois call it *orenda*; the Inuit call it *inua*; the Lakota call it *wakonda*; the Ojibwe call it *manitou*. Objects are created to represent that power and humankind's understanding of it; they are created to make use of it. Yet every object also serves to record its maker's presence on earth, to reaffirm an individual's place in the natural world.

I would like to close with an Iroquois thanksgiving address that is given whenever we have a meeting, dance, or ceremony. The Gonohonyohk reminds us of the spiritual forces that exist every day in our universe. These forces give us reasons to make beautiful things. They guide our hands while we work and inform our thoughts when we look at the creations of others.

We thank our Creator that we are gathered here, healthy in body and mind. We thank our Creator for creating Mother Earth for us to walk on and enjoy. We thank our Creator for creating plant life on Mother Earth for survival, especially the strawberry; the weeds for healing, some weeds for eating, and also as Earth's decoration. We give thanks for the underbrush; saplings for healing; the trees, especially the maple, that are a haven for the animals and birds, and that also give us heat for comfort and cooking. We give thanks for the animals, especially the deer, that give us food; the birds, that give us pleasure through their singing in the early morning hours. We give thanks for the large bodies of water, the running streams, the springs that we and Mother Earth survive on. We give thanks for our sustenance, the Three Sisters— Corn, Beans, and Squash—that give our breathing strength to strengthen our bodies. And for the gentle winds we breathe, which do not harm us. We thank the higher powers that maintain Earth's functions: the Thunders that carry water to wash the Earth, to keep waters new and fresh; the Sun that gives us light and heat for our comfort and also makes the plants grow; the Moon that gives us changing cycles for marking time, that controls conception of the female, human and animals, and also that replenishes moisture on Earth so plants will grow; the Stars that are markers for travelers and also replenish the Earth with moisture. We give thanks for our guardian spirits, who protect us in body and mind. And last comes the Creator: we give thanks to him for creating nothing but for the good of his people, and we give thanks to him for giving us the love of each other and his love. He forgives us for any wrongdoings and awaits us in his domain of everlasting happiness.

CONTRIBUTORS

Eulalie H. Bonar is an assistant curator at the National Museum of the American Indian. She is currently working with weaver D.Y. Begay and other weavers and scholars on an exhibition and book about nineteenth-century Navajo wearing blankets.

John C. Ewers, associate curator emeritus, National Museum of Natural History, Smithsonian Institution, is a recipient of two of the highest honors given by the Western History Association: the Oscar O. Winther Memorial Award and the Western History Association Prize. His many books include *The Horse in Blackfoot Indian Culture, Artists of the Old West, Plains Indian Sculpture,* and *Indian Life on the Upper Missouri.*

Diane Fraher (Osage/Cherokee) is collections move manager at the National Museum of the American Indian. A producer and screenwriter, she contributed to the award-winning public service campaign *You're Looking at the First Draft of the Constitution,* on the Iroquois Confederacy. She also makes traditional Osage appliqué ribbonwork.

Cécile R. Ganteaume is an assistant curator at the National Museum of the American Indian. Her essay "White Mountain Apache Dance: Expressions of Spirituality" appears in the National Museum of the American Indian's first major publication, *Native American Dance: Ceremonies and Social Traditions.* She has recently been directing a project to improve documentation of the museum's Apachean, Mohave, and Seminole collections.

Roger Gorman is the principal and creative director of Reiner Design Consultants in New York. His work has been honored with design awards from the Art Directors Clubs of New York and Los Angeles, the Society of Publication Designers, the American Institute of Graphic Arts, and *Print.* His design for David Bowie's *Sound+Vision* won the 1989 Grammy for best album package.

David Heald is head of the photography department at the Guggenheim Museum in New York City. He photographs fine art and architecture, and his work has been reproduced in numerous books and periodicals.

Richard W. Hill Sr. (Tuscarora) is special assistant to the director of the National Museum of the American Indian and a member of the faculty of the State University of New York at Buffalo. His essays and photographs on Native American life have been widely published.

Tom Hill (Seneca), museum director of the Woodland Cultural Centre in Brantford, Ontario, and co-chairperson of the Canadian Task Force on First Peoples and Museums, is the author of many books and exhibition catalogues, including, with Karen Duffek, *Beyond History* and, with Elizabeth McLuhan, *Norval Morrisseau and the Emergence of the Image Makers.* He is also a painter.

Duane King, assistant director of the National Museum of the American Indian, at the museum's George Gustav Heye Center in New York, has served as executive director of the Cherokee National Historical Society in Tahlequah, Oklahoma, and the Museum of the Cherokee Indian in Cherokee, North Carolina. He is founding editor of the *Journal of Cherokee Studies,* as well as author, editor, and contributing writer of a long and distinguished list of books and journals.

Mary Jane Lenz, associate curator at the National Museum of the American Indian, has produced several exhibitions, including shows on Northwest Coast art and Native Alaskan masks. She is a contributor to *Native American Dance* and the author of *The Stuff of Dreams: Native American Dolls.* She is currently doing research on Northwest Coast tourist art.

Ramiro Matos (Quechua), professor of archaeology at the University of San Marcos in Lima, Peru, is program specialist for Central and South America at the National Museum of the American Indian. He is the author of *Pumpu: Un Centro Inka de Administración* and a contributor, most recently, to *Timelines of the Ancient World.*

Elizabeth McKean is a painter and exhibition mountmaker who works independently and with Benchmark, Inc., in New York. *The Ottoman Empire,* at the Jewish Museum, is among her many mountmaking credits.

Dorie Reents-Budet is curator of pre-Columbian art at the Duke University Museum of Art and a research associate at the Smithsonian's Conservation Analytical Laboratory. Her book *Painting the Maya Universe: Royal Ceramics of the Classic Period* was recognized with a 1994 museum publications award from the American Association of Museums.

Nancy Rosoff, assistant curator at the National Museum of the American Indian, has conducted research and collaborative projects among native communities in Mexico, Ecuador, and Bolivia, and is currently working on an object-documentation project with the Shuar and Achuar of Ecuador. Her essay "The Fiesta: Rhythm of Life in the Sierras of Mexico and the Altiplano of Bolivia," written with Olivia Cadaval, appears in *Native American Dance.*

Mari Lynn Salvador is chief curator of the Maxwell Museum and associate professor of anthropology at the University of New Mexico, with a special interest in ethnoaesthetics. She is currently working on an exhibition about Hispanic *santos*—religious carvings and paintings on wood—at the Maxwell Museum and, as guest curator, on *The Art of Being Kuna* at the University of California, Los Angeles. She is also producing a television series for broadcast in Portugal and the United States on the aesthetics of ritual performance in the Azores.

The curators of the National Museum of the American Indian are indebted to colleagues and friends in universities, museums, and native communities who made many thoughtful contributions to this book. They wish to thank Margarita Alvarado and Gabriela Frings, Pontificia Universidad Católica de Chile; William Balée, Tulane University; José Barreiro (Taíno), Cornell University; Lowell John Bean; David Blackard, Ah-Tha-Thi-Ki Museum; J.J. Brody; Robert Carneiro, American Museum of Natural History; René Cibanacán Marcano and José Boriguex LaBoy, Nación Taína; Francisco Corrales, Museo Nacional de Costa Rica; Thomas Cummins, University of Chicago; Ross Day, Goldwater Library, Metropolitan Museum of Art; Christopher Donnan, UCLA; Gloria J. Fenner; Ann Fineup-Riordan; Catherine S. Fowler; Marjorie Halpin; Steve Henrickson; Bill Holm; Jonathon C.H. King; Keith W. Kintigh; Edmund J. Ladd and Randy Nahohai, Zuni Pueblo; Roger Mase, Dwight Mase, Myron Sekakuku, and Leigh Lomayestewa, the Hopi Tribe; Joan Lester; Stephen Loring; Sally McLendon; Betty J. Meggers, Smithsonian; Barbara J. Mills; Martha de Montaño; Francisco Pabón, SUNY Buffalo; Jay Van Orden, Arizona Historical Society; Marian Rodee; Douglas Rodgers, University of Montevallo; Stacy B. Schaefer, University of Texas, Pan-American; Anne-Louise Schaffer, Museum of Fine Arts, Houston; Margot Blum Schevill, Phoebe A. Hearst Museum, University of California, Berkeley; Inge Schjellerup, National Museum of Denmark; Brenda Shears; Martha H. Streuver; Edwin E. Sylvest, Southern Methodist University; Judy Thompson; Gaylord Torrence, Drake University; Javier Urcid, Smithsonian; Stefano Varese, University of California, Davis; Joe Ben Wheat; Laila Williamson, American Museum of Natural History; and many others.

5839

NOTES

Introduction, pp. 14–19
1. From Nancy Mitchell's presentation to the American Anthropological Association, 1992 (manuscript).
2. See Bea Medicine's "The Anthropologist as the Indian's Image Maker," *Indian Historian* 4, 1971.
3. See Vine Deloria's *Custer Died for Your Sins: An Indian Manifesto*, 1988, p. 2.
4. From Deborah Doxtator's thesis, "Iroquoian Museums and the Idea of the Indian: Aspects of the Political Role of Museums." Also see her book *Fluffs and Feathers: An Exhibit on the Symbols of Indianness* (Brantford), 1992.
5. Quoted by A.M. Josephy in *Red Power: The American Indian Fight for Freedom*, 1971.
6. See the account in *Native American Testimony: A Chronicle of Indian–White Relations from Prophecy to the Present*, P. Nabokov, ed., 1992, pp. 361–62.
7. Hanson, J., "The Reappearing Vanishing American," *Museum News* 59, October 1980, pp. 44–51.
8. Levi-Strauss, C., *The Savage Mind*, 1962.
9. From NMAI Collections Policy, 1992.

Growing Up Indian, pp. 20–25
1. See Standing Bear, L., *My Indian Boyhood*, 1928, and *My People the Sioux*, 1931.

pp. 26–27
Seminole birthing song is from Frances Densmore's *Seminole Music*, Bureau of American Ethnology Bulletin 161, 1956, p. 172.
1. For the development of patchwork designs, see Blackard, D., *Patchwork and Palmettos: Seminole–Miccosukee Folk Art Since 1820*, 1990.

pp. 28–29
1. Schaefer, S., "Huichol Weavers: Design Keepers of Sacred Knowledge," presented at the American Anthropological Association, 1990 (manuscript), p. 1.
2. Eger, S., "Huichol Women's Art," in *Art of the Huichol Indians*, K. Berrin, ed., 1978, p. 49.
3. Eger, p. 49. Schaefer, p. 28. See also Schaefer's "Becoming a Weaver: The Woman's Path in Huichol Culture," Ph.D. dissertation in anthropology, UCLA, 1990.

pp. 30–31
1. Whiteford, A.H., "The Origin of Great Lakes Beaded Bandolier Bags," *American Indian Art* 11:3, 1986, pp. 32–44. Whiteford suggests that beaded bandolier bags were not popular—perhaps did not even exist—before the mid-19th c.
2. Lanford, B.L., "Winnebago Bandolier Bags," *American Indian Art* 9:3, 1984, pp. 31–37. Lanford writes: "Three nearly identical Winnebago bandolier bags with American flag motifs repeated throughout the woven beadwork are known to exist, and were perhaps made by the same

person, suggesting the existence of specialized craftworkers." He credits M.G. Chandler with identifying the three features of Winnebago bandolier bags and discusses them in detail.

pp. 32–33 (Osage Childhood)
Chant of the Red Eagle Clan excerpted from a translation by J.O. Dorsey, Bureau of American Ethnology.

pp. 34–35
Yuma lullaby is from Frances Densmore's *Yuman and Yaqui Music*, Bureau of American Ethnology Bulletin 110, 1932, p. 198. "Narrative of an Arapaho Woman" by Truman Michelson appears in *American Anthropologist* 35:4, 1933, pp. 595–610.

pp. 36–37
Quotation is from the autobiography *Jim Whitewolf: The Life of a Kiowa Apache Indian*, 1969.

pp. 38–39
Oku'te is quoted in Frances Densmore's *Teton Sioux Music*, Bureau of American Ethnology Bulletin 61, 1918, p. 176.

pp. 40–41
The Alaskan girl is interviewed by Robert Coles in *The First and Last Eskimos*, 1978.
1. The Alaska State Museum owns a virtually identical model. According to Steve Henrikson, curator of collections, it was acquired in the 1880s by a sea captain who traveled throughout the Pacific Basin area. The two models may well be from the hand of the same maker.

pp. 42–43
This Iglulik poem appears in Knud Rasmussen's *Intellectual Culture of the Iglulik Eskimos*, Report of the Fifth Thule Expedition 1921–1924, p. 27. English translation by W.E. Calvert.

pp. 44–45
This Tlingit cradle song is translated by J.R. Swanton, Bureau of American Ethnology.
1. Cheryl Samuel gives extended descriptions and diagrams of twining techniques in *The Raven's Tail*, 1987. A weaver herself, she has been able to replicate yeil koowu robes.

pp. 46–47
This Haida cradle song appears in J.R. Swanton's *Haida Songs*, 1912.
1. The Haida people are divided into two "halves," the Ravens and the Eagles.
2. A house was rebuilt and rededicated as each new owner took his position, with ceremonies that brought pride to the lineage and added to the house's noble history.
3. This house model has virtually no documentation, but is strikingly similar to one in the British Museum commissioned around 1898 by J.H. Keen, a

missionary at the Haida village of Masset in the Queen Charlotte Islands. J.C.H. King, personal communication.

pp. 48–49
The Kwakiutl prayer is from Franz Boas's *Ethnology of the Kwakiutl*, 35th Annual Report of the Bureau of American Ethnology 1913–1914, p. 619.
1. Jensen, D., and P. Sargent, *Robes of Power: Totem Poles on Cloth*, 1986.

pp. 52–53
1. O'Neale, L., "Yurok-Karok Basket Weavers," *University of California Publications in American Archaeology and Ethnology* 32:1, 1952, p. 39.
2. Ibid., p. 13. Eisenhart, L.L., "Karok Basketry: Mrs. Phoebe Maddux and the Johnson Collection," in *The Hover Collection of Karok Baskets,* Clarke Memorial Museum, 1985.

pp. 54–55
R.A. Gould, in "The Wealth Quest Among the Tolowa Indians," *Proceedings of the American Philosophical Society* 110:1, 1966, pp. 67–89, defines Tolowa treasures as "all-purpose money" used to generate wealth as well as prestige, with women's labor providing the link between these two aspects of the economy.

pp. 58–59
This passage is quoted by D.K. Washburn in "Kachina: Window to the Hopi World," in *Hopi Kachina: Spirit of Life*, 1980, p 43. The slightly fuller version here is directly from Crow-Wing, *A Pueblo Indian Journal, 1920–1921*, American Anthropological Association Memoirs 32, 1925, p. 99.
1. Leigh Jenkins, Director, Cultural Preservation Office, Hopi, personal communication. Leigh Jenkins also provided the Hopi names for the tithu and the dances and collaborated on the text.
2. This tihu is illustrated in pl. LXXII of H.R. Voth's "The Oraibi Powamu Ceremony," *Field Columbian Museum Anthropological Series* 3:2, 1901, pp. 64–158. Voth was a turn-of-the-century Mennonite minister at Oraibi.

pp. 60–61
1. Ribeiro, D., and B.G. Ribeiro, *Arte Plumária dos Indios Kaapor* (Rio de Janeiro), 1957, pp. 148–49.
2. Ibid., p. 148.
3. Ibid., pp. 146–47.
4. Ibid., pp. 146–47.
5. Ibid., pp. 149–50.

pp. 62–63
This Andean folklore is from Salvador Guyasamin's "Cuentos de Tierradentro," in *Atawalpa* (Ecuador), 1980, p. 12.

Visual Prayers, pp. 64–69
1. Brasser, T.J., "Plains Indian Art" in *American Indian Art: Form and Tradition*, 1972.
2. Brassser (ibid.) identifies these five designs.

3. Snow, J., *These Mountains Are Our Sacred Places: The Story of the Stoney Indians*, 1977.
4. *From My Grandmother's Hands*, exhibition by the Glenbow Museum, 1979.
5. Lowie, R., *Indians of the Plains*, 1982, p. 139.

pp. 70–71
1. Whitehead, R.H., *Elitekey: Micmac Material Culture from 1600 A.D. to the Present*, 1980, p. 11.
2. St. Anne is the patron saint of the Micmac, and her festal day, July 26, has been described as "the most important date in the Micmac calendar." See Wallis, W.D., and R.S. Wallis, *The Micmac Indians of Eastern Canada*, 1955, p. 184.

pp. 72–73
1. By 1820, these peoples were becoming known as the Five Civilized Tribes because they had, in varying degrees, set up schools, adopted Christianity, and, in the case of the Cherokees, developed a written language and published a bilingual newspaper.

pp. 74–75
Elisapee Kiliutak is quoted in *Things Made by the Inuit*, 1980.
1. Boas, F., *The Eskimo of Baffin Land and Hudson Bay*, Bulletin of the American Museum of Natural History 15, 1901, p. 160.
2. The bottom of the pouch is secured with a strap, held under the mother's arms with toggles. On this parka the toggles, dangling at the front, are carved of ivory. Also of ivory are the needle case and thimble worn on a strap about the neck.
3. Driscoll, B., "Sapangat: Inuit Beadwork in the Canadian Arctic," *Expedition* 26:2, 1984, p. 42.
4. In traditional life, tattooing marked the change from girl to woman and held deep religious significance. Knud Rasmussen, an early-20th-c. student of the Inuit, reported that a woman with attractive tattooing always got on well with Nuliajuk, the Sea spirit, when she passed her on the way to the land of the dead. See Rasmussen's *Intellectual Culture of the Iglulik Eskimos*.

pp. 76–77
1. R.K. Wright, ed., identified these leggings as being made from a cornhusk bag in *A Time of Gathering: Native Heritage in Washington State*, 1991, p. 55.
2. Figurative motifs also appear on cornhusk bags. For a full description of the evolution of cornhusk bags, see Miller, L., "Basketry of the Plateau Region," in *A Time of Gathering*.

pp. 86–87
This Lakota Ghost Dance song appears in James Mooney's *The Ghost Dance Religion and the Sioux Outbreak of 1890*, 14th Annual Report of the Bureau of American Ethnology 1892–1893.

pp. 88–89 (The Symbolism of Feathers)
This Arapaho Ghost Dance song is from James Mooney's *The Ghost Dance Religion,* 14th Annual Report of the Bureau of American Ethnology 1892–1893.
1. Wooden Leg, *Wooden Leg: A Warrior who Fought Custer,* 1931.
2. Ibid.
3. Brochure, American Museum of Natural History, New York, undated.

pp. 90–91
1. In the 1889 Annual Report to the Secretary of the Interior, the Commissioner for Indian Affairs summarized U.S. policy: "The Indians must conform to 'the white man's ways,' peaceably if they will, forcibly if they must." See Hagan, W.T., "United States Indian Policies, 1860–1900," in *Handbook of North American Indians* 4, 1988, p. 61.
2. Arizona *Weekly Star* 1:1 (28 June 1877).

pp. 92–93
This Kuna love song is from Frances Densmore's *Music of the Tule Indians of Panama,* Smithsonian Miscellaneous Collections 77:11, 1926, p. 34.
1. Salvador, M.L., *Yer Dialege! Kuna Women's Art,* 1978, p. 10.
2. Wafer, L., *A New Voyage and Description of the Isthmus of America* II:73, L.E. Joyce, ed., 1934 (1st pub. 1899). Also Salvador, p. 12.
3. Sherzer, D., and J. Sherzer, "Mormaknamaloe: The Cuna Mola," in *Ritual and Symbol in Native Central America,* P. Young and J. Howe, eds., University of Oregon Anthropological Papers 9, 1978, p. 36.
4. See Howe, J., *The Kuna Gathering: Contemporary Village Politics in Panama,* 1986.
5. See Parker, A., and A. Neal, *Molas: Folk Art of the Cuna Indians,* 1977. See also Puls, H., *Textiles of the Kuna Indians of Panama,* 1988; and Helms, M., *Cuna Molas and Coclé Art Forms: Reflections on Panamanian Design Styles and Symbols,* Working Papers in Traditional Arts 7, 1981.

pp. 94–95
Rigoberta Menchú is quoted from her autobiography *I . . . Rigoberta Menchú: An Indian Woman in Guatemala,* A. Wright, trans., 1983, p. 81.
1. Conte, C., *Maya Culture and Costume,* 1984, p. 39. Also Wood, J., and L. de J. Osborne, *Indian Costumes of Guatemala,* 1966, p. 110.
2. Asturias de Barrios, L., *Comalapa: Native Dress and Its Significance* (Guatemala), 1985, p. 30.
3. Schevill, M.B., *Evolution in Textile Design from the Highlands of Guatemala,* 1985, pp. 3–4. Also Conte, p. 15.
4. Schevill, p.3.

pp. 96–97
Ruiz Blanco is quoted in Lizandro Alvarado, "Datos Etnográficos de Venezuela," *Obras Completas* IV (Caracas), 1956, p. 123.
1. de Civrieux, M., *Watunna: An Orinoco Creation Cycle,* 1980, pp. 1–2. Also Guss, D.M., *To Weave and Sing: Art, Symbol, and Narrative in the South American Rain Forest,* 1989, p. 7.
2. Wilbert, J., *Survivors of El Dorado: Four Indian Cultures of South America,* 1972, pp. 118–20.
3. Ibid. pp. 120, 125. Also de Civrieux, M., "Datos Antropológicos de los Indios Kunuhana," *Antropológica* 8, 1959, p. 134.
4. Guss, pp. 105–08. Wilbert, p. 125.

pp.98–99
1. Harner, M., *The Jivaro: People of the Sacred Waterfalls,* 1972, p. 107.
2. Ibid. p. 112.
3. Ibid. p. 117–21.

pp. 100–01
This Andean folklore is cited by Inge Schjellerup in "Gift-Exchange Ceremonies in the Northern Highlands of Peru," *Folk* 29 (Copenhagen), 1987,p. 47.

pp. 102–03
Andean folklore recorded by the author in Huancavelica, Peru, 1979.

pp. 104–05
1. Faron, L.C., *The Mapuche Indians of Chile,* 1968, pp. 1, 4.
2. Laczko, G., "The Weaver: The Araucanians of Chile," in *The Ancestors: Native Artisans of the Americas,* A.C. Roosevelt and J.G.E. Smith, eds., 1979, p 141.
3. For weaving terms, see Rowe, A.P., *Warp-Patterned Weaves of the Andes,* 1977.
4. Aldunate del Solar, C., *Mapuche: Seeds of the Chilean Soul,* 1992, pp. 88–91. Also Margarita Alvarado and Gabriela Frings, personal communication.
5. Laczko, pp. 137, 142–43.
6. Margarita Alvarado and Gabriela Frings, personal communication.
7. Laczko, pp. 136, 138.
8. Aldunate del Solar, C., "Reflexiones Acerca de la Platería Mapuche," in *Platería Araucana* (Santiago), 1983, p. 10.
9. Reccius, W., "Evolución y Caracterización de la Platería Araucana," in *Platería Araucana* (Santiago), 1983, pp. 18.
10. Ibid., p. 23.
11. Laczko, p. 139.

Vision and Virtuosity, pp. 106–10
1. Nemiroff, D., *Land Spirit Power,* 1992.
2. Ibid.
3. K. Varnedoe in *Primitivism in Twentieth Century Art,* W.S. Rubin, ed., 1984.
4. Duffek, K., "Northwest Coast Indian Art from 1950 to the Present," in *In the Shadow of the Sun,* 1993.

pp. 111–12
1. Collecting, washing, sorting, and dyeing moose hair is tedious and laborious. Sister Beatrice Leduc (1925–63) of the Order of the Grey Nuns in the Northwest Territories recalled: "How many times were we offered by hunters of the village to go and pluck the hair from hides of animals they had killed; it was hard and dirty work; we would come back home with painful blisters on our fingers . . . selection of the longest and whitest almost one by one, how many hours did I spend in that selection?" From *Out of the North: The Subarctic Collection of the Haffenreffer Museum of Anthropology,* B. Hail and K.C. Duncan, eds., 1989, p. 251.
2. For a thoughtful discussion of this issue, see J.C.H. King's "Tradition in Native Art," in *The Arts of the North American Indian: Native Traditions in Evolution,* E.L. Wade, ed., 1986. Barbeau, C.M., "The Origin of Floral and Other Designs Among the Canadian and Neighboring Indians," *Proceedings of the International Congress of Americanists* 23, 1928, p. 512.

pp. 114–15
1. Whitehead, R.H., *Micmac Porcupine Quillwork, 1750–1950,* 1978, p. 43.
2. This covered storage basket was made around 1840, before the introduction of labor-saving splint cutters and wooden molds; each splint is hand-cut with a knife. In *A Basketful of Indian Culture Change,* 1975, Ted Brasser contends that splint basketry was learned from Europeans. Others disagree: see J.A. Lester, "The Birchbark Art of Tomah Joseph," in *We're Still Here: Art of Indian New England,* 1987, p. 29; and *A Key into the Language of Woodsplint Baskets,* A. McMullen and R.G. Handsman, eds., 1987, p. 21.
3. See Richmond, T.L., "Spirituality and Survival in Schaghticoke Basket-Making," and G. Tantaquidgeon and J.G. Fawcett, "Symbolic Motifs on Painted Baskets of the Mohegan–Pequot," in McMullen and Handsman, pp. 94– 101.
4. McMullen and Handsman, p. 114.
5. Picture frames, card holders, glove boxes, and silverware trays were among the hundreds of pieces Joseph created during his long career.
6. Lester, p. 22. Other characters Joseph depicted include Mategwes, the pipe-smoking Northern Hare, often shown, as here, with his enemy the Wildcat.
7. Ibid., p. 25.

pp. 116–17
Agnes Thompson is quoted from *Interwoven Expression: Works of a Contemporary Alaska Native Basketmaker.*
1. An observer in 1791 wrote that the women of Unalaska split the rye grass with a fingernail grown "to a great length, until it is as sharp as a lancet." Ray, D.J., *Aleut and Eskimo Art: Tradition and Innovation in South Alaska,* 1981, p. 48.
2. Black, L.T., *Aleut Art,* 1982, p. 164.
3. See Hudson, R.L., "Designs in Aleut Basketry," in *Faces, Voices & Dreams,* P.L. Corey, ed., 1987, pp. 78 ff., for a description of ten distinct kinds of twining.
4. Ibid., p. 91.

pp. 118–19
The Eskimo song appears in Knud Rasmussen's *Intellectual Culture of the Copper Eskimo,* Report of the Fifth Thule Expedition 1921–1924 (Copenhagen), 1932, p. 53. English translation by W.E. Calvert.

pp. 120–21
1. The term Slavey has been used in the literature to refer to the Athapaskan people living near Great Slave Lake in northwestern Canada. There is, however, no evidence that these people ever formed a single tribal entity, rather preferring to identify themselves as smaller geographic groups. See Asch, M.I., "Slavey," in *Handbook of North American Indians* 6, 1981, pp. 38–49.
2. The origin of woven quillwork is lost in time, but the art form was fully developed by 1789 when Alexander Mackenzie encountered an encampment of Slavey and Dogrib people and described their belts as "the neatest thing of the kind that ever I saw." Helm, J., "Women's Work, Women's Art," in *Out of the North,* B. Hail and K.C. Duncan, eds., 1989, p. 120.
3. Sir John Franklin, cited by Helm, pp. 120–22.
4. Hail and Duncan, p. 144.

pp. 122–23
1. For a discussion of at.oow., see Dauenhauer, N.M., and R. Dauenhauer, *Haa Shuka, Our Ancestors: Tlingit Oral Narratives,* Classics of Tlingit Oral Literature 1, 1987.

2. Holm, B., *Spirit and Ancestor,* 1987, p. 208.

pp. 124–25
1. Holm, B., *Spirit and Ancestor,* 1987, p. 152.

pp. 126–27
The Tlingit song of Raven is translated by J.R. Swanton, Bureau of American Ethnology.

pp. 128–29
1. For a thoughtful discussion of the naxnox, see Guedon, M.-F., "An Introduction to the Tsimshian World View and its Practitioners" in *The Tsimshian: Images of the Past, Views for the Present,* M. Seguin, ed., 1993.
2. Boas, F., *Tsimshian Mythology,* 31st Annual Report of the Bureau of American Ethnology 1916, p. 543.
3. Halpin, M., "'Seeing' in Stone: Tsimshian Masking and the Twin Stone Masks," in *The World Is as Sharp as a Knife: An Anthology in Honour of Wilson Duff,* D.M. Abbott, ed., 1981.
4. For a discussion of the gitsontk, see Shane, A.P.M., "Power in Their Hands: The Gitsontk," in Seguin, pp. 160–173.

pp. 130–31
Elizabeth Hickox's letter is quoted in the Reese Bullen Gallery's *Elizabeth Conrad Hickox: Baskets from the Center of the World,* 1991, p. 11.
1. O'Neale, L.M., "Yurok–Karok Basket Weavers," *University of California Publications in American Archaeology and Ethnology* 32:1, 1932, p. 175.
2. See O'Neale for the most comprehensive account of Yurok/Karuk basketry materials, techniques, and design conventions based on interviews with the weavers themselves.
3. Lang, J., in *Elizabeth Conrad Hickox: Baskets from the Center of the World,* p. 9.
4. The term Pomo is misleading. There were actually at least 72 politically autonomous Pomoan tribes or groups living north of San Francisco and speaking 7 mutually unintelligible languages. McLendon, S., "California Baskets and Basketmakers," in *Basketmakers: Meaning and Form in Native American Baskets,* 1992, p. 59. Also S. McLendon and B.S. Holland, "The Basketmaker: The Pomoans of California," in *The Ancestors: Native Artisans of the Americas,* pp. 106–107.
5. McLendon and Holland, p. 191.
6. Benson, W., letters to Grace Nicholson, 1904–1906, NMAI archives.

pp. 132–33 (The Legacy of Baskets)
1. Allen, E., *Pomo Basketmaking: A Supreme Art for the Weaver,* 1972.

pp. 134–35
The Lakota song appears in Frances Densmore's *Teton Sioux Music,* Bureau of American Ethnology Bulletin 61, 1918, p. 337.
1. Denig, E.T., *Five Indian Tribes of the Upper Missouri,* J.C. Ewers, ed., 1961, p. 158.

pp. 138–39
This Sun Dance song appears in Frances Densmore's *Teton Sioux Music,* Bureau of American Ethnology Bulletin 61, 1918, p. 140

pp. 142–43
1. In 1984, Don Fowler of the University of Nevada-Reno submitted these radiocarbon dates for two of the decoys: 2,080 ± 330 BP (13.4513) and 2,250 ± 230 BP (13.4512B), placing them in the Transitional to early Late Lovelock phase (500 B.C.–A.D. 500). See D.R. Tuohy and L.K. Napton, "Duck

Decoys from Lovelock Cave, Nevada, Dated by 14C Accelerator Mass Spectrometry," *American Antiquity* 51:4, 1986, pp. 813–16. Also Tuohy's "Portable Art Objects," in *Handbook of North American Indians* 11, 1986, pp. 227–37.
2. Elston, R.G., "Prehistory of the Western Area," in *Handbook* 11, pp. 140, 141 (fig. 7).
3. Catherine S. Fowler, 1993, personal communication.
4. Lovelock culture may represent the "parent" of Northern Paiute culture, although it is more likely that Northern Paiute culture was intrusive into the area. Few differences existed in the economic activities of the two peoples. See Grosscup, G.L., "Lovelock, Northern Paiute and Culture Change," *Nevada State Museum Anthropological Papers* 9, 1963, pp. 70–71.
5. Wheat, M.M., *Survival Arts of the Primitive Paiutes*, 1967, p. 117.
6. The art/artifact distinction is becoming increasingly blurred. In *Handbook* 11, p. 228, Tuohy writes, "These decoys presumably had only a utilitarian function, but they are classic sculptural expressions deserving consideration as art forms." Fowler, C.S., *Tule Technology: Northern Paiute Uses of Marsh Resources in Western Nevada*, Smithsonian Folklife Studies 6, 1990.

pp. 144–45
1. Kabotie, F., and B. Belknap, *Fred Kabotie, Hopi Indian Artist*, 1977, p. 8.
2. Seymour, T.V.N., *When the Rainbow Touches Down: The Artists and Stories behind the Apache, Navajo, Rio Grande Pueblo and Hopi Paintings in the William and Leslie Van Ness Denman Collection*, 1988, pp. 245–46.
3. *Snake Dance* is almost identical to a painting from the collections of the Laboratory of Anthropology published in Hewett, E.L., "Native American Artists," *Art and Archaeology* 13:3, 1922, pp. 103–12 (fig. 8). J.J. Brody, 1994, personal communication.
4. Douglas, F.H., and R. d'Harnoncourt, *Indian Art of the United States*, 1941, p. 13.

pp. 146–47
1. Wheat, J.B., "Early Trade and Commerce in Southwestern Textiles before the Curio Shop," in *Reflections: Papers on Southwestern Culture History in Honor of Charles H. Lange*, A.V.S. Poore, ed., 1988, p. 60.
2. In 1844, Josiah Gregg, who chronicled his travels in the West, wrote that the Navajos wove "a singular species of blanket, known as the *Sarape Navajo* which is of so close and dense a texture that it will frequently hold water almost equal to gum-elastic cloth. . . . Some of the finer qualities are often sold among the Mexicans as high as 50 or 60 dollars each." Cited in Kent, K.P., *Navajo Weaving: Three Centuries of Change*, 1985, p. 10.
3. Scholars group Navajo textiles into the Classic, Transitional, Rug, and Recent periods. Weaving materials comprise the most reliable criteria; weaving styles frequently overlap in time—for example, revival pieces were made as early as the 1890s. See Hedlund, A.L., *Reflections of the Weaver's World: The Gloria F. Ross Collection of Contemporary Navajo Weaving*, 1992, pp. 17–19; and Kent.
4. The expression "It's up to her" is often heard in conversations with Navajo weavers; see Hedlund, p. 15. It is also a recurrent theme in Navajo life histories. In Left Handed, *Son of*

Old Man Hat: A Navajo Autobiography, W. Dyk, and R. Dyk, eds., 1980, pp. 65–66, Left Handed's father advises his wife to "work for your properties, work for the sheep, horses, and cattle. If you work for them, you will have them, and pretty soon you will have everything. So it's up to you."

pp. 148–49
1. Babcock, B.A., et al., *The Pueblo Storyteller: Development of a Figurative Ceramic Tradition*, 1986, pp. 10–11.

pp. 150–51
The poem excerpted here is attributed to Nezahualcóytl, 15th-c. king of the city-state of Texcoco. See Garibay, A., *Poesía Náhuatl* (Mexico), 1965.
1. Millon, R., "The Place Where Time Began: An Archaeologist's Interpretation of What Happened in Teotihuacan History," in *Teotihuacan: Art from the City of the Gods*, K. Berrin and E. Pasztory, eds., 1993, pp. 17, 33.
2. Serra Puche, M.C., "The Role of Teotihuacan in Mesoamerican Archaeology," in *Teotihuacan*, p. 65.
3. Millon, p. 17. Also Rattray, E.C., and E. Pasztory, in *Teotihuacan*, p. 258.
4. Pasztory, in *Teotihuacan*, p. 264.
5. Ibid., pp. 174–75.
6. Berrin, K., "Unknown Treasures: The Unexpected in Teotihuacan Art," in *Teotihuacan*, pp. 82–83. Also Rattray and Pasztory, p. 258.
7. Rattray and Pasztory, p. 258.

pp. 152–53
Ramón Medina is quoted by P. Furst in *The Ninth Level: Funerary Art from Ancient Mesoamerica*, 1978, p. 11.
1. Kan, M., et al., *Sculpture of Ancient West Mexico: Nayarit, Jalisco, Colima—The Proctor Stafford Collection*, 1970, p. 14. Also Gallagher, J. *Companions of the Dead: Ceramic Tomb Sculpture from Ancient West Mexico*, 1983, p. 39.
2. Gallagher, pp. 31, 41.
3. Furst, pp. 22,75.
4. Gallagher, pp. 32, 35.
5. Ibid., p. 35.
6. Furst, p. 75. Kan, p. 14.
7. Couch, N.C.C., *Pre-Columbian Art from the Ernest Erickson Collection*, 1988, p. 17. Also Gallagher, pp. 35, 41.

pp. 154–55
1. Wheat, J.B., "Saltillo Sarapes of Mexico," in *Spanish Textile Tradition of New Mexico and Colorado*, N. Fisher, ed. 1984, pp. 74–75.
2. The Spanish wool industry was well established in Mexico by the end of the 16th c. The large estate at Apizaco in Tlaxcala, for example, was a self-sufficient community with grazing land for cattle and sheep, houses for the owner and workers, and a textile shop and two mills. See Jeter, J., and P.M. Juelke, *The Saltillo Sarape*, 1978, p. 13.

pp. 156–57
1. Couch, N.C.C., *Pre-Columbian Art from the Ernest Erickson Collection*, 1988, p. 28.
2. Goldstein, M.M., *Ceremonial Sculpture of Ancient Veracruz*, 1988, p. 63.
3. Ibid.
4. Nicholson, H.B., "The Iconography of Classic Veracruz Ceramic Sculptures," in *The Ancient Art of Veracruz*, O. Hammer, ed., 1971, p. 14.
5. Heyden, D., "A New Interpretation of the Smiling Figures." in *The Ancient Art of Veracruz*, p. 37.
6. Goldstein, p. 38.
7. Wilkerson, S.J.K., "Cultural Time

and Space in Ancient Veracruz," in Goldstein, p. 169.
8. Couch, p. 31.
9. Wilkerson, p. 13. Also Wilkerson, S.J.K., "El Tajín: Great Center of the Northeast," in *Mexico: Splendors of Thirty Centuries*, 1990, p. 169; and Proskouriakoff, T., "Classic Art of Central Veracruz," in *Handbook of Middle American Indians* 11, 1971, p. 564.

pp. 158–59
1. MacLeod, B., "Deciphering the Primary Standard Sequence," Ph.D. dissertation, University of Texas, 1990. Also Reents-Budet, D., et. al. *Painting the Maya Universe: Royal Ceramics of the Classic Period*, 1994.
2. Houston, S., et al., "Folk Classification of Classic Maya Pottery," *American Anthropologist* 91:3, 1989, pp. 720–26.
3. Schele, L., and M.E. Miller, *Blood of Kings*, 1986.
4. Schele, L., and D. Friedel, *A Forest of Kings*, 1990.
5. Schele and Miller. Also Schele and Freidel.
6. Estrada, J., *La Música de México* (Mexico), 1984. Also Mendoza, V.T., "Música Precolombina de América," *Boletín Latinamericano de Música* (Mexico) 4, 1938.
7. Miller, M.E., *Jaina Figurines*, 1975.

pp. 160–61
1. Schele, L., and D. Freidel, *A Forest of Kings*, 1990.
2. Schele, L., and M.E. Miller, *Blood of Kings*, 1986.
3. Schaffer, A.-L., *On the Edge of the Maya World: Stone Vases from the Ulúa Valley, Honduras*, exhibition at the Museum of Fine Arts, Houston, 23 February–31 May 1992. Little has been published about Ulúa Valley stone vessels. What we do know is dependent on the work of Louise Schaffer, who was instrumental in preparing this text. Her exhibition was the first devoted solely to these vessels.

pp. 162–63
This Aztec poem is quoted by Elizabeth Carmichael in her book *Turquoise Mosaics from Mexico*, 1970, p. 26.
1. Stuart, G.S., and G.F. Stuart, *Lost Kingdoms of the Maya*, 1993, p. 102.

pp. 164–65
This quotation is from Cieza de León's *Crónica del Perú* (Lima), 1986 (1st pub. 1553).

pp. 168–169
1. Farabee, W.C., *Indian Tribes of Eastern Peru*, Papers of the Peabody Museum of American Archaeology and Ethnology 10, 1922. Also Steward, J.H., and A. Métraux, "Tribes of the Peruvian and Ecuadorian Montaña," in *Handbook of South American Indians* 3, 1948.
2. Román V., L., "Etica y Esthetica en el Arte Piro," *Anthropologica* 3:3 (Peru), 1985, p. 126.
3. Roe, P., *The Cosmic Zygote: Cosmology in the Amazon Basin*, 1982, p. 42.
4. Román V., p. 125.
5. Gebhart-Sayer, A., *The Cosmos Encoiled: Indian Art of the Peruvian Amazon*, 1984, p. 9. Also Farabee.

pp. 170–71
Quotation is from Francisco de Avila's *Dioses y Hombres de Huarochirí* (Lima), José María Arguedas, trans., 1966 (1st pub. 1608), p. 38.

Across the Generations, pp. 172–177
1. Cushing, F.H., *Zuni Breadstuff*,

Indian Notes and Monographs 8, 1974 (1st pub. 1920)
2. From Willie Hensley's speech at the 1981 conference "Seeing with the Native Eye" (manuscript).
3. Carl Sweezy is quoted from his autobiography *The Arapaho Way: A Memoir of an Indian Boyhood*.

pp. 182–83
1. Letter from Charles Foster dated 24 January 1967, NMAI archives.
2. The bonnet's headband is constructed of a ring of birchbark covered with black satin trade cloth. It is lavishly adorned with dozens of the small, silver ring brooches that were important trade items during the 18th c. The importance of silver in trade can be seen in the records of the post at Detroit, which, for the year 1782, requested 18,600 pieces for trade. See N.J. Fredrickson and S. Gibb, *The Covenant Chain: Indian Ceremonial and Trade Silver*, 1980, p. 46.
3. The Berne Historical Museum in Switzerland has in its collections a black silk scarf folded in the form of a band and decorated with rows of ring brooches and silver earrings very similar to the ones on the Foster headdress. See J. Thompson, *The North American Indian Collection of the Berne Historical Museum*, 1977, p. 124, for an illustration. Documentation is almost completely lacking but suggests a late-18th-c. date and an Ottawa provenience for at least some of the associated objects. The earliest feather bonnet that can be associated with a specific individual was acquired in 1833 by Maximilian along the upper Missouri River. It belonged to the Mandan chief Mato Tope and is very similar in style to the Foster bonnet.
4. In 1806, at the age of 38, Foster was killed in battle in Capetown, South Africa.
5. Phillips, R.B., "Like a Star, I Shine: Northern Woodlands Artistic Traditions," in *The Spirit Sings*, 1987, p. 87.

pp. 184–85
Earnest Spybuck's description of *Procession* is from Mark Harrington's notes for 1910 in the NMAI archives, OC 117, #5.
1. NMAI archives, OC 117, #5.
2. Harrington, M.R., "Spybuck, the Shawnee Artist," in *Indians at Work* V:8, 1938, pp.13–15.
3. NMAI archives, OC 117, #5.

pp. 192–93
1. In Innu religious belief, the Lord of the Caribou dwells in a high mountain and maintains dominion over all the caribou in the world. He releases caribou only to hunters with powerful spiritual medicine. See Speck, F.G., *Naskapi: The Savage Hunters of the Labrador Peninsula*, The Civilization of the American Indian 10, 1977 (1st pub. 1935), pp. 81ff., for several versions of this belief.
2. This coat includes very old elements such as dots and double curves, as well as a particularly rich use of leaf sprays, which some scholars suggest may reflect the influence of early-19th-c. European decorative arts; see Burnham, D.K., *To Please the Caribou*, 1992, p. 200. Burnham (p. 3) suggests that the "finest" painting was done on coats which predate the missionary period, when a man had several wives and a woman with a special talent for painting could be freed from household chores to devote full time to making her husband's coats.
3. Ibid., p. 3.

4. The basic paint was crushed fish roe, which produced the soft yellow seen on this coat outlining the smaller design elements and on the leggings in very fine crosshatching. Red was made by mixing red ocher (or, later, vermilion obtained in trade) with fish roe; browns, black, green, and blue were also used.
5. Stephen Loring, 1994, personal communication.

pp. 194–95
1. The construction of most Yup'ik masks is complex. One or several outer hoops of thin splints are mounted on the body with split willow roots, with appendages such as feathers, a tail, or wings. The rings, referred to as *ellanguat*—pretend cosmos or universe—are said to represent different levels of the universe, while the appendages complete the spirit of the mask. Yup'ik masks have also been interpreted as ringed centers that function as eyes into the unseen spirit world.
2. Mask-making and the accompanying dances and ceremonies were discouraged by missionaries in the late 19th and early 20th c., but they never died out completely. In recent years both dancing and mask-making have been revived, encouraged by the efforts of a few elders who remember the old ways. Much of the old religious symbolism is not as visible today, and masks are made for sale as well as for use. But many people still believe in the ritual treatment of animals, in the commonality of all life, and in the endless cycle of death and resurrection.

pp. 196–97
Makah elder Helma Ward is quoted in *A Time of Gathering,* R.K. Wright, ed., 1991.
1. Guedon, M.-F., "Tsimshian Shamanic Images," in *The Tsimshian: Images of the Past, Views for the Present,* M. Seguin, ed., 1993, p. 196.
2. Garfield, V.E., "Making a Bird or Chief's Rattle," *Davidson Journal of Anthropology* 1:11, 1955, p. 156.
3. Suttles, W., "Productivity and its Constraints: A Coast Salish Case," in *Indian Art Traditions of the Northwest Coast,* R.L. Carlson, ed., p. 71.
4. Holm, B., *Spirit and Ancestor,* p. 82.
5. Ibid.

pp. 198–99
1. The Nuxalk word for the Eagle Spirit is *sa.lpsta,* which T.F. McIlwraith translates as "incubus."
2. The Kusiut was one of two separate Nuxalk secret societies, each with its own songs, dramas, and ceremonies. The most prestigious of the many kinds of Kusiut names belonged to the Cannibals, whose songs and dances dramatized how an animal spirit entered their bodies and how, through drumming and songs, it was expelled. The spirit entering the dancer might be Eagle, Wolf, or Bear, depending on family titles and prerogatives.

pp. 200–01
The Makah song of a whale appears in Frances Densmore's *Nootka and Quileute Music,* Bureau of American Ethnology Bulletin 124, 1939, p. 68.
1. The 18th-c. explorer Captain James Cook should be credited (or blamed) for the name Nootka, which he used to refer to the people who live along the west coast of Vancouver Island. The combined Tribal Council in 1980 adopted the name Nuu-chah-nulth, meaning Those Living at the Foot of

the Mountains. See Holm, B., *Spirit and Ancestor,* 1987, p. 65.

pp. 202–03
Mary Azbill is quoted by Stewart Culin in his "Report on a Collecting Trip among the Indians of California, April 26–August 4, 1908," cited by C.D. Bates and B. Bibby, "Collecting among the Chico Maidu: The Stewart Culin Collection at the Brooklyn Museum," *American Indian Art* 8:4, 1983, p. 49. Also see I. Jacknis in *Objects of Myth and Memory: American Indian Art at the Brooklyn Museum,* D. Fane et al., eds., 1991, p. 231.
1. Dixon, R.B., "The Shasta," in *Bulletin of the American Museum of Natural History* XVII:V, 1907, p. 468.
2. Silver, S., "Shastan Peoples," in *Handbook of North American Indians* 8, 1978, p. 211.
3. Dixon, p. 389.
4. Bates, C.D., "Feather Belts of Central California," *American Indian Art* 7:1, 1981, p. 47.
5. Culin documented the symbolism of the design of a similar Maidu feather belt in the collections of the Brooklyn Museum. Only the red motifs differ. According to Culin, the red triangles represent wild grape leaves, the two narrow green stripes represent tongs used to remove hot stones from the fire for cooking acorn mush, and the green rectangle represents a large grasshopper. See Bates and Bibby, p. 49. Also Jacknis, pp. 230–231.
6. "Report on a Collecting Trip among the Indians of California," cited by Jacknis, p. 231.
7. Ibid, p. 284.

pp. 204–05
1. In 1911, the main pit at Cerillos measured 40 m. deep and 60 m. wide. See N.M. Judd, *The Material Culture of Pueblo Bonito,* Smithsonian Miscellaneous Collections 124, 1954, p. 81.
2. See Lekson, S.H., "Settlement Patterns and the Chaco Region," in *Chaco and Hohokam: Prehistoric Regional Systems in the American Southwest,* P.L. Crown and W.J. Judge, eds., 1991, pp. 31–57, for a reexamination of the criteria used to define the Chaco regional system.
3. Keith Kintigh, 1994, personal communication.
4. Hawikku was excavated by Frederick Webb Hodge for the Museum of the American Indian–Heye Foundation between 1917 and 1923. See W. Smith et al., *The Excavation of Hawikuh by Frederick Webb Hodge: Report of the Hendricks-Hodge Expedition 1917–1923,* Contributions from the Museum of the American Indian–Heye Foundation XX, 1966.

pp. 206–07
1. Randy Nahohai, 1993, personal communication.
2. Barbara Mills, 1993, personal communication.
3. Hardin, M.A., *Gifts of Mother Earth: Ceramics in the Zuni Tradition,* 1983, pp. 4.
4. Bunzel, R.L., *The Pueblo Potter: A Study of Creative Imagination in Primitive Art,* Columbia University Contributions to Anthropology 8, 1929, p. 106.
5. Hardin, p. 4.

pp. 208–09
1. Peterson, S., *The Living Tradition of Maria Martinez,* 1977, p. 83.
2. For an account of the development of the method for producing matte designs, see R.L. Spivey, *Maria,* 1979,

pp. 47–48.
3. Peterson, S., *Lucy M. Lewis: American Indian Potter,* 1984.
4. Martha H. Struever, 1994, personal communication. In about 1982, Struever recorded Dextra speaking about the migration design on one of her own pots: "It's from way back, the ancient people from way back that migrated. It's probably a whole Sikyatki design. The way my mother explained it is the way people moved around the continent from all over." Also see M.L. Cusick, *Nampeyo: A Gift Remembered.*

pp. 210–11
This quotation, the response of an anonymous Aztec priest told by the Spanish to renounce his religion, appears in R.F. Townsend, *The Aztecs,* 1992, p. 109.
1. Coe, M.D., "The Aztec Empire: Realm of the Smoking Mirror," in *Circa 1492: Art in the Age of Exploration,* J.A. Levenson, ed., 1991, p. 500.
2. Ibid., pp. 501, 552.
3. Ibid., pp. 502, 552. Townsend, pp. 204, 212.
4. Coe, p. 552.
5. Solis, F., in *Circa 1492,* pp. 556–57.

pp. 212–13
1. Sylvest, E.E., Jr., *Nuestra Señora de Guadalupe: Mother of God, Mother of the Americas,* 1992, p. 77.
2. Ibid., pp. 1, 77–78. Also Wolf, E.R., "The Virgin of Guadalupe: A Mexican National Symbol," *Journal of American Folklore* 71:279, 1958, pp. 701–02.
3. Sylvest, pp. 1, 15. Also Wolf, p. 702.
4. Sylvest, p. 2. Also Wolf, p. 704.

pp. 214–15
1. Spicer, E.H., "The Yaqui and Mayo," in *Handbook of Middle American Indians* 8, 1969, p. 830. Also Griffith, J., "Cáhitan *Pascola* Masks," *The Kiva* 37:4, 1972, p. 185.
2. Griffith, pp. 185–86. And Spicer, E.H., *The Yaquis: A Cultural History,* 1980, p. 102.
3. Griffith, pp. 196–97. And Painter, M.T., *With Good Heart: Yaqui Beliefs and Ceremonies in Pascua Village,* 1986, pp. 244, 247.
4. Conzemius, E., *Ethnographical Survey of the Moskito and Sumu Indians of Honduras and Nicaragua,* Bureau of American Ethnology Bulletin 106, 1932, pp. 161–63.

pp. 216–17
1. René Cibanacán Marcano, Nación Taína, 1994, personal communication. Also Rouse, I., *The Tainos: Rise and Decline of the People who Greeted Columbus,* 1992, p. 5.
2. Rouse, p. 13.
3. Ibid.
4. Stevens-Arroyo, A.M., *Cave of the Jagua: The Mythological World of the Taínos,* 1988, p. 59. And Rouse, I., and J.J. Arrom, "The Taínos," in *Circa 1492,* 1991, p. 512.
5. Rouse and Arrom, pp. 576–577.
6. Rouse, p. 123. Rouse and Arrom, p. 576.

pp. 218–19
Prayer recorded by the author in Ayacucho, Peru, 1980.

pp. 220–21 (Native Gold, Spanish Gold)
1. Milbrath, S., and J. Milanich, eds. *First Encounters: Spanish Explorations in the Caribbean and the United States, 1492–1570,* 1989. Also see K. Sale, *The Conquest of Paradise: Christopher Columbus and the Columbian Legacy,* 1991, pp. 259–60.

2. Massing, J.M., "Early Ethnographic Images of America, in *Circa 1492,* p. 515.
3. Vitoria, F. de, *De Indies et de Jure Belli Relectines,* in L. Hanke, *The Spanish Struggle for Justice in the Conquest of America,* 1949.
4. Sepúlveda, J.G. de, *Democrates II (Concerning the Just Cause of the War against the Indians),* in Hanke.
5. Cieza de León, Pedro de, *The Incas,* 1959 (1st pub. 1553).

pp. 222–23
1. Rostowrowski, M., *Etnía y Sociedad* (Lima), 1977, Craig Morris, trans., 1979, p. 242.

pp. 226–27
Quechua folklore recorded by the author in Cuzco, Peru, 1980.
1. Betanzos, J. de, *Suma y Narración de los Incas* (Madrid), M. del Carmen Rubio, transcription, 1987 (1st pub. 1551).
2. Donnan, C., *Moche Art of Peru: Pre-Columbian Symbolic Communication,* 1978, pp. 139–148. Also Benson, E.P., *The Mochica,* 1972, pp. 27–36.

pp. 228–29
1. Fawcett, D.M., "The Featherworkers: The Karajá of Brazil," in *The Ancestors: Native Artisans of the Americans,* A.C. Roosevelt and J.G.E. Smith, eds., 1979, pp. 30–31.
2. Ibid., p. 37.
3. Ibid., pp. 31–32. And Ehrenreich, P., "Contributions to the Ethnography of Brazil," Shelton Hicock, trans., *Veroffentlichungen aus dem Koniglichen Museum fur Volkerkunde* 2, 1891, p. 44.
4. Fawcett, pp. 28–29, 31.
5. Yde, J., *Material Culture of the Waiwái* (Copenhagen), 1965, pp. 166–68.
6. Ibid., pp. 260–62.

pp. 230–31
Shipibo folklore compiled by Margarita Mendizábal in Yarinacohas, Perú (manuscript).
1. Metraux, A., *The Native Tribes of Eastern Bolivia and Western Matto Grosso,* 1942. And Schultes, R., and Hoffmann, A., *Plantas de los Dioses. Orígenes del uso de Alucinógenos* (Mexico), 1982.

pp. 232–33
1. Cooper, J.M., "The Yahgan" in *Handbook of South American Indians* 1, 1946, pp. 81–84. Also Lothrop, S.K., *The Indians of Tierra del Fuego,* 1928, pp. 17, 32, 116.
2. Lothrop, p. 177. And Wilbert, J., ed., *Folk Literature of the Yamana Indians: Martin Gusinde's Collection of Yamana Narratives,* 1977, pp. 186–193.
3. Cooper, p. 104. Also Wilbert, pp. 191, 193.
4. Lothrop, p. 170.
5. Ibid., p. 171.

Epilogue, pp. 234–39.
There are many ways to say the Gonohonyohk. This version was written by Reg Henry (Cayuga) and is provided by the Woodland Cultural Centre, Brantford, Ontario.
1. Steltzer, U., *Indian Artists at Work,* 1977, back cover.

References
Delores Churchill, Haida spruce root basketmaker, is quoted in the *Newsletter of Native Arts,* November/December 1983, Institute of Alaskan Native Arts, Fairbanks.

REFERENCES

I started to notice the grasses around me, what kind of grasses were used for basketmaking. I read everything I could about basketry, and a lot of the grasses that were listed for basketry didn't work. And then I started thinking, well, some of these things that were written aren't even true.

—DELORES CHURCHILL, HAIDA

Introduction, pp. 14–19
Ames, M.M., *Cannibal Tours and Glass Boxes: The Anthropology of Museums.* Vancouver, 1992.

Deloria, V., *Custer Died for Your Sins: An Indian Manifesto.* Norman, Oklahoma, 1988.

Dickason, O.P., *Indian Arts in Canada.* Ottawa, 1972.

Douglas, F.H., and R. d'Harnoncourt, *Indian Art of the United States.* New York, 1941.

Doxtator, D., *Fluffs and Feathers: An Exhibit on the Symbols of Indianness.* Brantford, Ontario, 1992.

Duffek, K., and T. Hill, *Beyond History.* Vancouver, 1989.

Furst, P.T., and J.L. Furst, *North American Indian Art.* New York, 1992.

Hanson, J., "The Reappearing Vanishing American," *Museum News* 59, October 1980, pp. 44–51.

Hill, D., *As Snow Before the Summer Sun.* Brantford, Ontario, 1992.

Joe, J.R., *American Indian Policy and Cultural Values: Conflict and Accommodation.* Los Angeles, 1985.

Josephy, A.M., *Red Power: The American Indian Fight for Freedom.* New York, 1971.

Levi-Strauss, C., *The Savage Mind.* New York, 1962.

Medicine, B., "The Anthropologist as the Indian's Image Maker," *Indian Historian* 4, 1971.

Nabokov, P., ed., *Native American Testimony: A Chronicle of Indian–White Relations from Prophecy to the Present.* New York, 1992.

Schrader, R.F., *The Indian Arts and Crafts Board: An Aspect of New Deal Indian Policy.* Los Angeles, 1931.

Growing Up Indian, pp. 20–25
Standing Bear, L., *My Indian Boyhood.* New York, 1928.

———*My People the Sioux.* Lincoln, Nebraska, 1975 (1st pub. 1931).

pp. 26–27
Helm, J., "Seminole's Men's Clothing," in *Essays on the Verbal and Visual Arts,* J. Helm, ed. Seattle, 1967, pp. 160–74.

Blackard, D., *Patchwork and Palmettos: Seminole–Miccosukee Folk Art Since 1820.* Ft. Lauderdale, 1990.

Densmore, F., *Seminole Music,* Bureau of American Ethnology Bulletin 161, 1956.

West, P., "Glade Cross Mission: An Influence on Florida Seminole Arts and Crafts," *American Indian Art* 9:4, 1984, pp. 58–67.

pp. 28–29
Berrin, K., ed., *Art of the Huichol Indians.* New York, 1978

Clifton, J.A., *The Potawatomi.* New York, New York, 1987.

Grimes, J.E., and T.B. Hinton, "The Huichol and Cora," in *Handbook of Middle American Indians* 8, R. Wauchope, ed. Austin, 1969.

Phillips, R.B., *Patterns of Power: The Jasper Grant Collection and Great Lakes Indian Art of the Early Nineteenth Century.* Kleinburg, Ontario, 1984.

Schaefer, S., "Becoming a Weaver: The Woman's Path in Huichol Culture," PhD. dissertation, UCLA, 1990.

Skinner, A.B., "The Mascoutens or Prairie Potawatomi Indians," *Bulletin of the Public Museum of the City of Milwaukee* 5, 1924–27, pp. 1–30.

pp. 30–31
Flint Institute of Arts, *The American Indian/The American Flag.* Flint, Michigan, 1976.

Lanford, B.L., "Winnebago Bandolier Bags," *American Indian Art* 9:3, 1984, pp. 31–37.

Whiteford, A.H., "The Origin of Great Lakes Beaded Bandolier Bags," *American Indian Art* 11:3, 1986, pp. 32–44.

pp. 34–35
Densmore, F., *Yuman and Yaqui Music,* Bureau of American Ethnology Bulletin 110, 1932.

Greene, C.S., "Soft Cradles of the Central Plains," *Plains Anthropologist* 37, 1992, pp. 95–113.

Schneider, M.J., "Kiowa and Comanche Baby Carriers," *Plains Anthropologist* 28, 1983, pp. 305–14.

pp. 36–37
Conn, R., "Southern Plains Beadwork in the Fred Harvey Fine Arts Collection," in *The Fred Harvey Fine Arts Collection,* The Heard Museum. Phoenix, 1976.

Whitewolf, J., *The Life of a Kiowa Apache Indian.* New York, 1969.

pp. 38–39
Densmore, F., *Teton Sioux Music,* Bureau of American Ethnology Bulletin 61, 1918.

Lowie, R., *The Crow Indians.* Lincoln, Nebraska, 1983 (1st pub. 1935).

Hewitt, J.N.B., ed., *The Journal of Rudolph Frederick Kurz,* Bureau of American Ethnology Bulletin 115, 1937.

pp. 40–41
Black, L.T., *Aleut Art.* Anchorage, 1982.

———*Glory Remembered: Wooden Headgear of Alaskan Sea Hunters.* Juneau, 1991.

Coles, R., *The First and Last Eskimos.* Boston, 1978.

Heath, J.D., "Baidarka Bow Variations," in *Faces, Voices and Dreams.* Juneau, 1987.

Laughlin, W., *Aleuts: Survivors of the Bering Land Bridge.* New York, 1980.

pp. 42–43
Hoffman, W.J., *The Graphic Art of the Eskimos,* Report of the U.S. National Museum for 1895, 1897.

Maxwell, M.S., "A Contemporary Ethnography from the Thule Period," *Arctic Anthropology* 20:1, 1983, pp. 79–87.

Rasmussen, K., *Intellectual Culture of the Iglulik Eskimos,* Report of the Fifth Thule Expedition 1921–24. Copenhagen, 1927.

Ray, D.J., *Eskimo Art: Tradition and Innovation in North Alaska.* Seattle, 1977.

pp. 44–45
Holm, B., "A Wooling Mantle Neatly Wrought: The Early Historic Record of Northwest Coast Pattern-Twined Textiles, 1774–1850," *American Indian Art* 7:1, 1982, pp. 34–42.

Samuel, C., *The Chilkat Dancing Blanket.* Seattle, 1982.

———*The Raven's Tail.* Vancouver, 1987.

pp. 46–47
Jonaitis, A., *From the Land of the Totem Poles.* New York and Seattle, 1988.

MacDonald, G.F., *Haida Monumental Art: Villages of the Queen Charlotte Islands.* Vancouver, 1983.

Nabokov, P., and R. Easton, *Native American Architecture.* New York and Oxford, 1989.

Swanton, J.R., *Contributions to the Ethnology of the Haida,* Publications of the Jesup North Pacific Expedition 5, Memoirs of the American Museum of Natural History 8:1, 1905, pp. 1–300.

———*Haida Songs.* Washington, 1912.

Wyatt, V., *Shapes of Their Thoughts: Reflections of Culture Contact in Northwest Coast Indian Art.* New Haven and Norman, Oklahoma, 1984.

pp. 48–49
Assu, H., and J. Inglis, *Assu of Cape Mudge: Recollections of a Coastal Indian Chief.* Vancouver, 1989.

Boas, F., *Ethnology of the Kwakiutl,* 35th Annual Report of the Bureau of American Ethnology 1913–1914, 1921.

———*Social Organization and Secret Societies of the Kwakiutl Indians,* Report of the U.S. National Museum for 1895, 1897.

Holm, B., *Crooked Beak of Heaven.* Seattle, 1972.

———*Spirit and Ancestor: A Century of Northwest Coast Indian Art at the Burke Museum.* Seattle, 1987.

Jensen, D., and P. Sargent, *Robes of Power: Totem Poles on Cloth.* Vancouver, 1986.

pp. 52–53
Eisenhart, L.L., "Karok Basketry: Mrs. Phoebe Maddux and the Johnson Collection," in *The Hover Collection of Karok Baskets,* Clarke Memorial Museum. Eureka, California, 1985.

Goddard, P.E., "Life and Culture of the Hupa," *University of California Publications in American Archaeology and Ethnology* 1:1, 1903, pp. 1–88.

McLendon, S., "California Baskets and Basketmakers," in *Basketmakers: Meaning and Form in Native American Baskets,* L. Mowat, et al., eds. Oxford, 1992, pp. 50–75.

Moser, C.L., *American Indian Basketry of Northern California.* Riverside, California, 1989.

O'Neale, L., "Yurok-Karok Basket Weavers," *University of California Publications in American Archaeology and Ethnology* 32:1, 1932, pp. 1–179.

pp. 54–55
Drucker, P., "The Tolowa and their Southwest Oregon Kin," *University of California Publications in American Archaeology and Ethnology* 36:4, 1937, pp. 221– 300.

Goddard, P.E., "Life and Culture of the Hupa," *University of California Publications in American Archaeology and Ethnology* 1:1, 1903, pp. 1–88.

Gould, R.A., "The Wealth Quest Among the Tolowa Indians," *Proceedings of the American Philosophical Society* 110:1, 1966, pp. 67–89.

Kelly, I.T., "The Carver's Art of the Indians of Northwestern California," *University of California Publications in American Archaeology and Ethnology* 24:7, 1930, pp. 343–360.

Wallace, W.J, "Hupa, Chilula, and Whilkut," in *Handbook of North American Indians* 8, R.F. Heizer, ed. Washington, 1978, pp. 164–79.

pp. 56–57
Basso, K.H., *The Cibecue Apache: Case Studies in Cultural Anthropology.* Prospect Heights, Illinois, 1986.

————"The Gift of Changing Woman," *Anthropological Papers* 76, Bureau of American Ethnology Bulletin 196, 1966, pp. 113–73.

Goseyun, A.E., "Carla's Sunrise," *Native Peoples* 4:2, 1991, pp. 8–16.

Quintero, N., "Coming of Age the Apache Way," *National Geographic* 157:2, 1980, pp. 262–71.

pp. 58–59
Colton, H.S., *Hopi Kachina Dolls, with a Key to their Identification.* Albuquerque, 1959.

Crow-Wing, *A Pueblo Indian Journal, 1920–1921,* American Anthropological Association Memoirs 32, 1925.

Fewkes, J.W., *Hopi Katcinas Drawn by Native Artists,* 21st Annual Report of the Bureau of American Ethnology 1899–1900, 1903, pp. 3–126.

Voth, H.R., "The Oraibi Powamu Ceremony," *Field Columbian Museum Anthropological Series* 3:2, 1901, pp. 64–158.

Washburn, D.K., ed., *Hopi Kachina: Spirit of Life.* San Francisco, 1980.

Wright, B., *Hopi Kachinas: The Complete Guide to Collecting Kachina Dolls.* Flagstaff, 1977.

pp. 60–61
Dorta, S.F., *Brazilian Feather Art.* Brazil, 1982.

Huxley, F., *Affable Savages.* New York, 1957.

Ribeiro, D., and B.G. Ribeiro, *Arte Plumária dos Indios Kaapor.* Rio de Janeiro, 1957.

pp. 62–63
Guyasamin, S., "Cuentos de Tierradentro," *Atawalpa* (Ecuador), 1980.

Meggers, B.J., et al., *Early Formative Period of Coastal Ecuador: The Valdivia and Machalilla Phases,* Smithsonian Contributions to Anthropology, 1965.

Visual Prayers, pp. 64–69
Brasser, T.J., *Bo'jou Neejee.* Ottawa, 1976.

Brose, D.S., et al. *American Woodland Indians.* New York, 1985.

Hill, T., and E. McLuhan, *Norval Morrisseau and the Emergence of the Image Makers.* Toronto, 1984.

Schevill, M.B., *Costume as Communication.* Seattle, 1986.

Snow, J., *These Mountains Are our Sacred Places: The Story of the Stoney Indians.* Toronto, 1977.

Turner, G., *Hair Embroidery in Siberia and North America.* Oxford, 1955.

Walker Art Center, *American Indian Art: Form and Tradition.* New York, 1972.

pp. 70–71
Lester, J.A., *We're Still Here: Art of Indian New England.* Boston, 1987.

Schevill, M.B., *Costume as Communication.* Seattle, 1986.

Speck, F.G., *The Double-Curve Motive in Northeastern Algonkian Art,* Canada Department of Mines Geological Survey, Memoir 42:1, 1914.

Wallis, W.D., and R.S. Wallis, *The Micmac Indians of Eastern Canada.* Minneapolis, 1955.

Whitehead, R.H., *Elitekey: Micmac Material Culture from 1600 A.D. to the Present.* Halifax, 1980.

pp. 72–73
Howard, J.H., and M. Gettys, "The Harkins Choctaw Dolls as a Source of Choctaw Culture History," *Bulletin of the Oklahoma Anthropological Society* 32, 1983.

Peterson, J.H., "The Mississippi Choctaws: A Pattern of Persistence," in *Persistence of Pattern: In Mississippi Choctaw Culture.* Jackson, Mississippi, 1987.

pp. 74–75
Balikci, A., *The Netsilik Eskimo.* Garden City, New York, 1970.

Boas, F., *The Central Eskimo.* Lincoln, Nebraska, 1964 (1st pub. 1888).

————*The Eskimo of Baffin Land and Hudson Bay,* Bulletin of the American Museum of Natural History 15, 1901.

Driscoll, B., "Pretending to Be Caribou: The Inuit Parka as an Artistic Tradition," in *The Spirit Sings: Artistic Traditions of Canada's First Peoples,* The Glenbow Museum. Toronto, 1987.

————"Sapangat: Inuit Beadwork in the Canadian Arctic," *Expedition* 26:2, 1984, p. 42.

Mary-Rousseliere, G., "Iglulik," in *Handbook of North American Indians* 5, D. Damas, ed. Washington, 1984, pp. 431–46.

Orchard, W.C., *Beads and Beadwork of the American Indians,* Contributions from the Museum of the American Indian–Heye Foundation 11, 1975 (1st pub. 1929).

Rasmussen, K., *Intellectual Culture of the Iglulik Eskimos,* Report of the Fifth Thule Expedition 1921–24. Copenhagen, 1927.

pp. 76–77
Miller, L., "Basketry of the Plateau Region," in *A Time of Gathering: Native Heritage in Washington State,* Wright, R.K., ed. Seattle, 1991.

Shawley, S.D., "Hemp and Cornhusk Bags of the Plateau Indians," *Indian America* 9:1, 1975, pp. 25–29, 48–49.

pp. 78–79
Fawcett, D., and L.A. Callander, *Native American Painting: Selections from the Museum of the American Indian.* New York, 1982.

Ewers, J.C., et al., *Views of a Vanishing Frontier.* Omaha, 1984.

pp. 80–81
Ewers, J.C., "Assiniboine Antelope-Horn Headdresses," *American Indian Art* 7:4, 1982, pp. 44–45.

Truettner, W., *The Natural Man Observed: A Study of Catlin's Indian Gallery.* Washington, 1979.

pp. 82–83
Orchard, W.C., *The Technique of Porcupine Quill Decoration among the Indians of North America.* New York, 1971.

pp. 84–85
Ewers, J.C., et al., *Views of a Vanishing Frontier.* Omaha, 1984.

pp. 86–87
Ewers, J.C., "Climate, Acculturation, and Costume: A History of Women's Clothing among the Indians of the Southern Plains," *Plains Anthropologist* 25, 1980, pp. 63–82.

Mooney, J., *The Ghost Dance Religion and the Sioux Outbreak of 1890,* 14th Annual Report of the Bureau of American Ethnology 1892–1893, 1896.

pp. 88–89 (The Symbolism of Feathers)
Wooden Leg, *Wooden Leg: A Warrior who Fought Custer.* New York, 1931.

pp. 90–91
Bourke, J.G., *An Apache Campaign in the Sierra Madre: An Account of the Expedition in Pursuit of the Hostile Chiricahua Apaches in the Spring of 1883.* New York, 1958 (1st pub. 1886).

Hagan, W.T., "United States Indian Policies, 1860–1900," in *Handbook of North American Indians* 4, W.E. Washburn, ed. 1988, pp. 51–65.

Porter, J.C., *Paper Medicine Man: John Gregory Bourke and his American West.* Norman, 1986.

Viola, H.J., *Diplomats in Buckskin: A History of Indian Delegations in Washington City.* Washington, 1981.

pp. 92–93
Brown, Lady R., *Unknown Tribes, Uncharted Seas.* London, 1924.

Densmore, F., *Music of the Tule Indians of Panama,* Smithsonian Miscellaneous Collections 77:11, 1926.

Helms, M., *Cuna Molas and Coclé Art Forms: Reflections on Panamanian Design Styles and Symbols,* Working Papers in Traditional Arts 7, 1981.

Howe, J., *The Kuna Gathering: Contemporary Village Politics in Panama.* Austin, 1986.

Parker, A., and A. Neal, *Molas: Folk Art of the Cuna Indians.* Barre, Massachusetts, 1977.

Puls, H., *Textiles of the Kuna Indians of Panama.* United Kingdom, 1988.

Salvador, M.L., *Yer Dialege! Kuna Women's Art.* Albuquerque, 1978.

Sherzer, D., and J. Sherzer, "Mormaknamaloe: The Cuna Mola," in *Ritual and Symbol in Native Central America,* P. Young and J. Howe, eds., University of Oregon Anthropological Papers 9, 1978.

Wafer, L., *A New Voyage and Description of the Isthmus of America* II:73, L.E. Joyce, ed. Oxford, 1934 (1st pub. 1899).

pp. 94–95
Asturias de Barrios, L., *Comalapa: Native Dress and Its Significance.* Guatemala, 1985.

Conte, C., *Maya Culture and Costume.* Colorado, 1984.

Menchú, R., *I . . . Rigoberta Menchú: An Indian Woman in Guatemala,* A. Wright, trans. London, 1983.

Pancake, C.M., "Communicative Imagery in Guatemalan Indian Dress," in *Textile Traditions of Mesoamerica and the Andes,* M.B. Schevill, et al., eds. New York, 1991, pp. 45–62.

Schevill, M.B., *Evolution in Textile Design from the Highlands of Guatemala.* Berkeley, 1985.

Wood, J., and L. de J. Osborne, *Indian Costumes of Guatemala.* Austria, 1966.

pp. 96–97
Alvarado, L., "Datos Etnográficos de Venezuela," *Obras Completas* IV (Caracas), 1956.

Arroyo, M.G., et. al., *Arte Prehispánico de Venezuela.* Caracas, 1971.

de Civrieux, M., *Watunna: An Orinoco Creation Cycle.* San Francisco, 1980.

Guss, D.M., *To Weave and Sing: Art, Symbol, and Narrative in the South American Rain Forest.* Berkeley, 1989.

Wilbert, J., *Survivors of El Dorado: Four Indian Cultures of South America.* New York, 1972.

pp. 98–99
Bianchi, C., *Artesanias y Tecnicas Shuar.* Ecuador, 1982.

Harner, M., *The Jivaro: People of the Sacred Waterfalls.* Berkeley, 1972.

pp. 100–01
Donnan, C., "Moche-Huari Murals from Northern Peru," *Archaeology* 25:2, 1972, pp. 88–95.

————*Moche Art of Peru: Precolumbian Symbolic Communication.* Los Angeles, 1978.

Larco Hoyle, R., *Los Mochicas.* Lima, 1959.

Schjellerup, I., "Gift-Exchange Ceremonies in the Northern Highlands of Peru," *Folk* 29 (Copenhagen), 1987.

pp. 102–03
Anton, F., *Ancient Peruvian Textiles*. New York, 1987.

Feltham, J., *Peruvian Textiles*. United Kingdom, 1989.

Paul, A., *Paracas Art and Architecture: Object and Context in South Coastal Peru*. Iowa City, 1991.

————"Paracas Necropolis Textiles: Symbolic Visions of Coastal Peru," in *The Ancient Americas: Art from Sacred Landscapes*, R.F. Townsend, ed. Chicago, 1992, pp. 279–89.

Paul, A., ed., *Paracas Ritual Attire: Symbols of Authority in Ancient Peru.*, Norman, Oklahoma, 1990.

Rowe, A.P., *Costumes and Featherwork of the Lords of Chimor*. Washington, 1984.

Wasserman, T., and J. Hill, *Bolivian Indian Textiles: Traditional Design and Costume*. New York, 1981.

pp. 104–05
Aldunate del Solar, C., *Mapuche: Seeds of the Chilean Soul*, 1992.

————"Reflexiones Acerca de la Platería Mapuche," in *Platería Araucana*. Santiago, 1983.

Faron, L.C., *The Mapuche Indians of Chile*. New York, 1968.

Laczko, G., "The Weaver: The Araucanians of Chile," in *The Ancestors: Native Artisans of the Americas*, A.C. Roosevelt and J.G.E. Smith, eds. New York and Seattle, 1979.

Rowe, A.P., *Warp-Patterned Weaves of the Andes*. Washington, 1977.

Vision and Virtuosity, pp. 106–11
Duffek, K., "Northwest Coast Indian Art from 1950 to the Present," in *In the Shadow of the Sun*, Canadian Museum of Civilization. Ottawa, 1993.

Holm, B., and B. Reid, *Indian Art of the Northwest Coast*. Seattle and London, 1975.

Nemiroff, D., *Land Spirit Power*. Ottawa, 1992.

Rubin, W.S., ed., *Primitivism in Twentieth Century Art*. New York, 1984.

Shadbolt, D., *Bill Reid*. Toronto, 1986.

pp. 112–13
Barbeau, C.M., "The Origin of Floral and Other Designs among the Canadian and Neighboring Indians," *Proceedings of the International Congress of Americanists* 23, 1928.

Gerin, Leon, "The Hurons of Lorette," *Report of the 70th Meeting of the British Association for the Advancement of Science (Ethnological Survey of Canada)*, 1900, pp. 549–68.

Hail, B., and K.C. Duncan, eds., *Out of the North: The Subarctic Collection of the Haffenreffer Museum of Anthropology*. Bristol, Rhode Island, 1989.

King, J.C.H., "Tradition in Native Art," in *The Arts of the North American Indian: Native Traditions in Evolution*, E.L. Wade, ed., 1986.

Speck, F.G., "Huron Moose Hair Embroidery," *American Anthropologist* 13:1, 1911, pp. 1–14.

————"Notes on the Material Culture of the Huron," *American Anthropologist* 13:2, 1911, pp. 208–28.

Turner, G., "Hair Embroidery in Siberia and North America," *Occasional Papers on Technology* 7, T.K. Penniman and B.M. Blackwood, eds. Oxford, 1976.

pp. 114–15
Brasser, T., *A Basketful of Indian Culture Change*. Ottawa, 1975.

Lester, J.A., "The Birchbark Art of Tomah Joseph," in *We're Still Here: Art of Indian New England*. Boston, 1987.

McMullen, A., and R.G. Handsman, eds., *A Key Into the Language of Woodsplint Baskets*. Connecticut, 1987.

Whitehead, R.H., *Micmac Porcupine Quillwork, 1750–1950*. Ottawa, 1978.

pp. 116–17
Black, L.T., *Aleut Art*. Anchorage, 1982.

Hudson, R.L., "Designs in Aleut Basketry," in *Faces, Voices & Dreams*, P.L. Corey, ed., Sitka, Alaska, 1987.

Ray, D.J., *Aleut and Eskimo Art: Tradition and Innovation in South Alaska*, 1981.

Shapsnikoff, A.T., and R.L. Hudson, "Aleut Basketry," *Anthropological Papers of the University of Alaska* 16:2, 1974, pp. 41–69.

Thompson, A., *Interwoven Expression: Works of a Contemporary Alaska Native Basketmaker*. n.d.

pp. 118–19
Chance, N.A., *The Eskimo of North Alaska*. New York, 1966.

Cole, D., *Captured Heritage: The Scramble for Northwest Coast Artifacts*. Seattle, 1985.

Fitzhugh, W.W., and S.A. Kaplan, *Inua: Spirit World of the Bering Sea Eskimo*. Washington, 1982.

Nelson, E.W., *The Eskimo about Bering Strait*. Washington, 1983 (1st pub. 1899).

Rasmussen, K., *Intellectual Culture of the Copper Eskimo*, Report of the Fifth Thule Expedition 1921–1924. Copenhagen, 1932.

Zimmerly, D.W., *QAJAQ: Kayaks of Siberia and Alaska*. Juneau, 1986.

pp. 120–21
Asch, M.I., "Slavey," in *Handbook of North American Indians* 6, J. Helm, ed. Washington, 1981, pp. 38–49.

Hail, B., and K.C. Duncan, *Out of the North: The Subarctic Collection of the Haffenreffer Museum of Anthropology*. Bristol, Rhode Island, 1989.

Orchard, W.C., *The Technique of Porcupine Quill Decoration among the North American Indians*, 1971.

Osgood, C., *The Ethnology of the Tanaina*. New Haven, 1987.

Thompson, J., "No Little Variety of Ornament: Northern Athapaskan

Artistic Traditions," in *The Spirit Sings: Artistic Traditions of Canada's First Peoples*, The Glenbow Museum. Alberta, 1987.

pp. 122–23
Dauenhauer, N.M., and R. Dauenhauer, *Haa Shuka, Our Ancestors: Tlingit Oral Narratives*. Juneau, 1987.

De Laguna, F., *Under Mount Saint Elias: The History and Culture of the Yakutat Tlingit*, Smithsonian Contributions to Anthropology 7, 1972.

Milburn, M., "Louis Shotridge and the Objects of Everlasting Esteem," in *Raven's Journey: The World of Alaska's Native People*, S.A. Kaplan and K.J. Barsness, eds. Philadelphia, 1986, pp. 54–77.

Shotridge, L., "War Helmets and Clan Hats of the Tlingit Indians," *The Museum Journal* 10:1,2, 1919, pp. 43–48.

pp. 124–25
Holm, B., "Objects of Unique Artistry," in *Soft Gold: The Fur Trade and Cultural Exchange on the Northwest Coast of America*. Portland, 1982.

————*Spirit and Ancestor*. Seattle, 1987.

Sturtevant, W.C., *Boxes and Bowls: Decorated Containers by Nineteenth Century Haida, Tlingit, Bella Bella, and Tsimshian Indian Artists*. Washington, 1974.

Wright, R.K., ed., *A Time of Gathering: Native Heritage in Washington State*. Seattle, 1991.

pp. 126–27
Hall, E.S., Jr., et al., *Northwest Coast Indian Graphics: An Introduction to Silk Screen Prints*. Seattle, 1981.

Macnair, P.L., et al., *The Legacy: Continuing Traditions of Canadian Northwest Coast Indian Art*. Victoria, British Columbia, 1980.

Stewart, H., *Robert Davidson: Haida Printmaker*. Seattle, 1979.

pp. 128–29
Adams, J.W., *The Gitksan Potlatch: Population Flux, Resource Ownership and Reciprocity*. Toronto and Montreal, 1973.

Boas, F., *Tsimshian Mythology*, 31st Annual Report of the Bureau of American Ethnology, 1916.

Halpin, M., "'Seeing' in Stone: Tsimshian Masking and the Twin Stone Masks," in *The World Is as Sharp as a Knife: An Anthology in Honour of Wilson Duff*, D.M. Abbott, ed. Victoria, British Columbia, 1981.

Holm, B., *Northwest Coast Indian Art: An Analysis of Form*. Seattle and London, 1965.

King, J.C.H., *Portrait Masks from the Northwest Coast of America*. London, 1979.

Seguin, M., ed., *The Tsimshian: Images of the Past, Views for the Present*. Vancouver and Seattle, 1993.

pp. 130–31
Benson, W., letters, 1904–1906, archives of the National Museum of the American Indian.

Fields, V.M., *The Hover Collection of Karuk Baskets*. Eureka, California, 1985..

McLendon, S., "Pomo Baskets: The Legacy of William and Mary Benson," *Native Peoples* 4:1, 1990, pp. 26–33.

McLendon, S., "California Baskets and Basketmakers," in *Basketmakers: Meaning and Form in Native American Baskets*, 1992.

McLendon, S., and B.S. Holland, "The Basketmaker: The Pomoans of California," in *The Ancestors: Native Artisans of the Americas*, A.C. Roosevelt and J.G.E. Smith, eds. New York and Seattle, 1979, pp. 106–107.

O'Neale, L.M., "Yurok–Karok Basket Weavers," *University of California Publications in American Archaeology and Ethnology* 32:1, 1932, pp. 1–184.

The Reese Bullen Gallery, *Elizabeth Conrad Hickox: Baskets from the Center of the World*. Arcata, California, 1991

pp. 132–33 (The Legacy of Baskets)
Allen, E., *Pomo Basketmaking: A Supreme Art for the Weaver*. Seattle, 1972.

pp. 134–35
Denig, E.T., *Five Indian Tribes of the Upper Missouri*, J.C. Ewers, ed. Norman, Oklahoma, 1961.

Wildschut, W., and J.C. Ewers, *Crow Indian Beadwork: A Descriptive and Historical Study*, Contributions from the Museum of the American Indian–Heye Foundation 16, 1959.

pp. 136–37
Ewers, J.C., *The Horse in Blackfoot Indian Culture*. Washington, 1980 (1st pub. 1955).

Marriott, A., "The Trade Guild of the Southern Cheyenne Women," in *Native North American Art History*, Z. Mathews and A. Jonaitis, eds. Palo Alto, 1982 (1st pub. 1956).

pp. 138–39
Walker, J.R., *The Sun Dance and Other Ceremonies of the Oglala*, American Museum of Natural History, Anthropological Papers 16, 1917, pp. 51–221.

pp. 142–43
Elston, R.G., "Prehistory of the Western Area," in *Handbook of North American Indians* 11, W.L. d'Azevedo, ed. Washington, 1986, pp. 135–48.

Fowler, C.S., and S. Liljeblad, "Northern Paiute," in *Handbook* 11, pp. 435–65.

Grosscup, G.L., "Lovelock, Northern Paiute and Culture Change," *Nevada State Museum Anthropological Papers* 9, 1963, pp. 67–71.

Loud, L.L., and M.R. Harrington, "Lovelock Cave," *University of California Publications in American Archaeology and Ethnology* 25:1, 1929, pp. viii–183.

Taylor, S.L., "Paiute Family Keeps Tradition Alive," in *Native American Annual* 1: 17, 1985.

Tuohy, D.R., "Portable Art Objects," in *Handbook* 11, pp. 227–37.

Tuohy, D.R., and L.K. Napton, "Duck Decoys from Lovelock Cave, Nevada, Dated by 14C Accelerator Mass Spectrometry," *American Antiquity* 51:4, 1986, pp. 813–16.

Wheat, M.M., *Survival Arts of the Primitive Paiutes*. Reno, 1967.

pp. 144–45
Brody, J.J., *Indian Painters and White Patrons*. Albuquerque, 1971.

Douglas, F.H., and R. d'Harnoncourt, *Indian Art of the United States*. New York, 1941.

Kabotie, F., and B. Belknap, *Fred Kabotie, Hopi Indian Artist*. Flagstaff, 1977.

Seymour, T.V.N., *When the Rainbow Touches Down: The Artists and Stories Behind the Apache, Navajo, Rio Grande Pueblo and Hopi Paintings in the William and Leslie Van Ness Denman Collection*. Phoenix, 1988.

pp. 146–47
Hedlund, A.L., *Reflections of the Weaver's World: The Gloria F. Ross Collection of Contemporary Navajo Weaving*. Denver, 1992.

Kent, K.P., *Navajo Weaving: Three Centuries of Change*. Santa Fe, 1985.

Kluckhohn, C., and D. Leighton, *The Navajo*. Cambridge, Massachusetts, 1974.

Left Handed, *Son of Old Man Hat: A Navajo Autobiography*, W. Dyk and R. Dyk, eds. 1980.

Pepper, G.H., *Navaho Weaving*, 1923, manuscript in the NMAI archives.

Roessel, R., "Navajo Arts and Crafts," in *Handbook of North American Indians* 10, A. Ortiz, ed. Washington, 1983.

Wheat, J.B., "Early Navajo Weaving," *Plateau* 52:4, 1981, pp. 2–8.

———"Early Trade and Commerce in Southwestern Textiles before the Curio Shop," in *Reflections: Papers on Southwestern Culture History in Honor of Charles H. Lange*, A.V.S. Poore, ed. 1988.

———*Patterns and Sources of Navajo Weaving*. Denver, 1977.

pp. 148–49
Babcock, B.A., "'Those, They Called Them Monos': Cochiti Figurative Ceramics," *American Indian Art* 12:4, 1987, pp. 50–58.

Babcock, B.A., et al., *The Pueblo Storyteller: Development of a Figurative Ceramic Tradition*. Tucson, 1986.

Batkin, J., *Pottery of the Pueblos of New Mexico: 1700–1940*. Colorado Springs, 1987.

Di Peso, C., *Casas Grandes: A Fallen Trading Center of the Gran Chichimeca* 2. Dragoon, Arizona, 1974.

———"Casas Grandes Effigy Vessels," *American Indian Art* 2:4, 1977, pp. 32–37, 39.

Minnis, P., and M. Whalen, "Casas Grandes: Archaeology in Northern

Mexico," *Expedition* 35: 1, 1993, pp. 34–44.

pp. 150–51
Berrin, K. and E. Pasztory, eds., *Teotihuacan: Art from the City of the Gods*. San Francisco and New York, 1993.

Coe, M., *Mexico*. New York, 1962

pp. 152–53
Couch, N.C.C., *Pre-Columbian Art from the Ernest Erickson Collection*. New York, 1988.

Furst, P., *The Ninth Level: Funerary Art from Ancient Mesoamerica*. Iowa City, 1978.

Gallagher, J., *Companions of the Dead: Ceramic Tomb Sculpture from Ancient West Mexico*. Los Angeles, 1983.

Kan, M., et al., *Sculpture of Ancient West Mexico: Nayarit, Jalisco, Colima—The Proctor Stafford Collection*. Los Angeles, 1970.

pp. 154–55
Jeter, J., and P.M. Juelke, *The Saltillo Sarape*. Santa Barbara, 1978

Wheat, J.B., "Rio Grande, Pueblo, and Navajo Weavers: Cross Cultural Influence," in *Spanish Textile Tradition of New Mexico and Colorado*, N. Fisher, ed. Santa Fe, 1984, pp. 29–36.

———"Saltillo Sarapes of Mexico," in *Spanish Textile Tradition of New Mexico and Colorado*, N. Fisher, ed. 1984, pp. 74–82.

pp. 156–57
Couch, N.C.C., *Pre-Columbian Art from the Ernest Erickson Collection*. New York, 1988.

Goldstein, M.M., *Ceremonial Sculpture of Ancient Veracruz*. New York, 1988.

Hammer, O., ed., *The Ancient Art of Veracruz*. Los Angeles, 1971.

Medellin Zenil, A., and F. Peterson, "A Smiling Head Complex from Central Veracruz," in *American Antiquity* 20:2, 1954, pp. 162–69.

Proskouriakoff, T., "Classic Art of Central Veracruz," in *Handbook of Middle American Indians* 11, R. Wauchope, ed. Austin, 1971.

Wilkerson, S.J.K., "El Tajín: Great Center of the Northeast," in *Mexico: Splendors of Thirty Centuries*, Metropolitan Museum of Art. New York, 1990.

pp. 158–59
Coe, M., *The Maya Scribe and his World*. New York, 1973.

Estrada, J., *La Música de México*. Mexico, 1984.

Houston, S., et al., "Folk Classification of Classic Maya Pottery," *American Anthropologist* 91:3, 1989, pp. 720–26.

MacLeod, B., "Deciphering the Primary Standard Sequence," Ph.D. dissertation, University of Texas, 1990.

Martí, S., and G.P. Kurath, *Dances of the Anáhuac: The Choreography and Music of Precortesian Dances*. Chicago, 1964.

Mendoza, V.T., "Música Precolombina de América," *Boletín Latinamericano de Música* (Mexico) 4, 1938.

Miller, M.E., *Jaina Figurines*. Princeton , 1975.

Reents-Budet, D., et. al. *Painting the Maya Universe: Royal Ceramics of the Classic Period*. Durham, North Carolina, 1994.

Schele, L., and M.E. Miller, *Blood of Kings*. Ft. Worth, 1986.

Schele, L., and D. Friedel, *A Forest of Kings*. Ft. Worth, 1990.

pp. 160–61
Kerr, J., *The Maya Vase Book* 1–3. New York, 1989–1992.

Schaffer, A.-L., *On the Edge of the Maya World: Stone Vases from the Ulúa Valley, Honduras*, exhibition at the Museum of Fine Arts, Houston, 1992.

Schele, L., and M.E. Miller, *Blood of Kings*. Ft. Worth, 1986.

Schele, L., and D. Friedel, *A Forest of Kings*. Ft. Worth, 1990.

pp. 162–63
Bernal, I., *The Olmec World*. Berkeley, 1969.

Bonifaz Nuño, R., *Hombres y Serpientes: Iconografía Olmeca*. Mexico, 1989.

Carmichael, E., *Turquoise Mosaics from Mexico*, 1970.

Coe, M., "The Olmec Style and its Distribution," in *Handbook of Middle American Indians* 3, R. Wauchope and G. Willey, eds. Austin, 1965, pp. 739–75.

De la Fuente, B., *Los Hombres de Piedra: Escultura Olmeca*. Mexico, 1977.

Stuart, G.S., and G.F. Stuart, *Lost Kingdoms of the Maya*. Washington, 1993.

pp. 164–65
Bray, W., *Gold of El Dorado: The Heritage of Colombia*. New York, 1979.

Burger, R., *Chavin and the Origins of Andean Civilization*. New York, 1993.

Cieza de León, *Crónica del Perú*. Lima, 1986, (1st pub. 1553).

Cobo, B., *Inca Religion and Customs*, Roland B. Hamilton, trans. Austin, 1990 (1st pub. 1653).

Jones, J., ed., *El Dorado: The Gold of Ancient Colombia*. New York, 1974.

Reichel Domatoff, G., *Goldwork and Shamanism: An Iconographic Study of the Gold Museum*. Medillin, Colombia, 1988.

Rowe, J.H., *Chavín Art: An Inquiry into its Form and Meaning*. New York, 1962.

pp. 166–67
Proulx, D., "The Nasca Style," in *Art of the Andes: Precolumbian Sculptures and Painted Ceramics from the Arthur M. Sackler Collection*, L. Katz, ed. Washington, 1983.

Read, H., *Icon and Idea*. London, 1955.

Silverman, H., *Cahuachi in the Ancient Nasca World*. Iowa City, 1993.

Townsend, R.F., "Deciphering the Nazca World: Ceramic Images from Ancient Peru," *Art Institute of Chicago Museum Studies* 11:2, 1985, pp. 116–39.

pp. 168–169
Farabee, W.C., *Indian Tribes of Eastern Peru*, Papers of the Peabody Museum of American Archaeology and Ethnology 10, 1922.

Gebhart-Sayer, A., *The Cosmos Encoiled: Indian Art of the Peruvian Amazon*. New York, 1984.

Roe, P., *The Cosmic Zygote: Cosmology in the Amazon Basin*. New Brunswick, New Jersey, 1982.

Román V., L., "Etica y Esthetica en el Arte Piro," *Anthropologica* (Peru) 3:3, 1985, pp. 125–33.

Steward, J.H., and A. Métraux, "Tribes of the Peruvian and Ecuadorian Montaña," in *Handbook of South American Indians* 3, R. Wauchope and G. Willey, eds. Austin, 1948, pp. 535–656.

pp. 170–71
de Avila, F, *Dioses y Hombres de Huarochirí*, José María Arguedas, trans. Lima, 1966 (1st pub. 1608).

Pease G.Y., F., *Perú Hombre e Historia: Entre el siglo XVI y el XVIII*. Lima, 1993.

Sallnow, M.J., *Pilgrims of the Andes: Regional Cults in Cusco*. Washington, 1987.

Across the Generations, pp. 172–177
Cushing, F.H., *Zuni Breadstuff*, Indian Notes and Monographs 8, 1974 (1st pub. 1920).

Sweezy, C., *The Arapaho Way: A Memoir of an Indian Boyhood*. New York, 1966.

Walker, S., "Ancestral Art," The Toronto *Star*, 15 January 1994.

pp. 178–179
Brown, J.A., "Spiro Art and its Mortuary Contexts," in *Death and the Afterlife in Pre-Columbian America*, E.P. Benson, ed. Washington, 1975, pp. 19–22.

Emerson, T.E., "Mississippian Stone Images in Illinois," *Illinois Archaeological Survey* 6, p. 75.

———"Water, Serpents, and the Underworld: An Exploration into Cahokian Symbolism," in *The Southeastern Ceremonial Complex: Artifacts and Analysis*, P. Galloway, ed., 1989, pp. 44–92.

Fowler, M., ed., "The Cahokia Site," *Illinois Archaeological Survey* 7, 1969, pp. 1–30.

———*Cahokia, Ancient Capital of the Midwest*. Menlo Park, California, 1974.

Hudson, C., *The Southeastern Indians*. Knoxville, 1976.

pp. 180–81
Garcilasco de la Vega, G.S., *The Florida of the Inca*, J.G. Varner and J.J. Varner, eds. and trans. Austin, 1951.

Griffith, R.J., "Ramey Incised Pottery," *Illinois Archaeological Survey* 5, 1981.

Hall, R.L., "The Cahokia Presence outside of the American Bottom," paper for the Central State Anthropological Society, 1973 (manuscript).

Hudson, Charles, *The Southeastern Indians*. Knoxville, 1976.

pp. 182–83
Cleland, C.E., *Rites of Conquest: The History and Culture of Michigan's Native Americans*. Ann Arbor, Michigan, 1992.

Fredrickson, N.J., and S. Gibb, *The Covenant Chain: Indian Ceremonial and Trade Silver*. Ottawa, 1980.

The Glenbow Museum, *The Spirit Sings*. Alberta, 1987.

Innis, H.A., *The Fur Trade in Canada*. Toronto and Buffalo, 1970 (1st pub. 1930).

Thompson, J., *The North American Indian Collection of the Berne Historical Museum*. Berne, 1977.

pp. 184–85
Callander, L.A., and R. Slivka, *Shawnee Home Life: The Paintings of Earnest Spybuck*. New York, 1984.

Harrington, M.R., "Spybuck, the Shawnee Artist," in *Indians at Work* V:8, 1938, pp.13–15.

——— notes for 1910 in the archives of the National Museum of the American Indian, New York.

pp. 186–87
Archuleta, M., and R. Strickland, *Shared Visions: Native American Painters and Sculptors in the Twentieth Century*. New York, 1991.

pp. 188–89
Wildschut, W., *Crow Indian Medicine Bundles*, J.C. Ewers, ed., Contributions from the Museum of the American Indian–Heye Foundation 17, 1960.

pp. 190–91
Ewers, J.C., *The Blackfeet, Raiders of the Northwestern Plains*. Norman, Oklahoma, 1968.

Ewers, J.C., "The Bear Cult among the Assiniboine and their Neighbors of the Northern Plains," in *Indian Life on the Upper Missouri*, J.C. Ewers, ed. Norman Oklahoma, 1968.

pp. 192–93
Burnham, D.K., *To Please the Caribou*. Seattle, 1992.

Rogers, E.S., and E. Leacock, "Montagnais- Naskapi," in *Handbook of the North American Indians* 6, J. Helm, ed. Washington, 1981, pp. 169–89.

Speck, F.G., *Naskapi: The Savage Hunters of the Labrador Peninsula*. Norman, Oklahoma, 1977.

pp. 194–95
Carpenter, E., "Introduction" in *Form and Freedom*. Houston, 1975, pp. 9–29.

Fienup-Riordan, A., "Nick Charles, Sr.: Worker in Wood," in *The Artists Behind the Work*. Fairbanks, 1986, pp. 25–57.

———"Eye of the Dance: Spiritual Life of the Bering Sea Eskimo," in

Crossroads of Continents: Cultures of Siberia and Alaska, W.W. Fitzhugh and A. Crowell, eds. Washington, 1988, pp. 256–70.

Nelson, E., *The Eskimo about Bering Strait*, 18th Annual Report of the Bureau of American Ethnology 1896–1897, 1899.

Ray, D.J., *Eskimo Masks: Art and Ceremony*. Seattle, 1965.

Rubin, W., ed., *"Primitivism" in 20th Century Art: Affinity of the Tribal and the Modern*. New York, 1984.

Williams, E.A., "Art and Artifact at the Trocadero: Arts Americana and the Primitivist Revolution,'" in *Objects and Others: Essays on Museums and Material Culture*, G.W. Stocking, Jr., ed. Madison, Wisconsin, 1985.

pp. 196–97
Feder, N., "Incised Relief Carving of the Halkomelem and Straits Salish," *American Indian Art* 8:2, 1983, pp. 46–55.

Garfield, V.E., "Making a Bird or Chief's Rattle," *Davidson Journal of Anthropology* 1:11, 1955, p. 155–64.

Guedon, M.-F., "Tsimshian Shamanic Images," in *The Tsimshian: Images of the Past, Views for the Present*, M. Seguin, ed. Vancouver, 1993.

Suttles, W., "Productivity and its Constraints: A Coast Salish Case," in *Indian Art Traditions of the Northwest Coast*, R.L. Carlson, ed., pp. 67–87.

pp. 198–99
Kennedy, D.I.D., and R.T. Bouchard, "Bella Coola," in *Handbook of North American Indians* 7, W. Suttles, ed. Washington, 1990, pp. 323–39.

McIlwraith, T.F., *The Bella Coola Indians*. Toronto, 1948.

Stott, M.A., *Bella Coola Ceremony and Art*. Ottawa, 1975.

pp. 200–01
Densmore, F., *Nootka and Quileute Music*, Bureau of American Ethnology Bulletin 124, 1939.

Devine, S.F., "Nootka Basketry Hats: Two Special Types," *American Indian Basketry Magazine* 1:3, 1980, pp. 26–31.

Henry, J.F., *Early Maritime Artists of the Pacific Northwest Coast, 1741–1841*. Seattle, 1984.

Holm, B., *Spirit and Ancestor*. Seattle, 1987.

Jewitt, J.R., *The Adventures and Sufferings of John R. Jewett, Captive of Maquinna*. Vancouver, 1987 (1st pub. 1824).

Kaeppler, A.L., *Artificial Curiosities: An Exposition of Native Manufactures Collected on the Three Pacific Voyages of Captain James Cook, R.N.* Honolulu, 1978.

Moziño, J., *Noticias de Nutka, an Account of Nootka Sound in 1792*, I.H. Wilson, ed. and trans. Seattle and London, 1970.

pp. 202–03
Bates, C.D., "Feather Belts of Central California," *American Indian Art* 7:1,

1981, pp. 46–54.

Bates, C.D., and B. Bibby, "Collecting among the Chico Maidu: The Stewart Culin Collection at the Brooklyn Museum," *American Indian Art* 8:4, 1983, pp. 46–54.

Dixon, R.B., "The Northern Maidu," *Bulletin of the American Museum of Natural History* XVII:III, 1905, pp. 119–346.

———"The Shasta," in *Bulletin of the American Museum of Natural History* XVII:V, 1907, pp. 391–498.

Jacknis, I., "California," in *Objects of Myth and Memory: American Indian Art at the Brooklyn Museum*, D. Fane et al., eds., 1991, pp. 161–233.

Silver, S., "Shastan Peoples," in *Handbook of North American Indians* 8, R.F. Heizer, ed. Washington, 1978, pp. 211–24.

pp. 204–05
Adair, J., *The Navajo and Pueblo Silversmiths*. Norman, Oklahoma, 1944.

Ferguson, T.J., and E.R. Hart, *A Zuni Atlas*. Norman, Oklahoma, 1985.

Hodge, F.W., *History of Hawikuh, New Mexico*. Los Angeles, 1937.

Jernigan, E.W., *Jewelry of the Prehistoric Southwest*. Santa Fe, 1978.

Judd, N.M., *The Material Culture of Pueblo Bonito*, Smithsonian Miscellaneous Collections 124, 1954.

Lekson, S.H., "Settlement Patterns and the Chaco Region," in *Chaco and Hohokam: Prehistoric Regional Systems in the American Southwest*, P.L. Crown and W.J. Judge, eds. Santa Fe, 1991, pp. 31–57.

Lekson, S.H., et al., "The Chaco Canyon Community," in *Scientific American* 259:1, July 1988.

Smith, W., et al., *The Excavation of Hawikuh by Frederick Webb Hodge: Report of the Hendricks-Hodge Expedition 1917–1923*, Contributions from the Museum of the American Indian–Heye Foundation XX, 1966.

pp. 206–07
Batkin, J., *Pottery of the Pueblos of New Mexico: 1700–1940*. Colorado Springs, 1987.

Bunzel, R.L., *The Pueblo Potter: A Study of Creative Imagination in Primitive Art*, Columbia University Contributions to Anthropology 8, 1929.

Hardin, M.A., *Gifts of Mother Earth: Ceramics in the Zuni Tradition*. Phoenix, 1983.

Smith, W., et al., *The Excavation of Hawikuh by Frederick Webb Hodge: Report of the Hendricks–Hodge Expedition 1917–1923*, Contributions from the Museum of the American Indian–Heye Foundation XX, 1966.

pp. 208–09
Batkin, J., *Pottery of the Pueblos of New Mexico: 1700–1940*. Colorado Springs, 1987.

Cusick, M.L., *Nampeyo: A Gift Remembered*.

Dillingham, R., and M. Elliott, *Acoma and Laguna Pottery*. Santa Fe, 1992.

Marriott, A., *Maria: The Potter of San Ildefonso*. Norman, Oklahoma, 1948.

Maxwell Museum of Anthropology, *Seven Families in Pueblo Pottery*. Albuquerque, 1974.

Peterson, S., *The Living Tradition of Maria Martinez*. Tokyo, New York, and San Francisco, 1977.

———*Lucy M. Lewis: American Indian Potter*. Tokyo, New York, and San Francisco, 1984.

Spivey, R.L., *Maria*. Flagstaff, 1979.

pp. 210–11
Levenson, J.A., ed., *Circa 1492: Art in the Age of Exploration*. New Haven, 1991.

Townsend, R.F., *The Aztecs*. New York, 1992.

pp. 212–13
Sylvest, E.E., Jr., *Nuestra Señora de Guadalupe: Mother of God, Mother of the Americas*. Dallas, 1992.

Wolf, E.R., "The Virgin of Guadalupe: A Mexican National Symbol," *Journal of American Folklore* 71:279, 1958, pp. 701–02.

pp. 214–15
Conzemius, E., *Ethnographical Survey of the Moskito and Sumu Indians of Honduras and Nicaragua*, Bureau of American Ethnology Bulletin 106, 1932.

Griffith, J., "Cáhitan *Pascola* Masks," *The Kiva* 37:4, 1972, pp. 185–98.

Painter, M.T., *With Good Heart: Yaqui Beliefs and Ceremonies in Pascua Village*. Tucson, 1986.

Spicer, E.H., "The Yaqui and Mayo," in *Handbook of Middle American Indians* 8, R. Wauchope, ed. Austin, 1969, pp. 830–45.

———*The Yaquis: A Cultural History*. Tucson, 1980.

pp. 216–17
Rouse, I., *The Tainos: Rise and Decline of the People Who Greeted Columbus*. New Haven, 1992.

Rouse, I., and J.J. Arrom, "The Taínos," in *Circa 1492*, J.A. Levenson, ed. New Haven, 1991, pp. 509–13, 575–81.

Stevens-Arroyo, A.M., *Cave of the Jagua: The Mythological World of the Taínos*. Albuquerque, 1988, pp. 218–19.

p. 218–19
McEwan, C., and Van de Guchte, M., "Ancestral Time and Sacred Space in Inca State Ritual," in *The Ancient Americas*, R.F. Townsend, ed. Chicago, 1992, pp. 359–72.

Reinhard, J., *An Archaeological Investigation of Inca Ceremonial Platforms on the Volcano Copiapó, Central Chile*. Oxford, 1991.

———"Sacred Peaks of the Andes," *National Geographic*, March, 1992.

Schobinger, J., "Sacrifices of the High

Andes," *Natural History* 100:4, 1991, pp. 62–68.

p. 220–21 (Native Gold, Spanish Gold)
Cieza de León, *The Incas*, V.W. van Hagen, ed., H. de Onis, trans. Norman, Oklahoma, 1959 (1st pub. 1553).

Hanke, L., *The Spanish Struggle for Justice in the Conquest of America.* Philadelphia, 1949.

Milbrath, S., and J. Milanich, eds. *First Encounters: Spanish Explorations in the Caribbean and the United States, 1492–1570.* Gainesville, Florida, 1989.

Sale, K., *The Conquest of Paradise: Christopher Columbus and the Columbian Legacy.* New York, 1991

pp. 222–23
Cummins, T., "Abstraction to Narration: Kero Imagery of Peru and the Colonial Alteration of Native Identity," PhD. dissertation, UCLA, 1985.

Liebscher, V., *Iconografía de los Keros.* Lima, 1985.

Rostowrowski, M., *Etnía y Sociedad.* Lima, 1977. Craig Morris, trans., 1979.

pp. 224–25
Benson, E.P., *The Mochica: A Culture of Peru.* New York and Washington, 1972.

D'Harcourt, R., and M. D'Harcourt, *La musique des Incas et ses survivances.* Paris, 1925.

Legast, A., *El animal en el mundo míti-co Tairona.* Bogota, 1987.

Reichel-Dolmatoff, G., *Los Kogi.* Bogota, 1985.

pp. 226–27
Benson, E.P., *The Mochica: A Culture of Peru.* New York and Washington, 1972

Betanzos, J. de, *Suma y Narración de los Incas*, M. del Carmen Rubio, transcription. Madrid, 1987 (1st pub. 1551.

Donnan, C., *Moche Art of Peru: Pre-Columbian Symbolic Communication.* Los Angeles, 1978.

pp. 228–29
Ehrenreich, P., "Contributions to the Ethnography of Brazil," Shelton Hicock, trans., *Veroffentlichungen aus dem Koniglichen Museum fur Volkerkunde* 2, 1891, pp. 1–80.

Fawcett, D.M., "The Featherworkers: The Karajá of Brazil," in *The Ancestors: Native Artisans of the Americas,* A.C. Roosevelt and J.G.E. Smith, eds. New York, 1979, pp. 24–43.

Yde, J., *Material Culture of the Waiwái.* Copenhagen, 1965.

pp. 230–31
Metraux, A., *The Native Tribes of Eastern Bolivia and Western Matto Grosso.* Washington, 1942.

Pérez Gollán, J.A., and I. Gordillo, "Religión y alucinógenos en el antiguo Noroeste Argentino," *Ciencia Hoy* (Argentina) 4:22, 1993, pp. 51–64.

Schultes, R., and Hoffmann, A., *Plantas de los Dioses. Orígenes del uso de alucinógenos.* Mexico, 1982.

pp. 232–33
Cooper, J.M., "The Yahgan" in *Handbook of South American Indians* 1, J. Steward, ed. Washington, 1946, pp. 81–106.

Lothrop, S.K., *The Indians of Tierra del Fuego.* New York, 1928.

Lothrop, S.K., and Wilbert, J., ed., *Folk Literature of the Yamana Indians: Martin Gusinde's Collection of Yamana Narratives.* Berkeley, 1977.

Epilogue, pp. 234–39.
Steltzer, U., *Indian Artists at Work.* 1977.

PAGE 241: NATIVE ALASKAN WOMAN, EARLY 20TH C. PHOTOGRAPH BY F.H. NOWELL (36101)

PAGE 246: WEAVER USING BACKSTRAP LOOM. GUATEMALA

PAGES 252–253 SEAL HUNTERS, 1926. MOUTH OF THE KUSKOKWIM RIVER, ALASKA. PHOTOGRAPH BY CLARK M. BARBER (P20164)

PAGE 256: BRULE LAKOTA GIRL IN COWRIE-SHELL DRESS. NORTH DAKOTA (P23257)

The objects in this book were photographed by David Heald, except as noted below. Historical images from the Photo Archives of the National Museum of the American Indian are identified where they appear by photograph or negative numbers in parentheses after their captions. Sources and image numbers (again, in parentheses) for the remaining photographs are given here.

p. 16: National Anthropological Archives, Smithsonian Institution (NAA) (56202, 75-4541, and 57309).

p. 20: Museum of New Mexico (77536).

p. 21: amulets photographed by Karen Furth, National Museum of the American Indian (NMAI).

p. 22: gorget photographed by Carmelo Guadagno, NMAI.

p. 24: cradle photographed by Pamela Dewey, NMAI.

p. 25: NAA (56388).

p. 31: State Historical Society of North Dakota (Fiske-440).

p. 33: NAA (T13409).

p. 44: NAA (44-826-B).

p. 50: Winter and Pond Collection, Alaska State Library (PCA 87-017) and Buffalo and Erie County Historical Society (19-657-3).

p. 53: NAA (74-14715).

p. 54: NAA (43114).

p. 66: NAA (49383-A).

p. 68: NAA (53597) and Arizona Historical Society Library (25649).

p. 69: NAA (3318-B2).

p. 75: National Archives of Canada (PA 53606).

p. 78: National Archives (111-SC 85723).

p. 80: NAA (3510).

p. 83: NAA (3382).

p. 87: NAA (43906-D).

p. 89: Buffalo and Erie County Historical Society (19-657-4).

p. 91: NAA (2575-D-2).

p. 93: photograph by Andrew L. Young, Meria Obigandup, Kuna Yala, Panama, 1986;

courtesy of the photographer.

p. 100: The British Museum, drawing by Donna McClelland.

pp. 100-01: shirt photographed by Karen Furth, NMAI.

p. 109: NAA (72-489).

p. 110: NAA (56757).

p. 112: National Archives of Canada (C28553).

p. 117: Field Museum of Natural History (A13299).

p. 123: Winter and Pond Collection, Alaska State Library (PCA 87-1002).

p. 126: Eagle of the Dawn Artist, Ltd., White Rock, British Columbia.

p. 132: NAA (74-11863) and Winter and Pond Collection, Alaska State Library (PCA 87-1002).

p. 138: NAA (3642).

p. 141: ledger book drawings photographed by Pamela Dewey, NMAI.

p. 142: Churchill County Museum and Archive, Fallon, Nevada.

p. 149: School of American Research, collections in the Museum of New Mexico (16296).

p. 156: NMAI (P18270).

p. 168: NAA (79-14 767).

p. 171: NAA (S.A. 129).

p. 175: School of American Research, collections in the Museum of New Mexico (16212).

p. 177: NAA (2276).

p. 186: courtesy of the artist's family.

p. 189: NAA (55530).

p. 190: Glacier Studio, Browning, Montana.

p. 195: Library of Congress.

p. 202: NAA (2854A).

p. 206: NAA (2268A).

p. 213: courtesy of Max Stancari.

p. 226: courtesy of Ramiro Matos.

p. 229: NAA (G200).

p. 235: NAA (91-979).

p. 239: NAA (596-D2).

p. 246: NAA (94-8585).

INDEX